The MAILBOX®

The Idea Magazine For Teachers™

PRESCHOOL

1995–1996
YEARBOOK

Jayne M. Gammons, Editor

The Education Center, Inc.
Greensboro, North Carolina

The Mailbox® 1995–1996 Preschool Yearbook

Editor In Chief: Margaret Michel
Editorial Manager: Julie Peck
Early Childhood Editorial Director: Karen P. Shelton
Senior Editor: Jayne M. Gammons
Contributing Editors: Ada Hanley Goren, Marie Iannetti, Mackie Rhodes
Copy Editors: Lynn Bemer Coble, Jennifer Rudisill, Gina Sutphin
Contributing Artist: Lucia Kemp Henry
Staff Artists: Jennifer T. Bennett, Cathy Spangler Bruce, Pam Crane, Teresa Davidson, Clevell Harris, Susan Hodnett, Sheila Krill, Rebecca Saunders, Barry Slate, Donna K. Teal
Editorial Assistants: Elizabeth A. Findley, Wendy Svartz

ISBN 1-56234-135-9
ISSN 1088-5536

The Education Center®, *The Mailbox*®, *Teacher's Helper*®, *The Mailbox*® *Bookbag*™, *Learning*™, "the idea magazine for teachers,"™ and the mailbox/post/grass logo are trademarks of The Education Center, Inc., and may be the subject of one or more federal trademark registrations. All brand or product names are trademarks or registered trademarks of their respective companies.

Printed in the United States of America.

The Education Center, Inc.
P.O. Box 9753
Greensboro, NC 27429-0753

Look for *The Mailbox*® 1996–1997 Preschool Yearbook in the summer of 1997. The Education Center, Inc., is the publisher of *The Mailbox*®, *Teacher's Helper*®, *The Mailbox*® *Bookbag*™, and *Learning*™ magazines, as well as other fine products and clubs. Look for these wherever quality teacher materials are sold, or call 1-800-334-0298 for a catalog.

Contents

Thematic Units

Welcome To Preschool

Picnicking

Plan several picnics to ease preschool jitters. During the last weeks of summer, before school starts, invite small groups of incoming students to your home. Have children bring their own lunches. Provide decorations, drinks, and dessert for each picnic. Before departing, have each youngster decorate a nametag to be worn the first week of school. Isn't it about time you had a picnic?

A Surprise In The Mailbox

Before school begins, address a couple of postcards for each of your students. Stamp the postcards and tuck them away for later use. Whenever you observe something that is especially delightful about a particular child, jot a note on a postcard labeled with his name. Mail the postcard. When it arrives at his home, everyone will be delighted that you took the time to comment.

The Pick Of The Crop

If your newly enrolled preschoolers are invited to an Open House, here's a way to get them involved right then and there. Decorate a bulletin board with a large apple-tree design. For each child, place a personalized apple cutout on a tabletop near the bulletin board. Also provide art supplies so that each child can decorate his apple, if desired. During Open House, have each student decorate his apple and attach it to the bulletin-board apple tree with the help of his parent. When the evening is over, you'll be able to see at a glance which students were in attendance. The remaining youngsters may decorate and display their apples on the board when time permits.

Mary H. Case—Preschool
South Godwin Elementary School
Wyoming, MI

Balloons Abound

Make balloons the theme of your preschool class. Begin using the theme during registration or Open House. Send each young participant home with a Mylar® balloon (a regular balloon can pose a choking hazard) of his own. What a pleasant reminder of a first school visit!

A Napping Buddy

Enlist the help of a parent volunteer to make sure each of your youngsters has a warm and fuzzy impression of preschool. Using preprinted fabric pillow patterns (or your own designs) that resemble animals, make a soft, decorative pillow for each of your youngsters. When a child visits school for the first time, give him a pillow of his own to keep. With the animal pillow, provide a note (from the animal) that welcomes the child to school and says that he looks forward to being his napping buddy.

Hi! I'm your napping buddy. When it's time to rel...

Bring A
Preschool-Age Friend
To School

Tuesday, September 26

We'll have fun all day!

Call Miss Sarah for more
information.

Relaxing In A Rocker

One of the best ways to encourage relaxation and self-esteem is to provide one or more child-size rocking chairs. Each day, choose a different child to sit in each rocking chair during storytime. Encourage him to rock his favorite stuffed animal if he'd like to. It's impossible not to feel special when it's your very own rocking-chair day!

Friends Day

What a thrill it will be for each preschooler to have an opportunity to bring a preschool-age friend or relative to school with him one day! Establish a day for this purpose and notify parents. When Friends Day arrives, enjoy all of your usual preschool activities. Not only will this be a neat treat for each of your youngsters and their guests, it can be a great enrollment booster too.

School Books

Will You Come Back For Me?
Written by Ann Tompert
Illustrated by Robin Kramer
Published by Albert Whitman & Company

Starting School
Written by Allan Ahlberg
Illustrated by Janet Ahlberg
Published by Viking Children's Books

What Will Mommy Do When I'm At School?
Written & Illustrated by Dolores Johnson
Published by Macmillan Children's Books

All My Feelings At Preschool: Nathan's Day
Written by Susan Conlin and Susan Levine Friedman
Illustrated by M. Kathryn Smith
Published by Parenting Press

When I Was Little: A Four-Year-Old's Memoir Of Her Youth
Written by Jamie Lee Curtis
Illustrated by Laura Cornell
Published by HarperCollins Children's Books

Chatterbox Jamie
Written by Nancy Evans Cooney
Illustrated by Marylin Hafner
Published by Putnam Publishing Group

Reading About School

Young children often feel anxious about new school experiences. Show your youngsters that their feelings are not unusual by reading literature about new school experiences. (See "School Books.") After reading and discussing each of these books with your students, encourage parents to check them out and reread them to their youngsters. It's a great way to get kids and parents talking about their feelings about school.

Mascot's Journal

Imagine the delight of a preschooler who has just learned that the class mascot is going home with him for the evening! When it is a student's turn to take the mascot home, have him place the stuffed animal in a bookbag that has been labeled for this purpose. In the bookbag, include a notebook that contains a note asking parents to make a journal entry, along with a sample entry. Each time the mascot returns to school with a new journal entry, read the entry aloud to the class.

Speeding Recovery

Being in a new preschool setting is unsettling for many students. Consequently every little problem may seem like a big deal. Be prepared to give extra doses of tender, loving care and spread warm feelings. Label a bottle of hand lotion "Hurt Cream." Whenever a child is hurt or in despair, apply a small amount of the hurt cream to the affected area or to his hands. The one-on-one attention the youngster gets along with your caring touch has a way of making the discomfort associated with bumps, bruises, and hurt feelings disappear.

Collecting Hugs

There's nothing quite like a hug to show someone you care. Talk with your youngsters about friendship, hugs, and how they feel when they are embraced. Talk about how you give a hug. Give each of your children a lunch bag that has arms and hand cutouts already attached and is labeled "Hug Bag." Encourage each student to collect a hug from each of his classmates and pretend to tuck his hugs down in his hug bag to keep them forever.

I Need Some Attention

Little ones who find themselves in new preschool settings may not know how to express their need for attention. Help them get the attention they need and deserve with decorated wristbands. Cut, assemble, and decorate some felt wristbands that fit your preschoolers. Place them in an accessible location. Encourage each youngster to wear a wristband whenever he needs a little extra attention. When you see a child wearing a wristband, be sure to touch base with him to find out what's on his mind and how you can improve his day.

Decorative Carriers

It's easy to tell that school papers are special when they come home tucked in beautifully decorated tubes. Have students decorate toilet-tissue tubes using an assortment of art supplies. Label each child's tube with his name or have him label it. When artwork or notices need to go home, roll each student's papers and tuck them into his tube for transport.

My Buddy And Me

On his first day in your class, send a recent enrollee home with a special memento of the occasion. Using a Polaroid® camera, photograph the new student engaged in an activity with a buddy. This photograph is sure to give the newcomer and his parents a great deal of pleasure as they discuss the events of the child's first day.

You Ought To Be In Pictures

Give each of your students an ongoing opportunity to be the center of attention by exhibiting photographs of the children's choice. Caption a bulletin board "Say Cheese!" Then have students paint cardboard frames, cut to fit the most common size of prints that you get. Encourage students to bring photos from home, or select classroom-made pictures to frame. Whenever a student is ready to fill his frame or change the picture, offer him assistance. Tape the picture to the back of the opening and have the student attach the picture to the board. As pictures are removed from the board, ask the students' permission to add them to a class photo album. Allow each student to take the photo album home from time to time.

Book Bear

Students can take special pride in books they bring to school to share. Make some book bears to help students remember to bring books from home or a library. Use a permanent marker to write a student's name and "Bring a book" on a strip of poster board. Glue a cute bear-face cutout to the strip. Encourage each child who's given a book bear to have his bear help him find a good book to read. Whenever a book bear shows up with a book, take some time to discuss or read the book.

Good-bye Song

End your day with this cheerful call-and-response tune that also helps emphasize the order of the days of the week.

Good-Bye Song
(sung to the tune of "Are You Sleeping?")

Teacher: Good-bye, children.
Children: Good-bye, teacher.
Teacher: I'll see you soon.
Children: We'll see you soon.
Teacher: See you next on [name of next school day].
Children: See you next on [name of next school day].
Teacher: We'll work and play.
Children: We'll work and play.

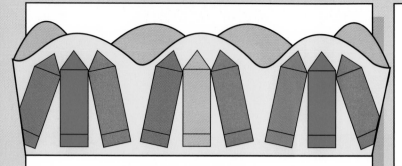

Crowns

Treat your preschoolers like royalty. Use a bulletin-board border to make a crown for each child. As you send him out the door wearing his crown, each youngster will stand a little taller.

Beautiful Bathroom

If your classroom bathroom is nothing to brag about, consider drafting the assistance of parent volunteers to turn it into a dream bath. After obtaining the necessary permission, ask parents to plan a scene for the bathroom walls; then work together to paint the room and add embellishments. Holographic or glow-in-the-dark cutouts, such as stars, may be used to give the bath a truly unique aura. Soon your little ones will be looking forward to the adventure of going to the bathroom.

Sonia M. Sims—Pre-K/Even Start
Parent & Child Co-op, Engelwood Elementary School
Orlando, FL

Furry Pals

During the first few days of preschool, encourage each youngster to bring a stuffed animal to school daily and mention that you will be bringing a cuddly friend of your own. Arrange to have a colleague assist you at the end of the week during your culminating activity. Each day for a week, bring a different stuffed animal to school and set aside time to discuss with your students all the furry pals in attendance. At the end of the week when it's time to talk about stuffed animals, explain that yours are missing! Take your students with you as you search for your furry pals in and around your school building. Along the way, stop to introduce your students to the people you meet and talk about the jobs they do at the school. Explain to each person along the way that you are looking for your furry pals. When your search brings you back to your own classroom, students will be delighted with what they will see—all five of your stuffed animals on a blanket, having a honey-and-biscuit picnic. Whisper in one of the furry animals' ears to get permission for you and your preschoolers to join the picnic.

Family Pennants

Three cheers for our families! Give each child a pennant-shaped piece of construction paper to decorate at home. Along with the pennant, send a note asking the child's parents to help convert the pennant into a work of art that represents their family. In the note, suggest that the pennant might be decorated with things such as family photos or the handprints of family members. Prominently display each of the pennants when it is returned to school. Soon lots of little ones will be crowded around. There's my family's pennant!

Beth Lemke, Heights Head Start, Coon Rapids, MN

Pam Crane

"MEOW, MEOW, MEOW!"

Encourage creativity and imagination with an integrated feline unit, and your students will soon be up to their whiskers in lively learning experiences. There will be cats cavorting in your block area, pawprints leading to your writing center, and "purr-fectly" delightful learning experiences *everywhere* in between.

The Cat's Out Of The Bag

Bring a kitty-cat gift bag to circle time to pique your little ones' curiosity about cats. Prior to circle time each day during your cat unit, place something associated with cats in a gift bag decorated with cat designs. For example, one day you might put a copy of *The Three Little Kittens* in the bag along with some mittens. On another day, you might fill the bag with a fiddle and other props for role-playing "Hey, Diddle, Diddle." Another day, you could place in the bag an announcement that explains that an animal-care professional will be bringing a cat to your classroom. Once you've established a pattern for the use of your kitty-cat bag at circle time, just producing the bag will create anticipation among your little ones.

Lisa Morrell Kohley, Liberal, MO

My cat's name is Tabby. She's the best cat in the whole wide world!

"Purr-fect" Excuses For Writing

Your writing center can be the cat's meow! Provide paper, stamp pads, and cat or pawprint rubber stamps for students to use to create their own stationery. (If you don't have commercially made stamps that are appropriate for this, make a pawprint potato printer and have children use it with tempera paint to decorate their stationery.) Include pencils with cat designs or cat-related pencil toppers. Set the tone for the center by adding a few stuffed toy cats and embellishing the tabletop and floor around the writing area with pawprint designs. Include pictures of your students' favorite cats on a bulletin board located at the center.

Encourage students to visit the center both to design stationery for general use and to "write" (or dictate) pertinent cat-related tidbits on pieces of the stationery as your cat theme continues.

Lisa Morrell Kohley, Liberal, MO

Kittens And Their Mittens

For "purr-fect" fun, have your students sing and dramatize the story of *The Three Little Kittens.* In advance, cut out two paper mittens for each child and consider purchasing a pie for the conclusion of this activity. Connect each pair of mittens with yarn and hide the pairs around the room. Tie a string between two chairs to serve as a clothesline for hanging the mittens later. To transform yourself into the mother cat, use face paint to paint your nose; then draw whiskers on your cheeks with eyeliner. Offer to similarly transform your students into kittens. Then read aloud and/or sing the story of *The Three Little Kittens.* Sing the story as each youngster searches for a pair of the hidden mittens to become his own. Label each pair of mittens with its owner's name; then, as the song continues, have each child "wash" his mittens and hang them on the clothesline "to dry." As you sing the final part of this song, produce a pie for your little kittens to sample.

Sara Bostelmann—Music for Preschool
Messiah Lambs
Richardson, TX

Meow, Meow

A feline variation of "Doggie, Doggie. Who Has The Bone?" will come as quite a delight during your cat unit. Instead of a bone, place a yarn ball behind a chair that is situated in front of and turned away from seated students. Designate one child to be the first kitten, and have him sit in the chair, facing away from his classmates and covering his eyes. Choose one student to silently approach the chair, take the yarn ball back to his place, and put it where it cannot be seen. When he is ready, have him chant with his classmates, "Meow, meow. Who has the ball?" On this signal the youngster in the chair can turn around and guess which of his classmates has the ball. Whether or not he guesses correctly, have the holder of the yarn ball sit in the chair for the next round of play.

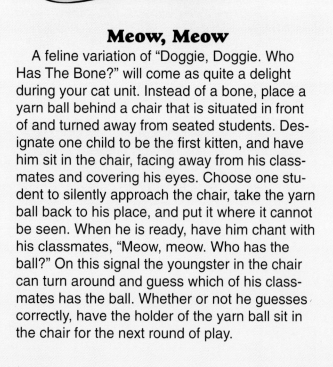

Cats Come In All Sizes And Shapes

Introduce your youngsters to some relatives of the ordinary house cat. One good way to do this is to start by reading aloud *Have You Seen My Cat?* by Eric Carle. Afterwards ask the students to study the illustrations of each cat in the book to decide whether it would make a good house pet. Encourage students to explain how they came to their conclusions. Talk about the fact that some cats, like house cats, are tame and that some are wild. Ask the students to contribute magazine pictures for a collage of wild cats and another of tame cats.

"Paws" For Poetry

Set aside bits of time during your study of cats to read aloud some related poetry. To establish the atmosphere for your poetry sessions, cut Con-Tact® covering into the shapes of pawprints. Arrange a trail of Con-Tact® pawprints so that they lead to, around, and onto a table. Place a stuffed toy cat or puppet at the end of the trail. Display one or more books containing cat poetry on the table. *Cats Sleep Anywhere* by Eleanor Farjeon (HarperCollins Children's Books) and *Cats Are Cats* compiled by Nancy Larrick (Putnam Publishing Group) are good books to feature. Whenever there's time to read a cat poem or two, start tiptoeing toward the table, softly saying, "Meow, meow." Encourage your little ones to join you at the table, meowing softly as they do. If you have a cat puppet, manipulate it so that the puppet appears to be reading the poetry. Once children become familiar with this gathering routine, they'll be excited to hear the meowing begin.

Cat Tales

On a crowded display shelf, cat books may be hard for your youngsters to find. But with a little fur, you can make sure youngsters can readily locate cat books. Begin by machine-stitching a strip of imitation fur into a tube that resembles a cat's tail. To one end of the tail, stitch a loop of elastic that fits nicely over one of the cat books in your collection. Make several of these cat tails. Then slip each tail into a book and each book onto the shelf. Since the cat tails will dangle from the shelf, your students will have no problem locating books that have cats in them.

They're slimy. They writhe and wiggle. They're short and fat one minute and long and skinny the next. Bring a few earthworms into your preschool classroom, and they're bound to generate grins, grimaces, giggles, and genuine curiosity. Use the ideas on pages 14–19 to introduce your little nature lovers to the underground gardeners that tend the soil and tend to go unnoticed.

by Marie E. Cecchini

Worm World

If you really want preschoolers to learn about worms, you're going to need to have some of the squirmy critters in the classroom. Have students help you create a worm habitat in an aquarium or large glass jar. Fill the container with alternate layers of damp soil and sand. Place three to six worms in your jar—depending on the size of the environment. Add some dead leaves to cover the surface of the soil, and cover the top of the container with perforated plastic. Cover the sides of the aquarium or jar with black paper.

When a week has passed, remove the black paper. Place your worm habitat on a low table along with magnifying glasses. How has the worm habitat changed? What can students learn about worms by looking at the jar?

Once your study of earthworms is winding down, be sure to release your worms where they can survive. A school flower bed may be a good choice. So long, friends!

Rain, Rain, Go Away!

People are probably not the only ones who sometimes wish for the rain to go away. In fact, if worms could talk, they might have an interesting perspective on the inconvenience of rain. Because they do not have lungs or gills, worms breathe through their moist skin. When rain floods worm tunnels, there is no air for them to breathe. When it rains, many worms come to the surface for air.

On a rainy day, take your youngsters outdoors in search of waterlogged worms. If the weather clears that same day, revisit the locations of any worms you saw. What do your youngsters believe happened to the worms? If the weather won't cooperate with you, use a worm habitat like the one described in "Worm World." Sprinkle or pour water into the container, and have students observe what happens.

Squish!

Read the poem "Mud" to your youngsters, adding lots of expression and acting out the words. Have some adult volunteers tape a vinyl tablecloth to the floor, slather it with brown finger paint, and supervise as your students take turns traipsing barefoot around in the paint as though it were mud. Encourage the adults to hold youngsters' hands until the little ones are surefooted in the paint. Also mention that youngsters can sit in chairs placed along the tablecloth's edge and create muddy-looking designs with their feet and toes. If having a few preschoolers ankle deep in finger paint is not your idea of fun, have your students finger-paint the tablecloth instead. Whether between the toes or between the fingers, the squish of imitation mud is a sensory experience that's sure to stimulate all kinds of expressive language!

When the tablecloth has dried, attach it to a bulletin board as a muddy-looking backdrop for the worm creations described in " 'Smoosh' Worms."

Mud

Sometimes after it rains,
If we go outside,
We can watch the worms,
As they slip and slide.

Wigglers dawdle in mud,
Squirming in and out.
Let's take off our shoes
To see what it's about.

First we'll tiptoe gently
Joining worms at play.
Slip, slide, squirm, and glide.
Let's stay here all day!

—by Marie E. Cecchini

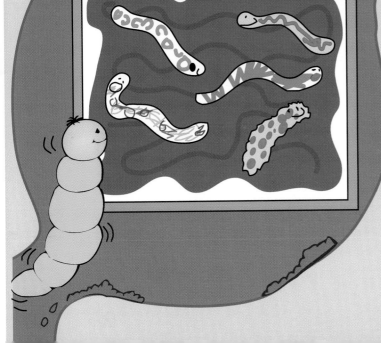

"Smoosh" Worms

If you prepared the muddy bulletin-board background described in "Squish!", you're going to need some worms to "wiggle" in the mud, the muck, and the mire! Set up an art station that contains scissors; panels cut from brown grocery bags; several different colors of thick, bright tempera paints in pots; cotton swabs; and large sheets of art paper. Encourage each child to visit the art station to create a worm for your muddy-looking bulletin board. To make a worm, have each child cut or tear a large worm shape from the brown grocery-bag paper. Then have him use the cotton swabs and the paint to decorate his worm cutout. While the paint is still wet, encourage him to press the worm painted-side-down onto a sheet of art paper to make a print. Then help him peel the worm off the paper and attach it to the bulletin board. The printed worm design may be taken home or cut out and added to the board as well.

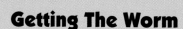

Worms In A Circle, Worms In A Row

You're going to want a large bucket of brightly colored worms for these manipulative activities. Purchase heavy gift-wrap yarn in four colors: red, yellow, blue, and green. Cut all but one yard of each color of yarn into five-inch lengths for imitation worms. Store the worms and the remaining yarn in a bucket until you're ready to use them. For a color-matching activity, use a yard-long length of yarn to make a large circle on a flannelboard. Then have children take worms from the bucket that match the color of the circle and place them within the circle. Continue play by substituting another color of circle on the flannelboard.

For patterning practice, have students establish and repeat a worm pattern on the flannelboard.

Getting The Worm

Few of us would probably think worms look very appetizing. However, it's a fact that they are included in the diets of moles, shrews, birds, snakes, frogs, toads, and salamanders. Find out how many of your youngsters have seen a bird with a beak full of worm. To simulate worms for this activity, cut heavy yarn into five-inch lengths and store them along with three spring-type clothespins in a resealable plastic bag. Glue shredded newspaper or brown, paper grocery bags in and around a shallow box to make a bird's nest. Place a toy baby bird inside the nest. To use this activity, have a child scatter the yarn lengths near the nest. Then have him use a clothespin to pick up the imitation worms one by one and place them in the nest. Afterward have him count how many worms he fed to the baby bird.

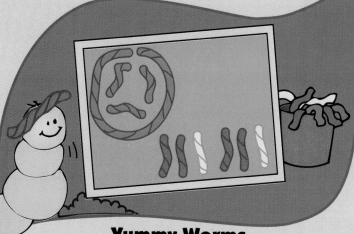

Yummy Worms

Squeaky-clean little hands get a fine-motor workout while creating these tasty worms. To make a peanut-butter dough, mix two cups of dry powdered milk, two cups of creamy peanut butter, and one-half cup of honey in a mixing bowl. When the dough has reached a smooth consistency, give each child a small ball to transform into a worm. Yum! Maybe birds have the right idea after all.

Wiggle Worm

Youngsters will very quickly observe that the way a worm moves is by wiggling. Tie one end of a length of rope to a table leg to simulate a worm. Gently move the free end of the rope so that it looks like a giant worm writhing on the floor. Invite each student to walk, crawl, or jump over the wiggling worm. Step with care! Don't squish the worm!

Wormy Books

No worm unit would be complete without some top-notch reading material to go along with it. If you're interested in reading aloud to your students, look for *Wonderful Worms* by Linda Glaser (The Millbrook Press). Sparse text and simple—but thought-provoking—illustrations make this book a perfect choice for preschool. There's an added bonus: light, factual information about worms is listed at the back of *Wonderful Worms.* If you're looking for a book that contains photos of earthworms, check out *Keeping Minibeasts: Earthworms* by Chris Henwood (Franklin Watts). It's filled with photographs and balanced with just the right amount of text to stimulate discussions. Top off your earthworm book collection by asking your librarian for these worm-related books: *Earthworm* by Andrienne Soutter-Perrot (American Education Publishing), *Squirmy Wormy Composters* by Bobbie Kalman & Janine Schaub (Crabtree Publishing Company), and *Earthworms: Underground Farmers* by Patricia Lauber (Henry Holt And Company, Inc.).

If you locate a copy of *National Worm Day* by James Stevenson (Greenwillow Books)—and dare to read aloud its first brief story of the same name— there's something you should know. You'll probably have to sing the worm national anthem and participate in a worm parade. But, hey! If you're up to it, locate *National Worm Day!*

Worms Invade The Writing Center

Fill a small bucket with an assortment of plastic fishing worms that have been washed and dried. Place the bucket of worms in an area stocked with cards bearing large manuscript letters, paper, and pencils. Encourage students to visit the center and use the worms to form letters, numerals, or words. Mention that paper and pencils are available for copying the formations, if desired.

On another day, provide a shallow pan of paint. When youngsters visit the center, suggest that they press a worm into the paint and use the worm to make a print on a sheet of paper. As students continue to add worm prints to their papers, they may observe interesting visual patterns or similarities to letter or numeral shapes.

Gayle Owens • Early Childhood Special Education
Johnson Elementary • Southlake, TX

The Long And Short Of It

No matter which materials you choose for these worms, your youngsters are going to be anxious to see how they measure up. Cut worms of noticeably varying lengths from brown paper-bag panels, rickrack, ribbon, felt, or vinyl. Decorate the worms as desired and store them in a bucket. On your classroom floor or a table-top, attach pieces of colored tape equal in length to each worm. If you have some wooden, self-standing flowers (or something similar), stand a few of them near the pieces of tape. To use this activity, have a child remove each worm from the bucket and place it on the piece of tape of equal length. For an additional challenge, ask the child to sequence the worms from shortest to longest.

Getting Out The Word About Worms

With all this wormy activity going on at school, parents are likely to want to get in on the action. To bring parents up to speed on the wormy goings-on at school, cut flattened, brown paper bags (or brown bulletin-board paper) into curvy strips. Trim to round the ends of the strips so that they resemble large earthworms. Using markers, add a smile design to one end of each strip. Then program each paper worm with interesting information about worms and a suggested activity (such as reading a book about worms) for a parent and child to complete together. Accordion-fold each paper worm so that it will peek out of a selected earthworm book. (See "Wormy Books" on page 17.) Send the worm-embellished book home with each student in turn. Who would have thought earthworms could strengthen the bonds between school and home?

Preschool has gone to the worms! We've been watching worms, wiggling like worms, and even eating worms (the Gummy kind)! When you stop to think about it, worms are very fascinating!

Did you know that... —one kind of earthworm in Australia can grow up to nine feet long?

—their tunneling, eating habits, waste elimination, make it easier lants to grow soil?

—worms don't have any eyes, but special cells in their skin sense light?

Read this worm book with your preschooler. Or talk about the pictures.

Soon you'll be a worm watcher too!

Mrs. Tussey

wiggle

squiggle

wiggle

Worms

Tunneling

What do earthworms do best? Tunnel, of course. If your youngsters had an opportunity to observe real earthworm tunnels (see "Worm World" on page 14), they'll be especially eager to do some tunneling of their own. To prepare for this activity, mix equal portions of Ivory Snow® and water in the bowl of a self-standing mixer. Add a small amount of brown tempera paint to the bowl. More paint can be added later, if a rich, dirtlike color isn't achieved at first. Whip until the soap forms stiff peaks. Make several large batches of whipped brown soap. Dump the soap onto a tabletop. Have students don their painting smocks, spread the soap out on the table, and use their fingers to make tunnels or pathways in it. Keep prints of the tunnels that your students create, if desired. To make individual prints, press art paper onto the area decorated by a particular child; then lift the paper to reveal the print. To make one giant print that shows the work of several students, press a length of bulletin-board paper onto the surface of the whipped soap; then peel the paper off the soap to reveal the print. Once the soap has completely dried on the paper, invite youngsters to glue rickrack worms onto the prints.

Walk The Walk

Our movement section, "Head, Shoulders, Knees, & Toes," contains a neat wiggle-worm walk. See page 132 for all the details.

19

Pumpkins, Squash, & Gourds

A bale of straw; some produce baskets; and a few dozen pumpkins, squash, and gourds can transform a corner of your preschool classroom into a bustling ever-changing farmers' market.

ideas contributed by Audrey Englehardt and Ruth Stanfill

Getting The Goods

Dig into this theme by starting out in a farmer's pumpkin, squash, or gourd patch. Encourage youngsters (with the farmer's permission, of course) to run their hands along the vines that nurtured their favorite vegetables and analyze the withered leaves that once shaded the immature vegetables. Have students examine and compare twisted lengths of vines. Best of all have them pull a few dozen pumpkins, squash, and/or gourds from the vines to bring back to their classroom.

Down On The Classroom Farm

Once you've returned from your trip to the farm (or otherwise collected a few baskets of pumpkins, squash, and gourds), help your youngsters set up a farmers' market in one corner of the classroom. To add to the market atmosphere, heap the produce in a wheelbarrow and place a bale or two of straw nearby. Label three produce baskets "pumpkins," "squash," and "gourds" respectively; then on each basket attach a picture of the corresponding vegetable. Place the baskets near the produce.

Discuss with students the fact that pumpkins, squash, and gourds are all in the same vegetable family. Explain that just as people in a human family have some characteristics that are similar and some that are different, the vegetables in your classroom market are alike in some ways and different in other ways. If desired, cut open one vegetable of each variety so that students can examine the interiors. After studying the vegetables using their senses of sight, smell, hearing, and touch, guide students in naming several similarities and several differences. Then give youngsters opportunities to sort the contents of the wheelbarrow into the three baskets by vegetable type.

Taking Produce Seriously

Invite your youngsters to man the farmers' market. Encourage volunteer produce peddlers to sort the vegetables into separate piles or baskets by type. Then ask them to line up each type of vegetable on a tabletop from largest to smallest. On another day ask students to line up each type of vegetable on a tabletop from lightest to darkest in color.

A Time To Weigh

Marketing such fine produce can be a weighty matter. Place a set of balance scales in your classroom farmers' market. Give students opportunities to explore the way that the balance scale works. Lead the discussion so that the children discover that the heavier tray of the scale will descend. Then encourage children to visit the center and select pairs of vegetables to compare. Before a child places a vegetable in each side of the balance scale, ask which of the two vegetables he believes will weigh the most. Then have him use the scales to determine which of the two selected  vegetables are actually heavier. Were the results what he expected, or was he surprised? Encourage lots of comparative exploration with the vegetables and the scale.

As students become increasingly comfortable in using the balance scale, have them use it to help answer more complex questions. For example, if one small pumpkin is placed on one side of the scale, how many squash would it take to weigh about the same as the pumpkin? Discuss the fact that when the trays of the scale are at even heights, the trays are holding similar weights.

Great Girth Estimates

What can your students do with string and the largest pumpkin in your collection? Practice estimating skills, of course! Attach three pieces of double-sided tape to a wall near the pumpkin. Label the tape sections "too short," "just right," and "too long." Cut a string length equal to the circumference of your pumpkin. Attach this string to the tape labeled "just right." Have each student cut a length of string to approximate the girth of the pumpkin. Then have him wrap his string around the pumpkin to see how close he was to the actual measurement. Is his string too short, just right, or too long? Have him attach his string to the tape in the appropriate category.

Zucchini
The Great Green Squash

Even those youngsters who think they don't like squash will be easily won over by these muffins. Have students help you in cleaning and shredding the zucchini, as well as in measuring and mixing the remaining ingredients.

Zucchini Muffins

2 cups shredded zucchini
3 eggs
2 cups sugar
3 cups flour
3 teaspoons salt

1/2 teaspoon baking powder
1 teaspoon baking soda
3 teaspoons cinnamon
1 cup oil

Combine the ingredients and beat well. Pour into greased muffin tins or cups. Bake at 375° for approximately 45 minutes, checking for doneness frequently. Makes 24 muffins.

Harvesttime Centerpieces

Pumpkins, gourds, and squash make beautiful centerpieces. With a nail poke several holes in a small pumpkin, squash, or gourd for each student. Allow each youngster to select the vegetable he would like to use to create a centerpiece. Have students collect greenery, leaves, and other natural items, then insert the selected items into the holes.

Getting A Feel For Vegetables

Challenge a small group of children with this fun guessing game. Place a few small pumpkins, gourds, and squash with significantly different shapes and textures in front of a small group of students. Blindfold a volunteer from the group; then pass her one of the vegetables. After giving her an opportunity to thoroughly investigate the vegetable using only her sense of touch, replace the vegetable in its original spot in your collection of vegetables. Then remove the volunteer's blindfold and ask her to identify the pumpkin, gourd, or squash that she examined with her sense of touch. When she identifies the vegetable that she felt, find out how she knows. Then ask for another volunteer to play the game.

Vine Times

On a blacktop or concrete playground surface, use sidewalk chalk to draw a simple network of imitation pumpkin, squash, or gourd vines. Draw a few leaves on the vines. Randomly position three children on the vine design. Ask them to walk heel-to-toe without getting off of the vine. When youngsters arrive at intersections simultaneously, encourage them to cooperate to get around one another without getting off the vine. After each student has had his turn walking on the vine, ask him to use chalk to draw a pumpkin, a squash, or a gourd growing on the vine.

Surprisingly Delicious

Rarely do youngsters get opportunities to sample pumpkin that hasn't been baked into a pie. So this recipe, which uses a pumpkin as an edible baking dish, will be quite an unusual treat!

Pumpkin-Apple Bake

1 small pumpkin
   suitable for baking
chopped apples
raisins

cranberries (optional)
sugar
cinnamon
butter

Preheat oven to 350°. Cut off the top of the pumpkin and scoop out the seeds. Mix chopped apples, raisins, cranberries, sugar, and cinnamon. Pour the mixture into the pumpkin and dot it with butter. Replace the top of the pumpkin. Bake it on a cookie sheet for one hour and 15 minutes to one hour and 30 minutes.

When the pumpkin has sufficiently cooled, scoop out some pumpkin with each serving of apple mixture. Although the pumpkin will darken slightly as it bakes, it will look great as a centerpiece surrounded by smaller pumpkins, squash, gourds, and brightly colored leaves.

Books That Really Grow On Kids

Finding books with just the right amount of text for preschoolers isn't always easy. Both Jeanne Titherington's *Pumpkin Pumpkin* (Greenwillow Books) and Zoe Hall's *It's Pumpkin Time!* (The Blue Sky Press) would complement this pumpkin, squash, and gourd unit. See pages 254 and 255 for a bumper crop of good ideas to use with *Pumpkin Pumpkin*.

Pizza Pizzazz!

Looking for a hot topic your youngsters can really sink their teeth into? Bring out the checkered tablecloths and slice into this spicy topic during October, National Pizza Month. *ideas by Lucia Kemp Henry*

Accept No Substitutes

Since there are no substitutes for actual hands-on experiences, contact a local pizza parlor and ask if they conduct field trips for preschoolers. Explain that it would be good for youngsters to see pizzas being made and/or to have an opportunity to make a pizza. Follow up a pizza-parlor field trip by mailing a student-autographed, pizza-shaped note of thanks to your field-trip guides.

Come Into The Kitchen

What fun it must be to toss a crust into the air, slop the sauce onto the crust, and sprinkle on handfuls of toppings! Set up this pizzeria kitchen center, so that each youngster will have an opportunity to put himself in the role of a pizza chef. Stock the center with appropriate props, such as aprons, chef hats, and photo-illustrated pizza menus. At the kitchen center, place utensils usually associated with pizza-making, such as varying sizes of pizza pans and rolling pins. Cut several imitation pizza crusts and corresponding sauce circles from felt to fit your pans. Use the patterns from page 29 to trace and cut toppings from appropriate colors of felt, other fabrics, or wallpaper samples. Cut felt into short, narrow strips to resemble shredded cheese. Label a container for each topping and place the corresponding cutouts inside.

Once the center is operational, a student dons an apron, rolls out and tosses the crust for his pizza, spreads the sauce onto the crust, and sprinkles on the toppings of his choice. Photograph each chef with his culinary masterpiece, before asking the student to sort his toppings into their original containers. When each student has been photographed with his pizza, attach the photos to a bulletin board to resemble a giant menu (like the one at the right). Near each photo write a student-dictated description of the pictured pizza.

Luigi's Menu

Pepperoni by Jacob

Jacob's pizza sauce is made from a secret family recipe. The pepperoni is good too.

Supreme by Jackie

Jackie's pizza is made with a thin, crunchy crust. It's loaded with peppers, pepperoni, and pineapple.

Cheese by Ryan

Ryan says his pizza is the best. It has lots and lots and lots of cheese.

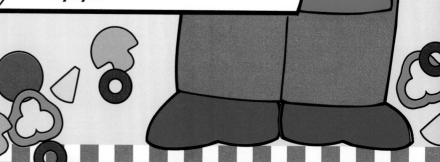

This pizza is spicy and hot because Sue likes it that way!

Culinary Masterpieces To Go

Concocting a pizza is so much fun, you may want to give students more than one opportunity to try it. At the center described in "Come Into The Kitchen" on page 24, replace the felt cutouts with paper ones and provide glue. Also include scissors and additional paper so that students can create their own toppings if they wish. Then give each student an opportunity to create a culinary masterpiece that he can take home. Since take-out pizzas are best transported in boxes, provide a piece of folded bulletin-board paper to serve as a pizza box for each student. When a student's pizza is ready for transport, slip it inside the folded paper. As the student dictates, write something about his pizza on the outside of the folded paper. "Guess what? The pizza dude is here!"

Pizza-Pie Chant

Here's a rhythmic movement activity that's not only good enough to sink your teeth into; you can also sink your whole body into it. Write the "Pizza Chant" in large letters on chart paper. Embellish the margins with colorful pizza stickers or sketches of pizza toppings. As your youngsters chorally say the first verse of the "Pizza Chant," have them clap to the beat. Once youngsters have mastered the combination of chanting and clapping, have them march in place and later march in a circle as they chant.

As youngsters move to the beat of this chant, begin to vary the wording to heighten their interest. Modify the second verse of the chant to indicate each student's topping preference.

Pizza Chant

Piz-za, piz-za. Let's have piz-za!
Let's have piz-za with cheese on top!

Piz-za, piz-za. Let's have piz-za!
[Student's name] wants piz-za with [child's favorite topping] on top!

Pizza-Box Puzzles

To get your pizza theme off to a zesty start, make several construction-paper pizzas to fit inside small pizza boxes. Using construction-paper copies of the patterns on page 29, decorate each paper pizza with a different construction-paper topping, such as pepperoni, mushrooms, black olives, pineapple tidbits, cheese, or green peppers. Laminate each pizza and cut it into several pieces to make a puzzle; then place the pieces inside a pizza box. Divide your students into small groups and give each group one of these pizza boxes. Encourage each group of students to assemble its pizza puzzle. When each group has completed its puzzle, have the students tell what toppings are on their pizzas. Then discuss your youngsters' favorite toppings. Make a bar or pie graph, if desired, to indicate your youngsters' topping preferences.

Peppy Pizza
855-0123

Strike Up The Band

Teach your youngsters the lyrics to this pizza tune. Then give each student an opportunity to take part in one of the world's most unusual bands. Provide youngsters with pizza-making utensils such as wooden spoons, pizza pans, rolling pins, measuring cups, and mixing bowls. Discuss with your youngsters the typical uses for the items. Encourage creative discussions about different ways that these utensils can be used to produce music. After giving the band an opportunity to warm up, have students sing "The Pizza Song" and accompany themselves with their highly unusual rhythm instruments. It's a "lotta" fun!

The Pizza Song

(sung to the tune of "Twinkle, Twinkle, Little Star")

Pizza, pizza. It's a treat.
Pizza pie is fun to eat!
Ooey-gooey cheese so yummy.
Crunchy crust goes in my tummy.
Pizza, pizza. It's a treat.
Pizza pie is fun to eat!

Poetic Pizza-Making

If you're going to make pizza from scratch, consider sharing this poem with your youngsters to introduce the basic steps of pizza-making.

Now We're Cookin'

Flour and water in a bowl.
Mix, mix, mix, and roll, roll, roll.
Roll the dough as flat as you can.
Put the dough in a pizza pan.
Spread the sauce; sprinkle with cheese.
Add some toppings, as you please.
Bake the pie until it's done.
Eat the pizza. Oh, what fun!
—*Lucia Kemp Henry*

Easy Minipizzas

If you're not quite up for making pizza from scratch, you'll love these quick-and-easy minipizzas. Encourage students to take turns grating mozzarella cheese and slicing some easy-to-slice pizza toppings. Have each student spoon a small amount of pizza sauce onto a bagel- or muffin-half and spread the sauce to the edges. Then have him add cheese and the toppings of his choice. Place several minipizzas on a baking sheet and broil them until the cheese melts. Cut each minipizza in half. When the pizzas are cool enough to eat, serve them to students. As students are enjoying their pizzas, discuss the meanings of *half* and *whole*.

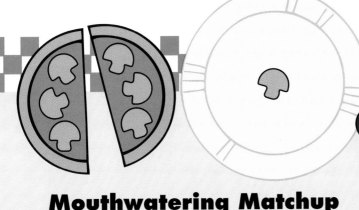

Mouthwatering Matchup

Duplicate and cut out copies of the patterns on pages 28 and 29. Assemble pairs of pizza halves, so that each pair features a different topping. Glue the pieces in place. For each set of pizza halves, glue a cutout of the featured topping to the middle of a paper plate. Place the pizza halves and the paper plates inside a clean pizza box, and place the box in a center. To use the center, a student finds two halves to match the topping on each plate; then he puts the matching halves in each plate.

Seriously Silly

This student-made book gets sillier with every slice. Begin by cutting finger-paint paper into large circular shapes. Have each student finger-paint his circle to resemble sauce-covered dough. While these papers are drying, ask your youngsters to dictate a list of toppings that are found on real pizzas. Then ask them to think of things that could be put on *make-believe* pizzas. Provide a wide range of duplicate pictures cut from flower, garden, or seed catalogs. Have each child select multiple pictures of the same kind of object for a silly make-believe pizza; then have him attach the pictures to his finger-painted circle. Attach each student's pizza to a different sheet of art paper. As the student dictates, write something on the art paper about the pizza that he has created. Bind these student-prepared pages between covers, before titling the booklet and decorating the front cover appropriately.

World's Best Pizza

Spirit your students away to the home of the world's best pizza. Read aloud Karen Barbour's *Little Nino's Pizzeria* (Harcourt Brace Jovanovich, Publishers). Discuss with the students what made Little Nino's Pizzeria and Little Tony's Pizzeria special. Talk in detail about what the world's best pizza would taste like. Discuss the crust, the sauce, the spices, and the toppings. Then ask each student to take a turn role-playing with you. Videotape the interviews if possible. Holding a microphone and playing the part of a television reporter, interview each child as though he has just come out of Little Nino's Pizzeria or Little Tony's Pizzeria. Introduce yourself and your network, and ask him to describe for your viewers what the world's best pizza tastes like. Lead the interviews so that each child has an opportunity to give a vivid description of the pizza to top all pizzas. Later send the video home for each child's parents in turn to enjoy; or invite parents to see a showing of the video before or after school.

Silly Pizza Pies

Jessica put flowers on a pizza!

Pam Crane

Pizza-Half Patterns
Use with "Mouthwatering Matchup" on page 27.

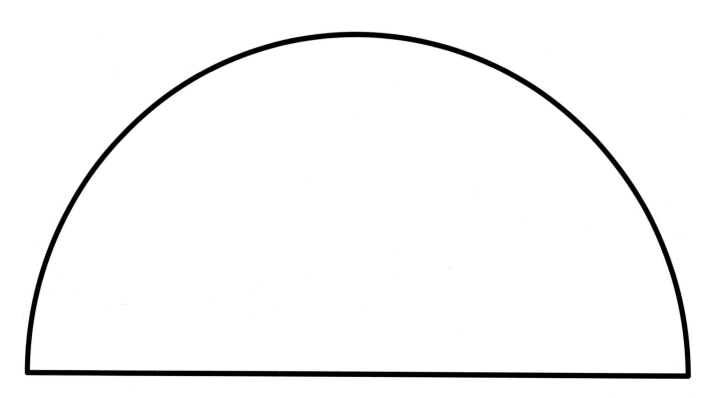

pizza crust

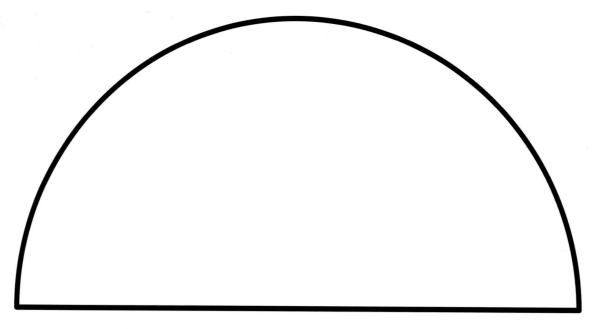

pizza sauce

Pizza Topping Patterns

Use with "Come Into The Kitchen" on page 24, "Culinary Masterpieces To Go" and "Pizza-Box Puzzles" on page 25, and "Mouthwatering Matchup" on page 27.

pepperoni

mushrooms

green pepper

olives

pineapple

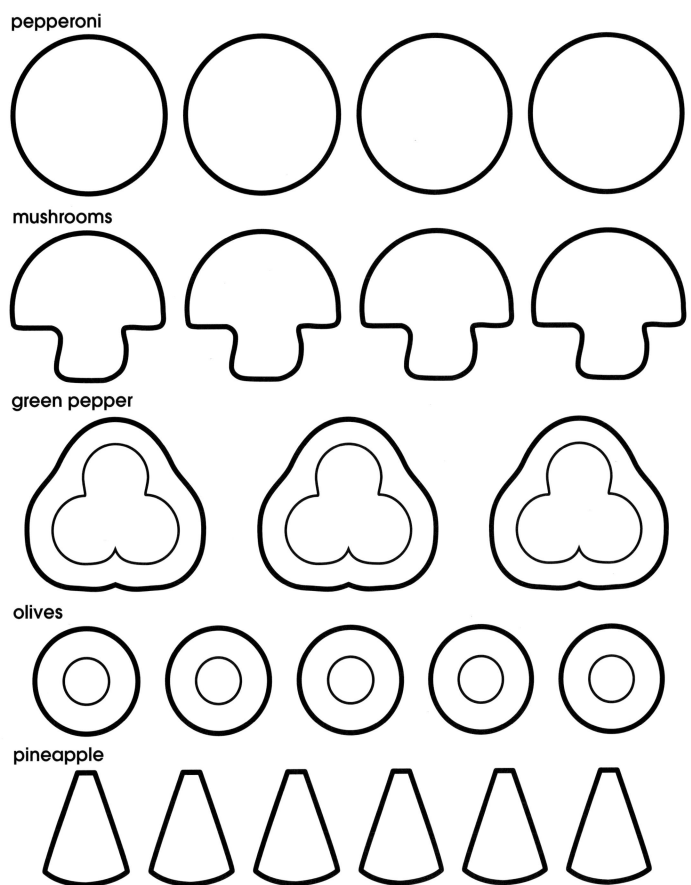

Note To Teacher: Cut small white paper or felt to resemble grated cheese.

DRESSED FOR SUCCESS

Zip-a-dee-doo-dah, Zip-a-dee-ay! These activities and tips for teaching self-help skills will save the day!

The Bunny-Ear Method

Share this story as you teach your youngsters how to tie.

Once there was a rabbit who was very sad because his ears were so long and narrow that he stepped on them all the time. One day a fairy landed on the bunny's head. She lifted up the bunny's ears and crossed them over. Then she put one end through the bottom of the X and pulled. Next she made each long ear into a loop and made another X like before and pulled. From then on the bunny remembered how to tie his ears into a bow, and he lived happily ever after.

All Tied Up!

Are you all tied up trying to keep your little ones' shoes tied? Try this colorful technique. Duplicate a class supply of the shoe pattern on page 32 onto tagboard. Cut out each shoe shape; then punch holes in the cutouts. Lace each cutout with a length of variegated yarn. Refer to the different colors on the yarn as you explain and demonstrate how to tie the shoelaces using the bunny-ear method (see "The Bunny-Ear Method"). Youngsters will learn to tie quickly with this visual help.

Linda Shute—Four-Year-Olds
Grace Day Care
Lafayette, IN

The Right Foot

Do your youngsters have trouble putting their shoes on the correct feet? Here is a helpful hint to get them off on the right foot! Using Super Glue™, glue a small piece of vinyl cloth tape to the inside sole of each shoe or boot as shown. Students will soon learn that when the two pieces of tape are together, the shoes are on the right feet. Your students will take great pride in doing this important task independently!

Tie Me Up

These shoes are always fit to be tied! Hot-glue an old pair of shoes to a board; then lace the shoes with brightly colored shoestrings. Place the board in a center so that children can practice their tying skills. Encourage two children to use the shoes cooperatively by asking one child to demonstrate how to tie as the second child copies his actions. When a child has learned to tie the shoes, write his name on the board with a marker.

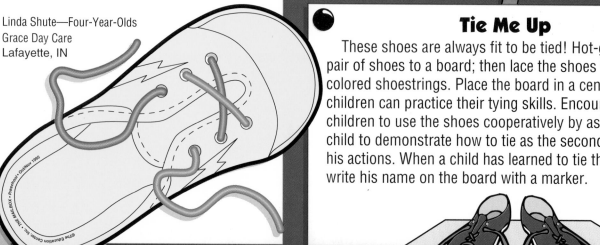

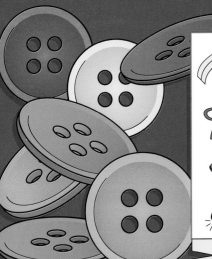

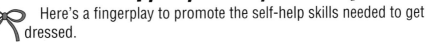

Zip, Tie, Button, And Snap

Here's a fingerplay to promote the self-help skills needed to get dressed.

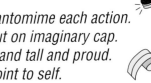

Zip, tie, button, and snap.
Last of all put on my cap.
You can be so proud of me.
I can dress myself, you see.

Pantomime each action.
Put on imaginary cap.
Stand tall and proud.
Point to self.

Dressed To Impress

Let imaginations soar with this fun dress-up center. Fill a chest or box with typical and novelty items of clothing. For example, you might include a shirt with buttons, a shirt with snaps, and a jacket with a zipper, as well as gloves, dressy scarves, and various types of hats. As each child visits the center, encourage him to dress to impress. Then, using a Polaroid® camera, take a picture of each child. Ask the child to dictate whom he is pretending to be or what he could imagine doing in his new attire. Display the photo along with the dictation in the center. Very impressive!

I am a builder. I will build a house.
Jeremy

Lace It Up!

Students will put their best feet forward when using this center that exercises fine-motor skills. Stock the center with shoes, boots, sneakers, and shoelaces of various colors and designs. To use this center, a child chooses a shoelace and uses it to lace a shoe, boot, or sneaker. He can then tie the shoe if desired.

Lacing Shapes

Give students additional fine-motor practice with these inexpensive lacing shapes. To make the lacing shapes, cut shapes from solid-colored plastic placemats. Using a hole puncher, punch holes around the perimeter of each shape. Place the shapes in a center along with a supply of brightly colored laces.

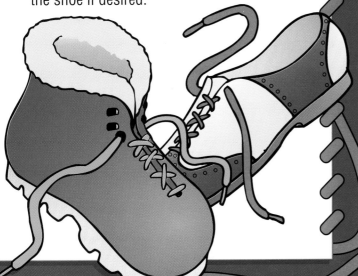

Shoe Pattern
Use with "All Tied Up!" on page 30.

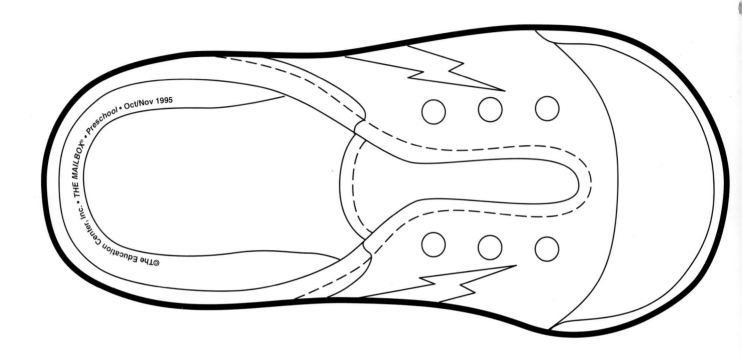

©The Education Center, Inc. • THE MAILBOX® • Preschool • Oct/Nov 1995

Award

can tie a shoe!

Note To Parent: Ask your child to demonstrate how he/she ties a shoe. Have him/her tie other shoes found at home.

©The Education Center, Inc. • THE MAILBOX® • Preschool • Oct/Nov 1995

Feeling Happy, Feeling Sad

Spirits are running high in your classroom at this time of year. Take this opportunity to explore the emotions of happiness and sadness.

by Ada Hamrick

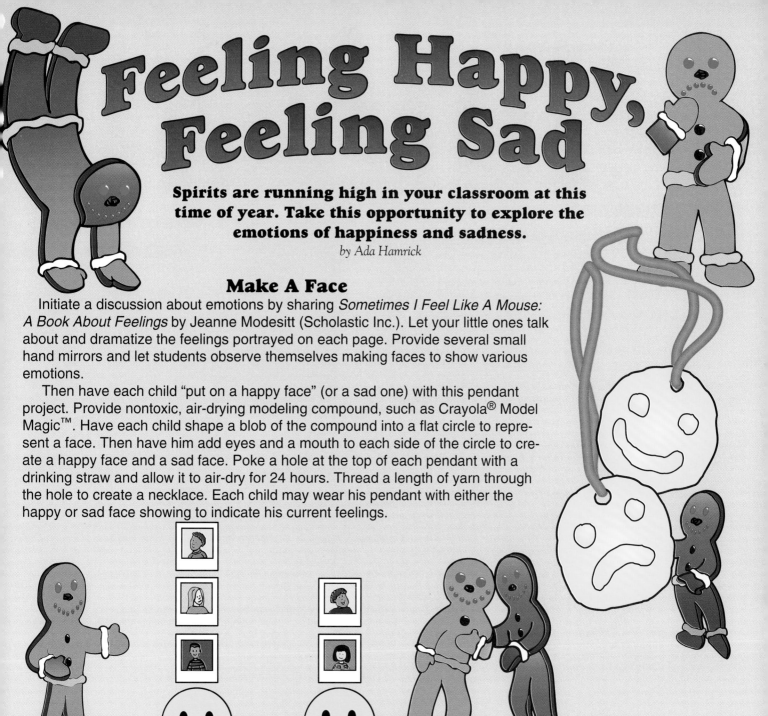

Make A Face

Initiate a discussion about emotions by sharing *Sometimes I Feel Like A Mouse: A Book About Feelings* by Jeanne Modesitt (Scholastic Inc.). Let your little ones talk about and dramatize the feelings portrayed on each page. Provide several small hand mirrors and let students observe themselves making faces to show various emotions.

Then have each child "put on a happy face" (or a sad one) with this pendant project. Provide nontoxic, air-drying modeling compound, such as Crayola® Model Magic™. Have each child shape a blob of the compound into a flat circle to represent a face. Then have him add eyes and a mouth to each side of the circle to create a happy face and a sad face. Poke a hole at the top of each pendant with a drinking straw and allow it to air-dry for 24 hours. Thread a length of yarn through the hole to create a necklace. Each child may wear his pendant with either the happy or sad face showing to indicate his current feelings.

How Are You Feeling Today?

Get a feel for each student's outlook with this daily attendance graph. Cut two large circles from poster board. Draw a happy face on one circle and a sad face on the other. Attach the faces to a bulletin board, chalkboard, or pocket chart. Provide a name or picture card to represent each student. As each child arrives at the beginning of your school day, have her place her name or picture above the face that indicates how she is feeling. When everyone has arrived, line up the cards to create a graph; then initiate a discussion based on the results. Help students count the cards in each category, and determine whether more people are happy or sad. Encourage your little ones to talk about the things that are affecting their feelings.

Sing A Song

Invite your students to show their feelings by singing the traditional song "If You're Happy And You Know It." Ask students to brainstorm ways to show happiness. Replace "clap your hands" with their suggestions—such as "stomp your feet"; "shout, 'Hooray!' "; or "wave your arms"—in subsequent verses of the song. Continue this activity by singing "If You're Sad And You Know It," having students suggest motions to display sadness. End on a happy note by repeating the first verse.

If You're Happy And You Know It

If you're happy and you know it, clap your hands!
If you're happy and you know it, clap your hands!
If you're happy and you know it,
Then your face will surely show it!
If you're happy and you know it, clap your hands!

For a variation, teach your students the sign language for *happy* and *sad.* Vary the words to the song to include the command "If you're happy [or sad] and you know it, sign the word." Your little ones can sign along as they sing along!

Kathy Martin—Pre-K and Kindergarten
Nellie Reed Elementary
Vernon, MI

happy

sad

Turn That Frown Upside Down

Help youngsters understand that feelings of sadness are valid. Share *I Am Not A Crybaby* by Norma Simon (Albert Whitman & Company). Discuss situations that might make someone sad.

Then help youngsters recall their own feelings of sadness with these unique props. Obtain two pairs of empty eyeglass frames. Create a pair of sad glasses by painting one set of frames blue and attaching blue construction-paper tears to them. Create a pair of happy glasses by painting the frames yellow and gluing on bright glitter. Let each student take a turn donning the sad glasses and recalling a time when she was sad. Then have her put on the happy glasses and tell (or speculate) how she helped herself or could have helped herself to feel better.

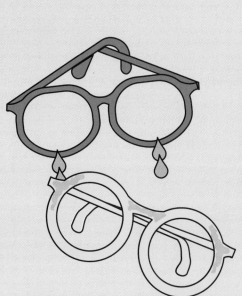

Solutions For Sadness

Have your youngsters brainstorm ways to help a friend who feels sad. Write and illustrate some of the children's suggestions on index cards. Place the cards in an inexpensive, plastic file box labeled "The Feel Better Box" and decorated with colorful stickers or paint pens. When a student is feeling sad, ask a volunteer to choose a card from the box and carry out the instructions to help his classmate feel better.

Give a hug.

The Feel Better Box

A Snack To Smile About
Your youngsters will grin from ear to ear when they devour this happy treat!

Apple Smiles
2 apple wedges (with the skin on and seeds removed)
creamy peanut butter
miniature marshmallows

Have each child use a craft stick to spread peanut butter on one side of an apple wedge. Have him place the miniature marshmallows atop the peanut butter, spread peanut butter on the other apple wedge, and place it over the marshmallows. Yum!

All Smiles
Follow up "Happy Talk" by creating a class book. Provide each child with a sheet of colored construction paper. Write each child's name on the top of his paper and draw a circle next to it. Have each youngster fill in the circle by drawing his smiling face, then search through magazines or old coloring books to find pictures of things that make him happy. Have him cut out these pictures and glue them onto his page. Attach the pages together with cellophane tape to create an accordion-folded book. Create a cover that reads "Miles And Miles Of Smiles."

Happy Talk
Encourage students to think of things that make them happy with this simple game. Have children sit in a circle, and give one child a ball. Ask him to tell about something that makes him happy, then roll the ball to another child. The child who receives the ball tells what makes him happy, then rolls the ball to another classmate. Continue until all children have had a turn.

Mary   Ryan   Julie

Miles
And
Miles
Of
Smiles

by Ms. Hamrick's Class

Photo Opportunities
Young children love to look at photos of themselves, so capitalize on this interest during your study of feelings. Bring in a camera and take two photos of each student, inviting her to make a happy face for one photo and a sad face for the other. After developing the pictures, mount each pair on a sheet of paper programmed as shown. Ask each child to dictate a situation that makes her happy and one that makes her sad. Write these comments below the photos. Display the completed projects on a bulletin board with the title "Happy And Sad: Feelings We've Had."

Ginger
is happy when

she plays with her toy farm.

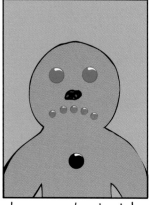

Ginger
is sad when

her grandpa is sick.

Tons Of Trucks

Vroom, vroom! Honk, honk! Get in gear with this truckload of learning activities. Your good buddies are sure to have tons of truckin' fun!

ideas by Lucia Kemp Henry

Let's Get Truckin'

Get your truck unit on the road by asking each youngster to bring in a toy truck or a magazine picture of a truck. During circle time, ask each youngster to describe the size and color of her truck or the truck in her picture. Help each child also brainstorm the kind of work for which her truck might be used. Use the toy trucks and pictures to help children identify similarities and differences in the trucks. Later assist small groups of children in sorting and classifying the trucks by type, size, and color. After each child has an opportunity to share her truck and sort the collection of trucks, display the toys on a table covered with a black, construction-paper road. Ask those youngsters who brought pictures to arrange and glue the pictures on a sheet of poster board or on a bulletin-board paper road.

A Song About My Truck

Follow up your circle-time sharing with this simple trucking song. Ask each youngster to think of two words that describe his truck. Sing the song below, replacing the words *big* and *shiny* with each child's chosen words.

(sung to the tune of "B-I-N-G-O")

Oh, look at my [big, shiny] truck!
I'm driving it today-o!
T-R-U-C-K
T-R-U-C-K
T-R-U-C-K
My truck is on its way-o!

Keep On Truckin'

Here's a song you can sing as you roll along. Each time you sing the song, replace the word *truckin'* with *drivin'*, *haulin'*, or *rollin'*. Encourage youngsters to develop their own movements for each verse.

(sung to the tune of "She'll Be Comin' 'Round the Mountain")

We'll be truckin' down the highway every day. Vroom! Vroom!
We'll be truckin' down the highway every day. Vroom! Vroom!
We'll be truckin' down the highway,
We'll be truckin' down the highway,
We'll be truckin' down the highway every day. Vroom! Vroom!

Up Close And Personal

Your preschoolers are sure to be fascinated with big trucks and their work. If possible watch some real trucks at work in your neighborhood. Or invite a truck driver to visit the school and give a tour of his own big rig. Whether or not you have the opportunity to check out real trucks, be sure to view the video *Close Up And Very Personal: Big Rigs* (available from Stage Fright Productions, 1-800-979-6800). Perfect for preschoolers, this video is all action with no narration. Your little ones will have the opportunity to fine-tune their listening skills and oral language as they hear, watch, and discuss how the big rigs hoot, honk, hiss, and roar.

Behind The Wheel

After watching the live action of a real truck or watching the suggested action video, give youngsters a chance to get their own big wheels in motion. Provide each child with her own big rig (chair). Encourage each student to imitate a truck's sounds and movements as she pretends to shut the door of her truck, buckle the seat belt, start the engine, turn on the lights, back up, honk the horn, turn on the windshield wipers, and drive away! After an appropriate length of time, direct your young drivers to put on the brakes and park at your own classroom truck stop for a snack and maybe a rest.

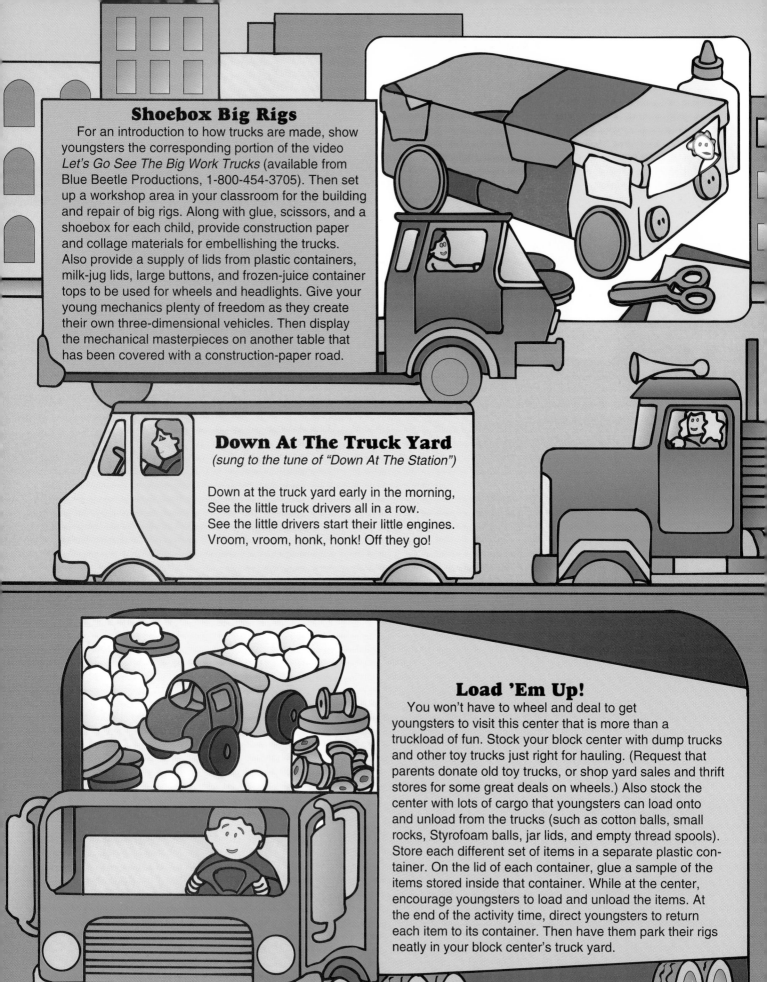

Shoebox Big Rigs

For an introduction to how trucks are made, show youngsters the corresponding portion of the video *Let's Go See The Big Work Trucks* (available from Blue Beetle Productions, 1-800-454-3705). Then set up a workshop area in your classroom for the building and repair of big rigs. Along with glue, scissors, and a shoebox for each child, provide construction paper and collage materials for embellishing the trucks. Also provide a supply of lids from plastic containers, milk-jug lids, large buttons, and frozen-juice container tops to be used for wheels and headlights. Give your young mechanics plenty of freedom as they create their own three-dimensional vehicles. Then display the mechanical masterpieces on another table that has been covered with a construction-paper road.

Down At The Truck Yard

(sung to the tune of "Down At The Station")

Down at the truck yard early in the morning,
See the little truck drivers all in a row.
See the little drivers start their little engines.
Vroom, vroom, honk, honk! Off they go!

Load 'Em Up!

You won't have to wheel and deal to get youngsters to visit this center that is more than a truckload of fun. Stock your block center with dump trucks and other toy trucks just right for hauling. (Request that parents donate old toy trucks, or shop yard sales and thrift stores for some great deals on wheels.) Also stock the center with lots of cargo that youngsters can load onto and unload from the trucks (such as cotton balls, small rocks, Styrofoam balls, jar lids, and empty thread spools). Store each different set of items in a separate plastic container. On the lid of each container, glue a sample of the items stored inside that container. While at the center, encourage youngsters to load and unload the items. At the end of the activity time, direct youngsters to return each item to its container. Then have them park their rigs neatly in your block center's truck yard.

Big Wheels Big Book

Your big-wheel watchers will want to look at and read this class big book over and over again. Enlarge and duplicate a dump truck pattern or a flatbed truck pattern (page 41) for each child. Cut out each truck pattern and glue it to a large sheet of light-colored construction paper. Gather a supply of shaped sponges and pour different colors of paint into pie pans. Instruct each child to select a sponge, dip it in paint, and press it onto her paper so that the truck appears to carry a load. When the paintings are dry, ask each child to dictate a sentence about her truck's load. Write each child's sentence on her page. Laminate the pages if desired; then bind them between titled pages. Send the class publication home for youngsters to share with their families.

Samantha's truck carries pumpkins.

Five Little Trucks

Teach this truck fingerplay to reinforce the basic colors and counting from one to five. In advance, duplicate the truck patterns (page 41) onto white construction paper; then color each numbered truck as indicated in the poem. Laminate the truck patterns; then cut on the bold lines. Back each truck pattern with felt. Use the truck patterns to accompany the poem "Five Little Trucks."

Five little trucks drive down the road.
Five little trucks each carry a load.

The **blue** truck is number **one**.
This truck can carry a ton!

The **red** truck is number **two**.
This truck can carry you!

The **yellow** truck is number **three**.
This truck can carry a tree.

The **green** truck is number **four**.
This truck can carry much more!

The **orange** truck is number **five**.
This truck is fun to drive!

—Lucia Kemp Henry

Trucks, Trucks, And More Trucks

If your youngsters are really on a roll learning about trucks, try these additional uses for the patterns on page 41.

• To make individual truck-shaped books, enlarge and duplicate any of the truck patterns. Staple each truck pattern to a supply of blank paper that has been cut to match the size or shape of the pattern. On the blank pages, encourage youngsters to attach truck stickers, glue magazine pictures of trucks, or draw pictures of their favorite trucks.

• Duplicate the set of patterns onto several different colors of construction paper. Laminate the truck patterns; then cut on the bold lines. Encourage youngsters to sort the trucks into groups by color or type.

• To create three or more different-sized trucks, reduce and enlarge one type of truck several times. Encourage youngsters to arrange the trucks by size.

• Use your choice of truck patterns to create nametags or to label students' truck projects.

On The Road Again

Give this art idea a ride and you'll arrive at the destination of a delightful display. Using books about trucks (see the suggestions below), show students pictures of the side view of a truck. Then provide each child with a large sheet of white construction paper and a supply of colorful, precut, construction-paper shapes including different sizes of circles, squares, rectangles, and triangles. Ask each child to arrange the shapes of his choice to create a truck on the paper. Assist each child in gluing his arranged shapes on the paper. When the glue is dry, cut around the overall shape of each truck. Mount the projects on a bulletin board along with paper roads and road signs. Way to go!

On The Move

Grease your wheels and start your engines! Youngsters are sure to enjoy moving to this action poem about the parts of a truck.

Here is the tractor so big and strong.	*Stand on toes and flex arm muscles.*
Here is the trailer so wide and long.	*Stretch arms out very wide.*
Here is the cab where the driver will be.	*Pretend to sit in driver's seat.*
Here is the window so the driver can see.	*Pretend to look out a window.*
Here is the steering wheel that's round.	*Pretend to steer.*
Here are the tires that roll on the ground.	*Make a rolling motion with arms.*
Here is the load that the truck will take.	*Pretend to hold a big box.*
Here is the engine that can roar and shake.	*Wiggle body and make engine noise.*
Here is the truck that's on its way;	*Pretend to drive.*
Off to work for another day.	*Wave good-bye.*

—Lucia Kemp Henry

Tons Of Truck Books

Truck
Written & Illustrated by Donald Crews
Published by Puffin Books

Trucks
Written & Illustrated by Byron Barton
Published by HarperCollins Children's Books

Trucks
Written & Illustrated by Anne F. Rockwell
Published by Dutton Children's Books

Trucks
Written & Illustrated by Gail Gibbons
Published by HarperCollins Children's Books

Truck Song
Written by Diane Siebert
Illustrated by Byron Barton
Published by HarperCollins Children's Books

Sam Goes Trucking
Written & Photographed by Henry Horenstein
Published by Houghton Mifflin Company

Eye Openers: Trucks
A Dorling Kindersley Book
Published by Aladdin Books

The Dump Truck
Written by Arlene Blanchard
Illustrated by Tony Wells
Published by Candlewick Press

Bernie Drives A Truck
Written & Illustrated by Derek Radford
Published by Candlewick Press

Mighty Machines: Truck
Written by Claire Llewellyn
Published by Dorling Kindersley

Truck Patterns

Use with "Five Little Trucks," "Big Wheels Big Book,"
and "Trucks, Trucks, And More Trucks" on page 39.

1. Dump truck
2. Pickup truck
3. Flatbed truck
4. Panel truck
5. Child's truck

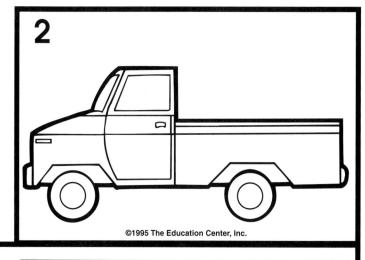

©1995 The Education Center, Inc.

©1995 The Education Center, Inc.

©1995 The Education Center, Inc.

©1995 The Education Center, Inc.

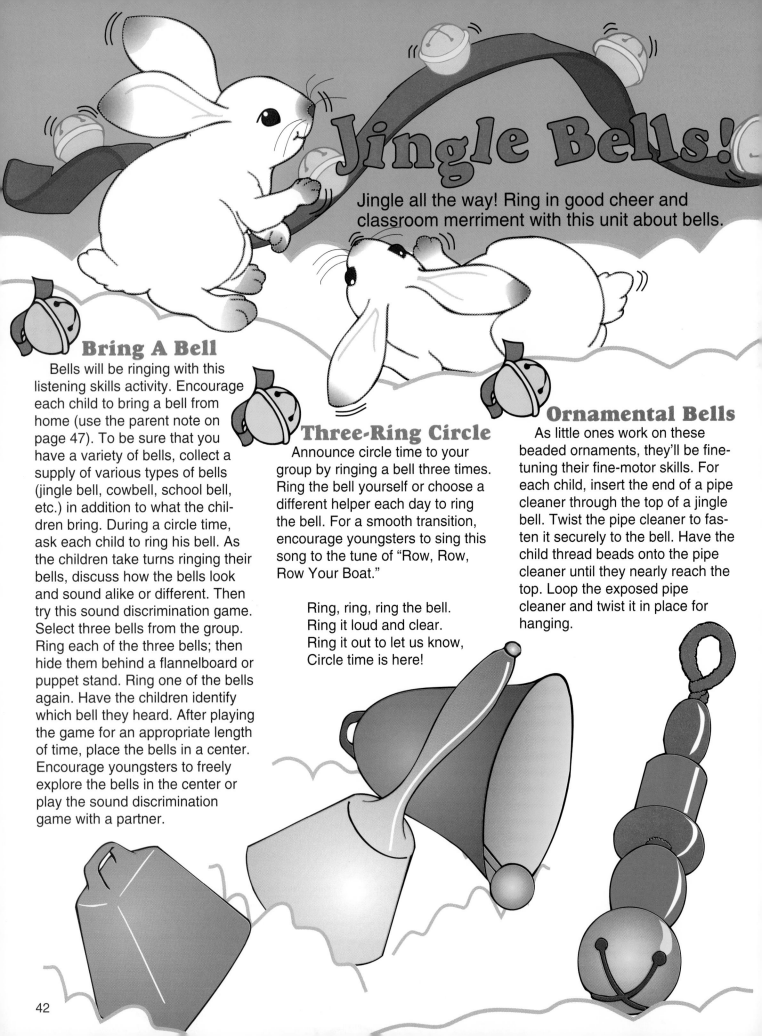

Jingle Bells!

Jingle all the way! Ring in good cheer and classroom merriment with this unit about bells.

Bring A Bell

Bells will be ringing with this listening skills activity. Encourage each child to bring a bell from home (use the parent note on page 47). To be sure that you have a variety of bells, collect a supply of various types of bells (jingle bell, cowbell, school bell, etc.) in addition to what the children bring. During a circle time, ask each child to ring his bell. As the children take turns ringing their bells, discuss how the bells look and sound alike or different. Then try this sound discrimination game. Select three bells from the group. Ring each of the three bells; then hide them behind a flannelboard or puppet stand. Ring one of the bells again. Have the children identify which bell they heard. After playing the game for an appropriate length of time, place the bells in a center. Encourage youngsters to freely explore the bells in the center or play the sound discrimination game with a partner.

Three-Ring Circle

Announce circle time to your group by ringing a bell three times. Ring the bell yourself or choose a different helper each day to ring the bell. For a smooth transition, encourage youngsters to sing this song to the tune of "Row, Row, Row Your Boat."

Ring, ring, ring the bell.
Ring it loud and clear.
Ring it out to let us know,
Circle time is here!

Ornamental Bells

As little ones work on these beaded ornaments, they'll be fine-tuning their fine-motor skills. For each child, insert the end of a pipe cleaner through the top of a jingle bell. Twist the pipe cleaner to fasten it securely to the bell. Have the child thread beads onto the pipe cleaner until they nearly reach the top. Loop the exposed pipe cleaner and twist it in place for hanging.

Jingle Bells!

Ideas contributed by Jean Huff—Four-Year-Olds, Bethel Presbyterian Weekday Program, Cornelius, NC, and Eva Murdock—Preschool, Children's Center, Shenandoah Baptist Church, Roanoke, VA

Jingle Bell Rock

Make these bells to ensure all of your little ones have their own bells to ring during group movement and music activities. Cut bell shapes from poster board. Have students decorate the bell shapes with markers; then laminate them, if desired. Hot glue a jingle bell to the bottom of each bell shape and a craft stick to the back of the bell shape. As you play a selection of lively holiday music, encourage youngsters to shake their bells. Get ready for jingle bell rock!

Jingle, Jingle, Little Bells

Youngsters will enjoy singing and ringing to this jingle bell tune. Give each child a bell as described in "Jingle Bell Rock." As the class sings this song, encourage them to use the bells to accompany the suggested actions.

(sung to the tune of "Twinkle, Twinkle, Little Star")

Jingle, jingle, little bell.
I can ring my little bell.
Ring it high.
Ring it low.
Ring it fast.
Ring it slow.
Jingle, jingle, little bell.
I can ring my little bell.

Jingle, jingle, little bell.
I can ring my little bell.
Ring it left.
Ring it right.
Even ring it
Out of sight.
Jingle, jingle, little bell.
I can ring my little bell.

Jingle Bells Rhythm

Jiggle out the wiggles—and strengthen rhythm and listening skills—with this echo chant. Chant a line of the poem, ringing a jingle bell to keep a steady beat as indicated. Direct the children to copy your words and actions. After completing the poem once, ring your bell one to five times, counting aloud as you ring. Then have the children copy you by ringing and counting the same number of times.

(Teacher:) Hear the mu-sic.

Use your ears.

Now re-peat just

What you hear.

(Children:) Hear the mu-sic.

Use your ears.

Now re-peat just

What you hear.

43

Bells In Baskets

Visit a craft store during the holiday season and you are sure to find a variety of bells. Purchase several colors and sizes of bells and store them in baskets. Encourage children to sort the bells by color, size, and loudness. Also assist children in counting sets of bells.

Cinnamon-Bread Bells

Ingredients:
1 slice of bread per child
a tub of margarine
cinnamon-sugar mixture in a shaker

For a tasty treat, have your little ones make cinnamon-bread bells. In advance place a toaster oven in your classroom housekeeping area. For each child, cut and personalize a square of aluminum foil that is slightly larger than a bell-shaped cookie cutter. Invite a small group of children to the center. Using the cookie cutter, have each child cut a bell shape from a piece of bread. Have him place his shape on his foil square. Next have him spread margarine over the shape and sprinkle it with the cinnamon-sugar mixture. Place the shapes in the oven and bake. Once the bread has cooled, invite youngsters to sit down at your housekeeping center table and enjoy!

Silver Bells

Use pears, paint, paper, and glitter to create these beautiful silver bells. Place several damp paper towels in a tray or pan. Spread white tempera paint over the paper towels. Slice a pear lengthwise, almost to the center. Slice the rounded bottom off the pear, leaving a piece in the center to resemble the bell clapper. Invite each child to press the pear into the paint and then onto construction paper. Have her continue in this manner until she has the desired number of prints on her paper. While the paint is wet, have her sprinkle glitter over the prints. Allow the prints to dry; then shake off the excess glitter.

Mopsy

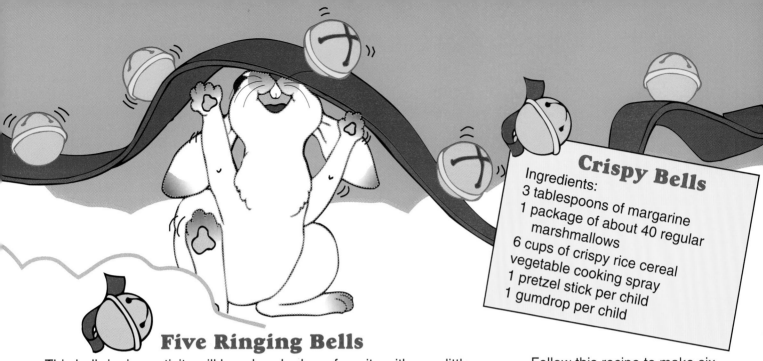

Crispy Bells

Ingredients:
3 tablespoons of margarine
1 package of about 40 regular marshmallows
6 cups of crispy rice cereal
vegetable cooking spray
1 pretzel stick per child
1 gumdrop per child

Five Ringing Bells

This bell-ringing activity will be a hands-down favorite with your little ones. In advance collect one glove for each child in your class (check your school's Lost and Found or a local thrift store). Sew a silver jingle bell to each fingertip of each glove. Have your students wear the gloves as you recite this poem together.

Five silver bells, ringing in the air.
The first one said, "Ring me everywhere."
The second one said, "Ring me every day."
The third one said, "Ring me on a sleigh."
The fourth one said, "Ring me loud and clear."
The fifth one said, "Wintertime is here!"

Hold up five fingers.
Hold up one finger.
Hold up two fingers.
Hold up three fingers.
Hold up four fingers.
Hold up five fingers and shake hand.

Follow this recipe to make six crispy bells. Melt the margarine in a large saucepan over low heat. Stir in the marshmallows. When the marshmallows have melted, remove the pan from the heat. Add the rice cereal, stirring well. Allow the mixture to cool but not harden. Spray the inside of a nine-ounce plastic cup and a child's hands with vegetable spray. Have her fill the cup with the mixture. Have her push a gumdrop into the top of the mixture to resemble the bell clapper. After approximately ten minutes, carefully take the mixture out of the cup. Next have the child push a pretzel in the top of the bell to resemble the handle. These crispy bells are really swell!

The Polar Express

In *The Polar Express* by Chris Van Allsburg (Houghton Mifflin Company), a boy boards a mysterious train that transports him to the North Pole. When Santa offers the boy any gift he desires, the boy asks him for a bell from a reindeer's harness. Read the book aloud; then present each child with a bell on a ribbon to wear. Remind the children that only if they believe in Santa will they hear the bells ring. Ring-a-ling! Do you believe?

Sleigh Ride

Oh, what fun it is to ride in this student-painted sleigh! Enlarge the sleigh pattern on page 47 onto a large piece of bulletin-board paper. Cut out the sleigh; then place it on the floor. Encourage children to paint the sleigh cutout with various colors of paint. When the sleigh is dry, tape it to two chairs that have been placed one behind the other. Place two additional chairs beside the first two chairs. Place one chair in front of the sleigh to represent a horse. To create reins, sew bells to two lengths of ribbon and tie the ribbon to the chair that represents the horse. Encourage students to sit on the chairs of the sleigh and hold onto the ribbon reins. With a little imagination, youngsters will soon be dashing through the snow!

All Aboard!

After reading aloud *The Polar Express* and distributing the bell necklaces, have students line up to form a train. Encourage youngsters to jingle their bells as you lead the train through the school. During your absence from the classroom, have an adult volunteer prepare a cup of warm cocoa for each child. When your crew arrives back at the classroom, have them sit down and enjoy the cocoa treat.

Books With Jingle

Jingle Bells: A Holiday Book With Lights And Music
Illustrated by Carolyn Ewing
Published by Aladdin Books

Jingle Bells
Written & Illustrated by Maryann Kovalski
Published by Little, Brown and Company

Jingle Bugs
Written & Illustrated by David Carter
Published by Simon & Schuster

Bells are really ringing in our class!

Please allow your child to bring a bell to school to share with the class.

Thank you!

_____

©The Education Center, Inc. • *THE MAILBOX®* • *Preschool* • Dec/Jan 1995–96

Sleigh Pattern
Use with "Sleigh Ride" on page 46.

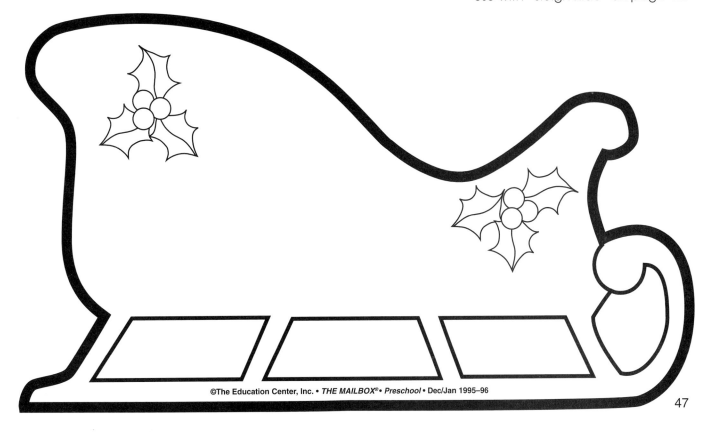

©The Education Center, Inc. • *THE MAILBOX®* • *Preschool* • Dec/Jan 1995–96

The Preschool Post Office

Look what's in the mailbox! It's a post office unit signed, sealed, and delivered to you! Introduce your youngsters to the postal service with these first-class ideas.

by Lucia Kemp Henry

Moving The Mail

Teacher:
Let's send some letters.
But how will they go?
How will they go?
Oh, do you know?

Children:

One letter goes on a great big plane.   Spread out arms to imitate a plane.
One letter goes on a choo-choo train.   Say, "Choo-choo."
One letter goes on a truck so wide.   Pretend to drive.
One letter goes on a horseback ride!   Gallop in place and neigh.
One letter goes in a boat on the sea.   Make wave motions with hand.
One letter goes to me!   Point to self and smile.

All About The Post Office

Ask your little ones what they already know about mail and how it moves from here and there to everywhere. Why not begin now making plans to visit your local post office to see the postal system in action? In the meantime, share with the class Gail Gibbons's *The Post Office Book* (Thomas Y. Crowell). If necessary, paraphrase the text to match your students' level of understanding while sharing the illustrations. Follow up your discussion on how the mail moves with this fun action poem.

Post Office Workshop Center

Set up a post office workshop center in your preschool classroom and fill it with all sorts of mail paraphernalia. Cover a table with bulletin-board paper and designate it as the mail sorting and weighing station. Place a toy cash register on the table along with a set of balance scales. Place a supply of promotional stamps, stickers, ink stamps, and ink pads in the center. Wrap boxes of varying sizes and weights in brown paper and tie them with twine. Collect a quantity of unopened junk mail, used magazines with mailing labels, and old catalogs. Label four baskets, each with a different picture indicating the types of mail collected—letters, magazines, catalogs, and packages.
To ensure that youngsters have an opportunity to wear postal uniforms, provide blue baseball-style caps and adult shirts with painted-on postal emblems. Encourage your young postal workers to don the postal attire, then sort and weigh the packages and mail. Need a mailbox? Paint a tall box blue. When the paint is dry, attach cutout letters that read "U.S. MAIL." Use an X-acto® knife to cut the box as shown.

Wait A Minute, Mr. Postman!

Every successful postal carrier needs her own personalized mailbag! Collect a paper grocery bag for each child. Fold the bags and cut them as shown. Trim the sides of the bag evenly if desired. Tape the narrow portions of the cut bag together to create a shoulder strap. Provide students with various art supplies including markers, glue, colored paper, and stamps used in promotional mailings for decorating the bags.

Sherry L. Petrik
Love And Tender Care
Dell Rapids, SD

Milk-Carton Mailboxes

To provide each child with a personalized mailbox, collect a paper milk carton for each child in your class. Wash the cartons; then cut off the tops. Cover each carton with colored paper. To make a connected row of mailboxes, staple or glue the cartons together. Stand the row upright and write a different child's name and a different numeral on each box. Glue a photo of each youngster to her box. To reinforce name and numeral recognition, write each child's name and numeral on several envelopes. Encourage children to hand-deliver the numbered envelopes to the correct milk-carton mailbox addresses.

Neighborhood Mail Delivery

Here's a hands-on color-matching activity to add to your post-office workshop center. Gather clean milk cartons, jugs, or plastic tubs. Cut a simple house shape from as many different colors of construction paper as you have cartons and add details with a marker. Staple each house shape to a carton. Using a commercial envelope as a pattern, cut and glue several envelopes to match each different color of house. To use this center, youngsters deliver each colored envelope to its matching house.

49

Students will get stuck on learning with this activity that reinforces one-to-one correspondence, matching, and fine-motor skills. Duplicate the envelope and stamp patterns on pages 52 and 53 onto construction paper. Color, laminate, and cut out the patterns. Attach the hook side of a small piece of adhesive Velcro® to each stamp cutout. Attach the loop side of a small piece of adhesive Velcro® to each envelope cutout. During a group time, give each child either an envelope or a stamp. Direct each child to find his postal partner by matching the picture on his envelope or stamp to the stamp or envelope of one of his classmates. Each set of partners should attach the stamp to the corresponding envelope. When everyone has a postal partner, ask the children to bring the envelopes to your classroom post office for inspection. Be sure to place the envelopes and stamps in a container in the post office for students to use independently when visiting the center.

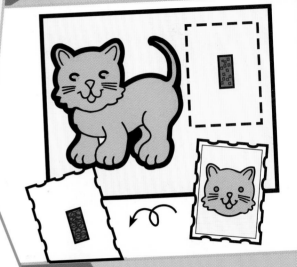

Tamara's stamp is blue and gre[en]

Ja'Quincy's lion stamp.

Stunning Stamp Art

Seen any interesting stamps "phi-lately"? Introduce your little ones to the hobby of stamp collecting, or *philately*, by showing them a collection of real stamps. Show youngsters stamps on envelopes or remove them from the envelopes. (Tear the top corner of an envelope. Place the paper, stamp side down, in a pan of warm water. After a few minutes, the stamp will sink to the bottom.) Packages of stamps may also be purchased from hobby shops. After discussing the stamps and choosing class favorites, give youngsters a chance to create their own stunning stamps. For each child, use pinking shears to cut a rectangle from white construction paper. Have each child paint or draw a design on his rectangle. Glue the rectangle to a larger piece of construction paper, and write the child's name and a description of the stamp design on the paper. If desired bind the pages to create a "Stunning Stamp Art" class book.

U.S. MAIL

Sponge-Art Stationery

With this letter-decorating and writing project, your students will learn about the postal system firsthand! For each child, personalize the back of a brightly colored piece of stationery or copier paper. To create sponge-art stationery, invite each child to use small sponges and different colors of tempera paint to print a top and bottom border on her paper. If desired, have youngsters sprinkle the wet prints with glitter. At a later time, write on each child's stationery as she dictates a letter to a parent or caregiver. Have her write her name at the bottom of the letter; then address the envelope. If you have scheduled a visit to the post office, have the children take the letters with them on the trip. If a trip is not possible, take your letters to a nearby mailbox so that each child can put her letter in the mail. Or make arrangements for the postal worker who visits your school to meet your children and collect their letters.

Dear Grandma,
You are my
bestest
grandmama!
Love,
Tanika

Special Delivery

Enlarge the mailbox pattern on page 53 to create a take-home special-delivery mail pouch. Duplicate and personalize a copy of the enlarged pattern for each child. Have each child color his paper. Cut out and glue each child's colored mailbox to a 10" x 13" envelope. Laminate each envelope with the flap open; then use an X-acto® knife to cut the laminating film at the opening. Attach adhesive-backed Velcro® to the flap and to the back of the envelope. Use these envelopes to transport student work and newsletters home to parents. If desired, label the pouches "Return To Sender" to encourage parents to use these special-delivery pouches for sending important messages to school.

First-Class Books About Mail

A Letter To Amy
Written & Illustrated by Ezra Jack Keats
Published by HarperCollins

Mr. Griggs' Work
Written by Cynthia Rylant
Illustrated by Julie Downing
Published by Orchard Books

LOCAL

Envelope Patterns

Use with "Stuck On Stamps" on page 50.

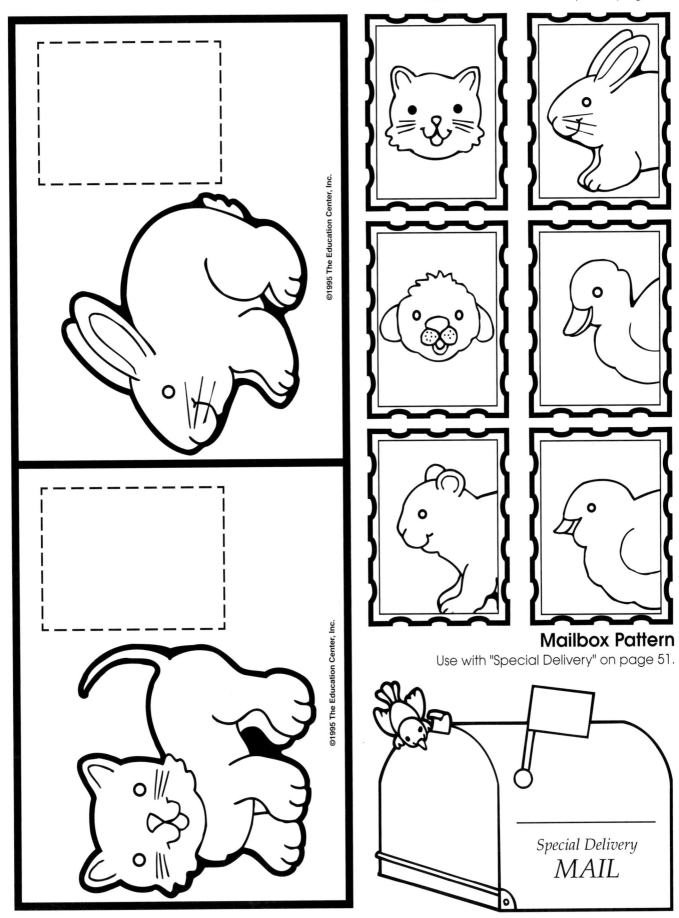

Envelope And Stamp Patterns
Use with "Stuck On Stamps" on page 50.

Mailbox Pattern
Use with "Special Delivery" on page 51.

Special Delivery
MAIL

©1995 The Education Center, Inc.

FABULOUS FRIENDSHIPS

Even though your little ones seem fairly focused on themselves, their interest in others may be just about to blossom. Help youngsters discover the fabulous fun of friends with these activities and book suggestions about friendship.

ideas contributed by Marie E. Cecchini

FRIENDS DO THINGS TOGETHER.

THE GET-ALONG GAME

Children, like adults, usually have special friends they enjoy being with the most. If you'd like to encourage youngsters to play with different and perhaps new friends, introduce "The Get-Along Game." To play, group youngsters in pairs. Ask each pair to play together until they hear a signal such as a bell or a whistle. After an appropriate length of time, give the signal and ask youngsters to find a new partner. So long! It's time to get along!

MAKING MUSIC

Use musical instruments to demonstrate how some activities that are fun alone are even more fun with friends. One at a time, provide each child with an instrument. Ask the child to play his instrument alone; then direct him to let his instrument rest on the floor. When each child has had an opportunity to play his instrument alone, ask the children to play their instruments at the same time. Discuss the difference in the sound of the instruments when played alone and when played together. If desired take your young musicians outside and have a marching band parade!

WE GO TOGETHER

Gather a collection of items that go together—such as a vase and artificial flowers, a baseball and a bat, and a toy dog and a bone. Discuss the items that go together; then place the items in a box. Have each child close his eyes and take one item from the box. When each child has an object, ask him to find his partner by finding the person with the corresponding object. After playing the game, place the box of objects in a center for children to match independently.

LITERATURE LINK

Rooster's Off To See The World
Written & Illustrated by
Eric Carle
Published by
Picture Book Studio

Step By Step
Written by Diane Wolkstein
Illustrated by Joseph A. Smith
Published by
Morrow Junior Books

FRIENDS ARE ALIKE AND DIFFERENT.

ALIKE AND DIFFERENT

Ask the children to describe their friends. Point out that some friends are very much alike while others are very different. Ask the children if they have friends who are older, younger, or perhaps are pets. Ask each child to draw a picture of an unusual friend with this unusual art technique. Provide the children with drawing chalk, colored paper, and a small bowl of milk. Direct each child to use the chalk to draw a picture of a friend who is very different from himself. To prevent smearing of the dried chalk, instruct the children to dip the tip of the chalk in the milk before drawing.

FRIENDSHIP GARDEN

By now your youngsters' social skills are probably blooming. This display is a beautiful way to show the diversity that exists in your classroom garden of friendship. Attach green, fringed paper to the bottom of a blue paper background. Provide children with various colors of construction paper and encourage them to cut out flowers, stems, and leaves. Have each child glue her flower parts together; then attach a photo of the child to the center of the flower. Mount the flowers onto the background along with the title "Our Friendship Garden."

LITERATURE LINK

Do You Want To Be My Friend?
Written & Illustrated by Eric Carle
Published by
HarperCollins Children's Books

My Friends
Written & Illustrated by Taro Gomi
Published by
Chronicle Books

FRIENDS HELP EACH OTHER.

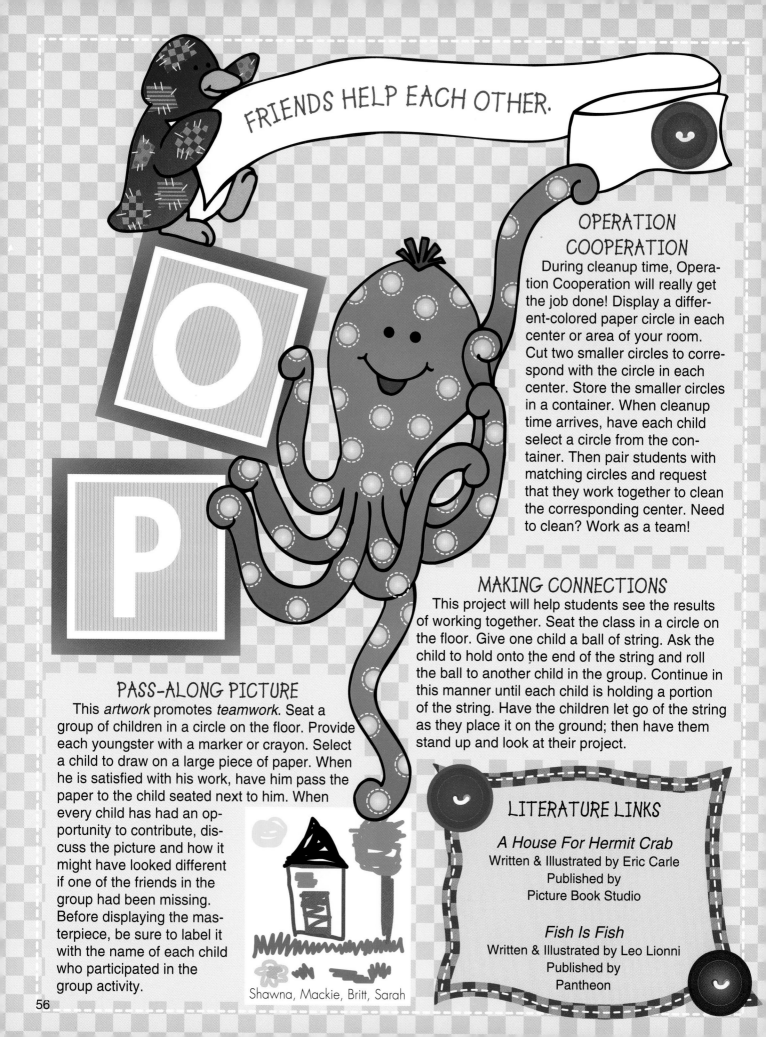

OPERATION COOPERATION

During cleanup time, Operation Cooperation will really get the job done! Display a different-colored paper circle in each center or area of your room. Cut two smaller circles to correspond with the circle in each center. Store the smaller circles in a container. When cleanup time arrives, have each child select a circle from the container. Then pair students with matching circles and request that they work together to clean the corresponding center. Need to clean? Work as a team!

MAKING CONNECTIONS

This project will help students see the results of working together. Seat the class in a circle on the floor. Give one child a ball of string. Ask the child to hold onto the end of the string and roll the ball to another child in the group. Continue in this manner until each child is holding a portion of the string. Have the children let go of the string as they place it on the ground; then have them stand up and look at their project.

PASS-ALONG PICTURE

This *artwork* promotes *teamwork*. Seat a group of children in a circle on the floor. Provide each youngster with a marker or crayon. Select a child to draw on a large piece of paper. When he is satisfied with his work, have him pass the paper to the child seated next to him. When every child has had an opportunity to contribute, discuss the picture and how it might have looked different if one of the friends in the group had been missing. Before displaying the masterpiece, be sure to label it with the name of each child who participated in the group activity.

Shawna, Mackie, Britt, Sarah

LITERATURE LINKS

A House For Hermit Crab
Written & Illustrated by Eric Carle
Published by
Picture Book Studio

Fish Is Fish
Written & Illustrated by Leo Lionni
Published by
Pantheon

FRIENDS LIKE EACH OTHER.

FRIENDLY PHONE CALLS

Ring! Ring! Hello? Stay on the line for a fun idea. Collect phones from thrift shops or yard sales. Place the phones in your classroom housekeeping center. During a group time, discuss with youngsters proper use of the telephone. During the discussion, remind them to always ask an adult for permission to use the phone. Then encourage youngsters to practice what they have learned by "calling" each other when they visit the housekeeping center. Consider sending a note home to parents making them aware of this life-skills lesson.

IT'S PARTY TIME!

Celebrate your unit on friendship with a party. If desired have the children plan to invite another class to join them. Ask the children to decorate with stickers and glitter a supply of folded, construction-paper invitations. As a class plan and prepare the party refreshments. When the guests arrive, encourage the children to provide each guest with a plate of the prepared goodies. Later play a group game or organize a group activity such as mural painting. At the close of the celebration, be sure to remind the hosts to thank their guests for coming!

LITERATURE LINK

The Very Quiet Cricket
Written & Illustrated by Eric Carle
Published by
Philomel Books

A Vegetable Variety Show

Now appearing—a showcase of vivacious vegetable ideas! Dig into this crisp and crunchy collection of produce projects and get your little ones involved in a vegetable exploration!
compiled by Ada Hamrick

Looking At Vegetables

Introduce your youngsters to a variety of vegetables by simulating a farmer's market display in your classroom. Bring in a child's wagon and some baskets. Ask several parents to send in different fresh vegetables such as carrots, peppers, lettuce, beans, corn, zucchini, radishes, potatoes, and cucumbers. Include some unusual vegetables such as artichokes or rutabagas. Fill the wagon and baskets with the produce. Dress the part of a farmer by wearing a straw hat, jeans, and a bandana.

Allow your students to touch and examine all of the vegetables. Assist them in identifying each food. Discuss the various colors, textures, and sizes. Cut several of the vegetables open, and discuss with the children internal differences and similarities.

Dip And Dig In

After your vegetable exploration, host a veggie-tasting party! Have little ones help you wash some of the vegetables from the display such as the carrots, lettuce, peppers, and cucumbers. Peel as needed and cut the vegetables into small pieces. Provide a mild-flavored dip and invite your young vegetable connoisseurs to eat up!

Vegetable Verse

Encourage your students to crunch into healthful eating habits with this song.

Oh, Do You Eat Your Vegetables?
(sung to the tune of "Oh, Do You Know The Muffin Man?")

Oh, do you eat your vegetables, vegetables, vegetables?
Oh, do you eat your vegetables—each and every day?

Oh yes, we eat our vegetables, vegetables, vegetables;
Oh yes, we eat our vegetables—each and every day!

To continue the song, ask each child in turn to name a vegetable. Substitute the child's name and her vegetable choice, and have everyone sing the new words. For example:

Oh, Janet eats green beans, green beans, green beans;
Oh, Janet eats green beans—each and every day!

Adapted from an idea by Kay Dawson, Atlanta, GA

Grow A Vegetable Sandwich

Teach young learners about seed growth by sprouting alfalfa seeds. Begin by sharing the book *Growing Vegetable Soup* by Lois Ehlert (Scholastic Inc.). Discuss the care needed in order for plants to grow. Then explain that you and the students are going to grow a vegetable *sandwich*. Follow the steps below to sprout some alfalfa seeds. (Purchase the seeds from a natural foods store. Do not use general agricultural alfalfa.)

You will need:

alfalfa seeds
3 widemouthed jars of different volumes
a strainer
a cake pan
paper towels
a rubber band

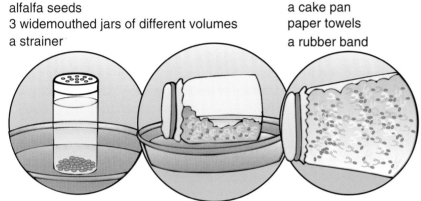

1. Place 1/4 cup of alfalfa seeds in the smallest jar. Cover them with water and soak them overnight.
2. The next day, pour off the water. Put the seeds in the strainer and rinse them with fresh water. Put the damp seeds back in the jar; then use a rubber band to secure a paper towel over the mouth of the jar.
3. Lay the jar on its side in the cake pan. Place the pan near a window.
4. Rinse the seeds once or twice a day, making sure they do not dry out.
5. You should begin to see growth by the third day. Transfer the sprouting seeds to the larger jars as they grow.
6. On the fourth or fifth day, you should see little green leaves. The sprouts are then ready to eat.

Make vegetable sandwiches by putting a generous amount of sprouts between slices of buttered bread. No doubt your young gardeners will enjoy this homegrown treat!

Betty Kobes, West Hancock Elementary School, Kanawha, IA

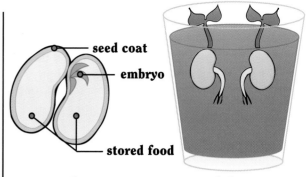

Where Do Vegetables Come From?

Give little ones more experience with the growth process by planting lima beans. Soak a few handfuls of lima beans in water overnight. The next day split open a few of the beans. Allow youngsters to observe the insides and outsides of the seeds with magnifying glasses. Encourage them to look for the tiny "baby" plant in the seed.

Provide clear plastic cups, potting soil, and plastic spoons. Punch several holes in the bottom of each cup. Have each child fill a cup with soil. Then have him push three or four beans into the soil next to the sides of the cup. This will enable him to see the roots and stems as they develop. Help students care for the seeds in the classroom for one or two weeks, providing them with light and water. Have your youngsters observe the plants daily and discuss the changes they see happening.

Adapted from an idea by Kay Dawson, Atlanta, GA

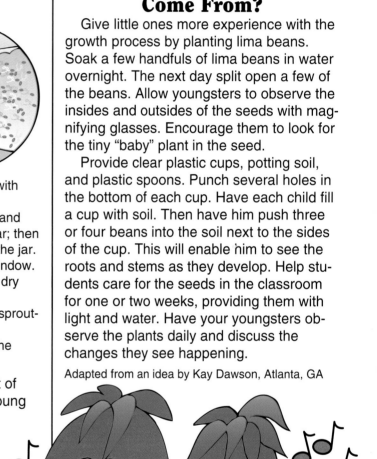

In The Garden Of Make-Believe

Plant seeds of imagination with this pretending activity! Invite your youngsters to pretend they are seeds planted in a garden. Have each child find a space on the floor and curl up into a ball. Turn off the classroom lights. Say, "You are a vegetable seed, planted in the dark ground. Don't tell us yet what kind of vegetable you are. When I turn on the lights, pretend warm sunshine is shining on you. I'm going to be the gardener. When I come by, I'll sprinkle some water on you to help you begin growing." Turn on the lights. Walk through your imaginary garden and gently tap each child on the back to "water" the seeds. Encourage the children to pretend to grow bigger and bigger. Afterward have each child share what kind of vegetable she dramatized.

Kay Dawson, Atlanta, GA

Colorful Veggies

Gather students together to discuss the colors of vegetables. Read *Growing Colors* by Bruce McMillan (Lothrop, Lee & Shepard Books). Then have students sit in a circle. Place a large basket containing at least one vegetable per child in the center of the circle. (Use some of the vegetables from "Looking At Vegetables" on page 58.) Have each child choose a vegetable to hold. Go around the circle, inviting each child to name the color of his vegetable and something else that is also that color. For example, a child might say, "Corn is yellow. The sun is yellow, too." He can then place his vegetable back in the basket. Continue until all the children have had a turn.

Kay Dawson, Atlanta, GA

Carrot Colors

Read about the planting of vegetable seeds by sharing the book *The Carrot Seed* by Ruth Krauss (Scholastic Inc.). Then have your little ones investigate color combinations as they finger-paint their own gigantic carrots. Cut a carrot shape (about 21 inches long) from finger-paint paper for each child. Place a few spoonfuls of red finger paint and a few spoonfuls of yellow finger paint on each student's carrot shape. Have her observe and verbalize what happens when she mixes the colors together while finger-painting. Have each child clean her hands with a moistened towelette. Then place blue and yellow finger paints on a 9" x 12" sheet of art paper for each child. Ask the children to predict what will happen when the paint colors are mixed. Then let students finger-paint the paper. When the papers are dry, accordion-fold each sheet. Staple the folded papers to the tops of the carrot shapes to create leaves. You'll want to display this enormous artwork for all to see!

Gail Moody—Preschool
Atascadero Parent Education Preschool, Atascadero, CA

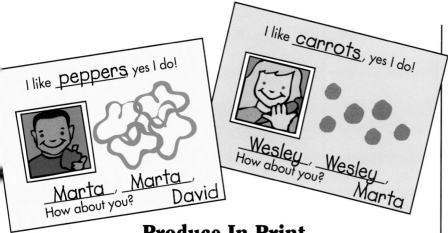

I like _peppers_, yes I do!
Marta, Marta,
How about you? David

I like _carrots_, yes I do!
Wesley, Wesley,
How about you? Marta

Produce In Print

Let students further explore the colors and shapes of vegetables with this art activity. Prepare vegetables for printing by washing and cutting them if necessary. Cover a table with bulletin-board paper and pour several colors of tempera paint into shallow containers (such as Styrofoam meat trays). To discover the print created by each vegetable, allow small groups of children to dip the vegetables into paint, then press them onto the paper. Take a photograph of each child holding or printing with his favorite vegetable. Then have each child make prints of his favorite vegetable on a sheet of art paper. When the paint is dry, program the papers with the incomplete sentence shown. Fill in the blanks, allowing each child to choose a different classmate to mention. Glue the photo of each child with his favorite vegetable near or on top of the vegetable prints. Put the pages in order and bind them into a class book titled "We Like Vegetables, Yes We Do!"

A Plant Play

Give your youngsters an enriching experience with a favorite story about a troublesome harvest. Read aloud *The Enormous Turnip,* retold and illustrated by Kathy Parkinson (Albert Whitman & Company). Then allow students to act out the story with the props you've prepared.

Create a giant turnip with a white, plastic garbage bag. Stuff some purple tissue paper into the bottom of the bag; then fill it with crumpled, white tissue paper. Secure the bag with a rubber band and fringe the open end of the bag to create the roots of the turnip plant. Fold in the two bottom corners of the stuffed bag and staple them together to give the bag a rounded shape. Staple some pieces of green tissue paper to the stuffed end of the bag to simulate the turnip's leafy top.

Supply simple costumes for students, such as a straw hat for the farmer or a headband with construction-paper ears for the dog. Then act as narrator while your young actors perform the story. Consider performing for another class or videotaping the performance to share at a Parents' Night.

To Market, To Market

Now that little ones have experience with how vegetables are grown, take a trip to the grocery store to examine vegetables in a more familiar setting. Arrange to visit the produce department of your local supermarket. Workers there can tell students about the various vegetables and where they are grown, demonstrate the produce scales, and may even give students free samples! While you're at the store, purchase a bag of potatoes to use with the "Mash 'Em And Smash 'Em" activity.

Mash 'Em And Smash 'Em

What could be more fun than making mashed potatoes? This cooking activity will allow your young learners to observe changes in matter and to practice motor skills. Begin by opening a bag of potatoes and allowing students to touch and examine them up close. Then let youngsters help you wash and peel the potatoes with safety peelers. Cut the potatoes into pieces as students watch. Pass around a few slices of raw potato so students can examine the texture. Boil the remaining potato pieces in a safe kitchen area; then drain and cool them.

Then mash 'em and smash 'em! Provide potato mashers and have students mash the potatoes. Have little ones help with adding butter and milk to the cooked potatoes. Discuss how the potatoes changed when they were cooked. Finish the activity by devouring this ever-popular vegetable dish!

Be A Farmer

Are your little farmers ready to bring in the harvest? Then turn your sand table into a vegetable garden! Place the plastic vegetables from your housekeeping center in the sand table, burying the carrots, potatoes, and other root vegetables under the sand. Then provide toy gardening tools such as rakes, hoes, shovels, watering cans, and baskets. Your youngsters will enjoy weeding, watering, and harvesting the vegetables. This center is sure to be considered the cream of the crop!

I Can Build; Can You?

Your little ones may be most familiar with vegetables in cans. Have each child bring in a small can of vegetables from home for some fun with building and sorting. Ask the children to sort the cans by the type of vegetables they contain or by similar brand logos. Then challenge them to use the cans for building activities. Invite them to build a long road or to create various shapes, using the cans as they would blocks. (Supervise the building activities and prevent students from building tall structures that might topple over.) When you're finished with your canned creations, donate the cans to a local food bank or shelter for the homeless.

How Does Your Garden Grow?

Culminate your study of vegetables by planting a vegetable garden on your school grounds. Refer to the "Growing In And Out" idea in our "Out And About" section (page 272) for instructions on starting a class garden. Your little ones will gain valuable hands-on experience by caring for the plants over an extended period of time. And when it's time for your first harvest, your young vegetable lovers will be delighted to see the results of their hard work!

Pam Crane

Vegetable Books To Grow On

Lunch
Written & Illustrated by Denise Fleming
Published by Scholastic Inc.

Eating The Alphabet: Fruits And Vegetables From A To Z
Written & Illustrated by Lois Ehlert
Published by Harcourt Brace Jovanovich

Vegetable Soup
Written by Jeanne Modesitt
Illustrated by Robin Spowart
Published by Macmillan Publishing Company

Eat Your Peas, Louise!
Written by Pegeen Snow
Illustrated by Mike Venezia™
Published by Childrens Press™

The Giant Vegetable Garden
Written & Illustrated by Nadine Bernard Westcott
Published by Little, Brown & Company

Vegetable Garden
Written & Illustrated by Douglas Flourian
Published by Harcourt Brace Jovanovich

All Cracked Up!

What's the story behind the chicken and the egg? About this time of year, your little ones just might want to know. That's why we've laid out this Grade-A unit about chicks hatching from eggs. With these activities, you can count on hatching up a barnyard full of fun!

ideas by Lucia Kemp Henry

What Is An Egg?

Before introducing this "egg-citing" topic to your students, hard-boil an egg. Then cut a piece of white bulletin-board paper into a large egg shape. During a group time, give each child an opportunity to hold the egg; then ask volunteers to describe it. Give students an opportunity to share what they think an egg is. Record their responses on the egg-shaped paper. Complete the activity by sharing the poem "What Is An Egg?"

What Is An Egg?

What is an egg?
It's a special place.
It's warm and it's safe.
It's a cozy space.

What is an egg?
It's a place to start
Growing bones and a beak
And feathers and a heart.

What is an egg?
It's a place to grow
For a chick and a duck
And an owl and a crow.

What is an egg?
It's a place to begin
For all sorts of birds;
For a rooster and hen.
—Lucia Kemp Henry

How Hatching Happens

Here's a basketful of good books to choose from when explaining to preschoolers how hatching happens.

The Egg: A First Discovery Book
Written by Gallimard Jeunesse and
Pascale de Bourgoing
Illustrated by René Mettler
Published by Scholastic Inc.

Egg: A Photographic Story Of Hatching
Written by Robert Burton
Photographed by Jane Burton and Kim Taylor
Published by Dorling Kindersley

Egg Story
Written & Illustrated by Anca Hariton
(Out of print. Check your local library.)

Sequencing The Story

After sharing the hatching story, ask your children to help you sequence the events using the sequence cards on page 68. To prepare, duplicate page 68 on white construction paper. Color and cut out the cards; then laminate them if desired. As youngsters help you sequence the cards, ask them to describe what is happening in each picture.

Excellent Eggs And Nifty Nests

Help youngsters put together these simple projects; then encourage them to use the manipulatives to describe how a chick hatches from an egg. For each child, cut two five-inch-tall egg shapes from white construction paper. Have each child cut one of his two egg shapes in half so that it appears that the egg has cracked open. Staple the top egg half atop the whole egg shape only at the top; then staple the bottom egg half to the whole egg shape along the sides and the bottom. To create a chick for each child, cut one three-inch-tall yellow chick shape. Have each child use crayons to add eyes and a beak to his chick. Then have him place his chick inside the egg. To make a nest for each child's egg and chick, cut a paper plate in half. Staple the halves together along the rim to form a pocket. Provide strips of brown and yellow paper or small twigs and straw for each child to glue to the outside of his nest. Invite students to retell the hatching story using these manipulatives.

What's Next? A Nest!

Before a hen starts to lay eggs, she gathers soft materials around her to make a nest. Set up this crafty center and get ready for some creative nest building right in your classroom. As a class, brainstorm a list of things that a hen might use to build a nest, such as twigs, feathers, hay, and leaves. Stock a center with the listed items, as well as other soft materials such as cotton batting, dryer lint, crinkled paper strips, dried grass, and cotton balls. Collect a plastic strawberry basket or cardboard mushroom container for each child. Place them in the center along with several glue sticks. As each child visits the center, encourage her to build a nest with the provided materials.

"Egg-citing" Egg Sorting

It's time to gather the eggs from the henhouse! Enlarge the barn pattern on page 69 on red construction paper. Cut out the barn and glue it onto one side of a box. Fill the box with straw or yellow plastic grass. Gather together a selection of large and small plastic eggs; then place them in the box. Label two baskets each with the word "large" or "small," and attach a corresponding egg shape. Encourage youngsters to take the eggs from the barn and sort them by size into the labeled baskets.

Old MacDonald's Barn

Tap, Tap, Tap...

Chicks certainly know what to do when it's time to hatch from their eggs. For a movement activity that's all it's cracked up to be, turn to our movement section on page 138. C-r-a-c-k!

Nine, Ten...A Big Fat Hen

Counting is fun with the big fat hen and all her friends. Read aloud *Big Fat Hen* (Harcourt Brace & Company). Keith Baker's version of the traditional nursery rhyme is so delightful, your little chicks won't be able to resist joining in! As a follow-up, make this counting-chicks game. Following the directions in "Excellent Eggs And Nifty Nests," make as many egg-and-chick sets as desired. Glue sets of eggs to brightly colored construction-paper strips; then sequentially number the eggs on each strip. To use the game, a child counts each chick as she removes it from or places it in an egg. Who says you can't count your chickens before they hatch?

Wait! There's More!
Can't get enough of Big Fat Hen? Turn to "Once Upon A Story" on page 239 for more hands-on counting activities related to this "egg-ceptional" book.

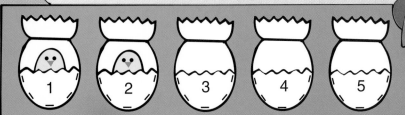

E-I-E-I-O

Did you know that Old MacDonald had a *chicken* farm? Yep! It's true. Put an interesting twist on a well-known song with this chicken-flavored version of "Old MacDonald."

Old MacDonald had a farm. E-I-E-I-O.
And on that farm he had a barn. E-I-E-I-O.
With a big barn here and a big barn there.
Here a barn, there a barn, everywhere a big barn.
Old MacDonald had a barn. E-I-E-I-O.

Old MacDonald had a barn. E-I-E-I-O.
And in that barn he had a hen. E-I-E-I-O.
With a cluck, cluck here and a cluck, cluck there.
Here a cluck, there a cluck, everywhere a cluck, cluck.
Old MacDonald had a hen. E-I-E-I-O.

Old MacDonald had a hen. E-I-E-I-O.
And under that hen he had a nest. E-I-E-I-O.
With a nice nest here and a nice nest there,
Here a nest, there a nest, everywhere a nice nest.
Old MacDonald had a nest. E-I-E-I-O.

Old MacDonald had a nest. E-I-E-I-O.
And in that nest he had an egg. E-I-E-I-O.
With a wee egg here and a wee egg there.
Here an egg, there an egg, everywhere a wee egg.
Old MacDonald had an egg. E-I-E-I-O.

Old MacDonald had an egg. E-I-E-I-O.
And in that egg he had a chick. E-I-E-I-O.
With a chick, chick here and a chick, chick there.
Here a chick, there a chick, everywhere a chick, chick.
Old MacDonald had a chick. E-I-E-I-O.

Old MacDonald's Barn Book

Singing about Old MacDonald's chicken farm is even more fun with these barn books. Assemble an Old MacDonald's Barn book for each child to manipulate while he is singing the song. To make a barn book, reproduce the patterns on page 69 on white construction paper. Cut out each picture, making sure to cut along the dotted lines of the barn pattern. From red construction paper, cut a rectangle identical in size to the barn pattern. Glue the barn pattern to the red paper only along the top and sides. Fold open the barn door. Center the hen pattern on the red paper; then glue it only along the left side. Fold the hen pattern along the solid line. In a similar manner, glue the nest pattern under the hen pattern and fold; then glue the egg pattern under the nest pattern and fold. Glue the entire chick pattern to the red backing paper. Have each child personalize and color his book. E-I-E-I-O!

Henhouse Hullabaloo!

What's all the fuss about? Chicks hatching, of course. With this creative craft and display idea, you'll soon have a whole henhouse full of artistic chicks. Provide each child with a large sheet of finger-painting paper. Encourage her to paint her paper with yellow finger paint. Next give her several feathers to press onto the center of her painting. When the paint is dry, cut a large chick shape from the paper. Have the child glue sequin or button eyes, a paper beak, and paper feet to her chick. Display the artistic chicks along a hall with the title "Henhouse Hullabaloo!"

Peek-A-Boo!

Watching a chick hatch from an egg is a sight your preschoolers will not soon forget. For information about hatching eggs, call your local Agricultural Extension Agency. It may be helpful to note that several types of incubators are available through school supply catalogs. Before beginning the project, be sure to arrange a future home for the chicks. During the 21-day incubation period, have your students share the responsibility of caring for the eggs. Keep a camera nearby to capture the group's efforts as well as their reactions when the chicks finally hatch. Now that's a "Kodak® moment"!

Pecking and peeping—
What can it be?
A chick is hatching.
Quick! Come and see!

Take A Peek

Check out these "eggs-traspecial" chicken and egg books.

Gemma And The Baby Chick
Written by Antonia Barber
Illustrated by Karin Littlewood
Published by Scholastic Inc.

Hatch, Egg, Hatch! A Touch-And-Feel Action Flap Book
Written by Shen Roddie
Illustrated by Frances Cony
Published by Little, Brown and Company

The Chick And The Duckling
Written by Mirra Ginsburg
Illustrated by Jose & Ariane Aruego
Published by Macmillan Publishing Company

Good Morning, Chick
Written by Mirra Ginsburg
Illustrated by Byron Barton
Published by Greenwillow Books

Zinnia And Dot
Written & Illustrated by Lisa Campbell Ernst
Published by Viking Children's Books

Sequence Cards

Use with "Sequencing The Story" on page 64.

Use with " 'Egg-citing' Egg Sorting" on page 65 and "Old MacDonald's Barn Book" on page 66.

egg

chick

hen

nest

Old MacDonald's Barn

The Wonder Of Butterflies

What's that flitting and fluttering around gardens and backyards at this time of year? The beautiful butterfly, of course! Introduce your little ones to this graceful creature with these activities. They'll be all aflutter over butterflies!

ideas contributed by Marie E. Cecchini

Butterfly Journeys

Ask your youngsters to close their eyes and pretend that they are butterflies. Read aloud the poem "If I Were A Butterfly." After sharing the poem, have the children open their eyes. Invite them to use colored chalk and large sheets of drawing paper to draw a picture that answers the question, "Where would you go if you were a butterfly?" Set the mood for this activity by playing soft, instrumental music as the children work. Encourage your youngsters to use their fingers to blend the colors of chalk to create soft effects in their drawings. (Keep a supply of moist towelettes handy for easy cleanup.) Write as each child dictates a sentence about her imaginary journey.

Write the poem on a large butterfly shape cut from bulletin-board paper. Display the poem along with the children's daydreamlike drawings. To complete the display, add the title "Butterfly Journeys." Beautiful!

I would fly near all the grass.

If I Were A Butterfly

If I were a butterfly,
Then no one would know
Wherever it was
I decided to go.

I could visit a farm,
A lake, or a zoo.
You just never know
What it is I might do.

Maybe I'd flit
From flower to flower
Drawing up nectar
To drink by the hour.

I might like to go
To the park or the beach,
Or soar to the sky
Where no one could reach.

I think I would like it,
At least I would try.
But I don't have wings
Like a butterfly.
—Marie E. Cecchini

The Beginnings Of A Butterfly

Your little ones will be fascinated to learn about the growth cycle of the butterfly. Share a nonfiction book about butterfly growth, such as *Monarch Butterfly* by Gail Gibbons (Holiday House, Inc.). As youngsters view the pictures, paraphrase the text to suit your students' interest level.

After discussing the growth cycle of a butterfly, prepare a sheet of chart paper with the story-starter sentence, "Once upon a time, there was a little egg." Ask the children to help you write a story about the growth of a butterfly. Personalize the story by naming the caterpillar in your tale. When the story has taken your caterpillar character from egg to butterfly, reread it to the class and invite them to share their comments. Display the story on a wall or bulletin board.

Then invite students to become illustrators as well as authors. Give each child a turn at a painting easel that is supplied with large sheets of art paper and several colors of paint. Have each child paint her favorite part of the caterpillar's story. When everyone has had an opportunity to create an illustration, mount the finished artwork around the chart story.

Counting Caterpillars

What could be more fun than a wriggly rhyme? Create a pair of storytelling gloves to wear that will delight your youngsters as you tell this tale of metamorphosis. Purchase a pair of canvas work gloves. Paint the palms of the gloves with bright colors of fabric paint; then allow the paint to dry thoroughly. To the top of each glove's fingertips, attach the hook side of a small piece of self-adhesive Velcro®. Prepare the eggs by attaching the loop side of a piece of Velcro® to each of five small, white pom-poms. To prepare each of the caterpillars, use hot glue to attach four small, green pom-poms together. Hot glue two wiggle eyes to one end of each caterpillar. Attach the loop side of a piece of Velcro® to the underside of each caterpillar. Attach each egg to the left glove and each caterpillar to the right glove. Put on the gloves; then follow the directions to make this story come to life!

Five Little Caterpillars

Five little eggs
Sitting on a leaf.
Will they ever hatch?
Oh my! Good grief!   *Hide right fingers under left hand.*

Then before you know it,   *Extend and wiggle fingers of right hand.*
Quick as a wink,
Out come caterpillars—
Five, I think.   *Count "1-2-3-4-5."*

They're eating and eating   *Wiggle fingers.*
And eating some more.
One crawls away,   *Remove caterpillar from pinky.*
And then there are four.

Four little caterpillars
Happy as can be.
One crawls away,   *Remove caterpillar from ring finger.*
And then there are three.

Three little caterpillars
Wondering what to do.
One crawls away,   *Remove caterpillar from middle finger.*
And then there are two.

Two little caterpillars
Just having fun.
One crawls away,   *Remove caterpillar from index finger.*
And then there is one.

One little caterpillar…
Now, what's this?
Just like magic,   *Wrap fingers around thumb.*
He's formed a chrysalis!

Just watch and see.   *Remove caterpillar from thumb.*
Don't blink an eye.
The chrysalis opens.
He's become a butterfly!   *Lock thumbs; extend and wiggle fingers.*

—Marie E. Cecchini

Spread Your Wings

Encourage your little ones to dramatize the metamorphosis of an egg into a butterfly with this movement activity. Before beginning the activity, make a pair of butterfly wings for each child. To make a pair of wings, simply gather a large sheet of colorful tissue paper in the center and secure it with a spring-type clothespin. Set the wings aside for students to use at the end of the activity.

To begin, invite each child to pretend that she is an un-hatched caterpillar, curled tightly inside an egg. Ask each child to "hatch" from her egg. Then encourage each wiggling, hungry caterpillar to crawl about, search for food, and "munch" on her favorite plants. When each caterpillar decides she is so full she can hardly move, have her pretend to form a chrysalis. Then visit each "sleeping" caterpillar to clip a pair of butterfly wings to the back of her clothing. When each caterpillar has received her wings, tell her to begin "breaking" from her chrysalis. Encourage each little butterfly to crawl out of her chrysalis, then rest as her wings dry and stretch out in the sun. Invite the newborn butterflies to "fly" gently around the room and out to the playground. Fly away!

adapted from an idea by Marsha Feffer—Pre-K
Salem Early Childhood Center
Salem, MA

Barefoot Butterflies

Let these butterflies do a springtime two-step across your classroom walls! Begin by spreading newspaper over a tabletop and the surrounding floor area. Working with one student at a time, ask each child to remove his shoe and sock from one foot. Use a paintbrush to cover the bottom of the child's foot with a bright color of washable paint. Then have him press a footprint onto the center of a 12" x 18" sheet of white drawing paper. (Have a tub of warm water and some paper towels handy for immediate cleanup.) Have the child replace his sock and shoe. Using several different colors of washable paint, paint the palms and fingers of both his hands. Ask him to make a set of handprints on each side of the footprint. Then instruct him to wash and dry his hands. Allow the footprint and handprints to dry. When the paint is dry, have each child cut around the shape of his butterfly. Give each child two wiggle eyes to glue onto his butterfly. Tape two pipe-cleaner antennae to the butterfly. Then invite each child to flutter his butterfly to a chosen spot on a classroom wall. Use masking tape to mount the butterflies in place for a springtime parade!

Kathleen Lademan—Pre-K
Noah's Ark Child Care Center, Portland, ME

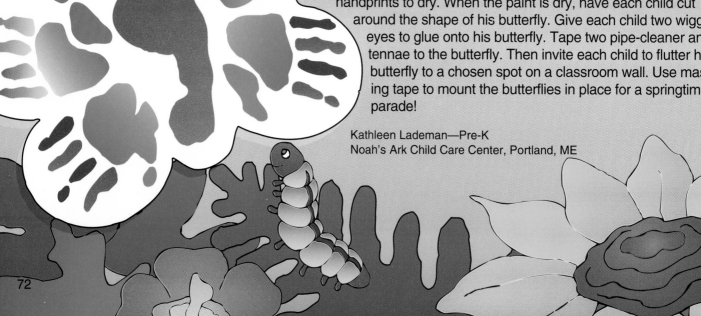

Clay Creations

Explore the shapes and colors of caterpillars and butterflies with this sculpting and painting activity. Begin by collecting photographs of colorful caterpillars and butterflies to inspire the children. Look through nature magazines, such as *Ranger Rick* or *National Geographic,* or check out a good nonfiction book, such as *Butterflies And Moths* by Bobbie Kalman and Tammy Everts (Crabtree Publishing Company). Discuss the various types of butterflies pictured, noting their coloring and markings. Then have the children assist in preparing a batch of baker's dough using the recipe provided. Give each child a small amount of dough. Ask her to begin by pulling off a ball of dough and rolling it into a caterpillar. Then have her use a small rolling pin to flatten the remainder of her dough. Provide a butterfly-shaped cookie cutter and ask each child to cut a butterfly from her dough. Place the shapes on waxed-paper-covered cookie sheets. Use a permanent marker to print each child's name on the waxed paper next to her shapes. Bake the children's creations in a 300˚ oven for 30 to 60 minutes or until dry. When the shapes have cooled, provide paints and brushes. Have the children decorate their clay figures using the photographs as inspiration.

Baker's Dough

(enough for approximately 16 students)
2 cups flour
1 cup salt
3/4 cup water
Mix all the ingredients together, adding additional water if necessary.
Knead until the mixture forms a smooth dough.

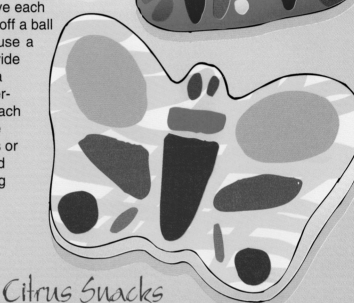

Citrus Snacks

Serve a springtime snack that resembles a beautiful butterfly. Peel several oranges and divide them into halves. Separate each half into sections containing two segments each. Being careful not to pull the segments completely apart, pull each section partially apart, starting from the inside where the seeds are and going toward the outside where the peel was. Lay each set of orange segments on a small paper plate; then give one plate to each student. Have each youngster add two short lengths of string licorice to resemble the butterfly's antennae. What a juicy creation!

Tammy Bruhn—Pre-K
Temperance, MI

Butterfly Books

Where Butterflies Grow
Written by Joanne Ryder
Illustrated by Lynne Cherry
Published by Lodestar Books

Hi, Butterfly!
Written & Illustrated by Taro Gomi
Published by William Morrow & Company
(This book is out of print.
Check your local library.)

The Lamb And The Butterfly
Written by Arnold Sundgaard
Illustrated by Eric Carle
Published by Orchard Books

Dandy Dandelions

Here's a dandy unit about everyone's favorite weed—the dandelion. Whether you're of the opinion that this bright yellow flower is a pest or a posy, you'll find the art, science, movement, and cooking activities to be delightfully fun. And we're not "lion"!

ideas contributed by Deborah Burleson

Dandy *Lion?*

Your little ones may wonder about the name of this bright yellow-and-orange flower. Some folks like to think that the dandelion looks like a lion's mane. The truth is, the word *dandelion* comes from the French *dent de lion* which means "lion's tooth." It was probably named this because of the dandelion's toothed leaves.

Take A Closer Look

Spring has sprung—and so have the dandelions! If you're going to be studying dandelions, you're going to need a bountiful supply of this wildflower. Take youngsters out for a dandelion hunt. Or request that parents help children look for dandelions in their own yards. Be sure to collect or request individual dandelion blossoms, blossoms that have lost their petals and turned to seed, as well as entire plants including the flower, stem, leaves, and root system. It may be helpful to know that dandelions blossom from May through June, and sometimes later, into the fall. And there's no need to worry about picking too many. Dandelions grow almost as quickly as the sun spreads its shine!

When you have a supply of the dainty dandelion, provide youngsters with hand magnifiers for taking a closer look. As a class, take the time to look at, smell, and feel the plants or flowers. You may discover that the blossom is actually made of more than 100 tiny flowers and that the stems are slightly hairy. Encourage careful observation with open questions such as, "How many fluffy seeds do you think this dandelion has?" or "Why do you think the leaves have jagged edges?"

Flower Or Fluff?

Is a dandelion still a dandelion when its flower turns to fluff? Absolutely! Use this crafty idea to discuss the stages and changes of a dandelion's growth cycle. Reproduce, color, and cut out the growth-cycle pattern on page 77. Sponge-paint a paper plate yellow. Paint a paper-towel tube green. When the paint is dry, attach the pattern to the center of the plate with a brad. Cut out construction-paper dandelion leaves; then glue them to the paper-towel tube. Tape the tube to the back of the paper plate.

Beginning with the picture of the seed in the ground, explain to youngsters how a dandelion seed grows, blossoms into a flower, turns into many seeds, and blows away to begin the process again. If desired, assist youngsters in making similar dandelions of their very own.

I'm A Dandelion

(sung to the tune of "I'm A Little Teapot")

I'm a dandelion,
Oh, so small.
I'm growing bigger;
Now I'm tall.

Soon my yellow blossom
Will turn to fluff.
Along will come the wind
With a great big huff.

Then my dandy seeds
Will dance around—
Traveling to places;
Floating to the ground.

Crouch down.
Slowly rise.
Stand.

Round arms over head.

Turn in a circle.
Blow.

Wiggle fingers above head.

Lower fingers to the ground.
—Deborah Burleson

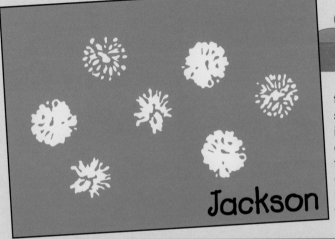

Jackson

Dandy Prints

Use a bunch of blossoms to make dandelion prints. In separate trays, pour yellow and white tempera paints. Clip the dandelion stems to about an inch below the flower. For each child, personalize a sheet of green and a sheet of blue construction paper. Guide each child to dip a dandelion into the yellow paint and press it onto the green paper to represent dandelions growing in the grass. Guide him to then dip another dandelion into white paint and press it onto the blue paper to represent the dandelion seeds floating through the air.

Puff Cookies And Dandelion Drink

Dandelion pizza? Dandelion jelly? Believe it or not, dandelions are actually as useful as they are pretty. Dandelions can be raised in gardens for use as greens to eat. Some health-food stores sell dehydrated dandelions for making tea and other products. Since many dandelions in populated areas have been sprayed with weed killer, cooking with fresh dandelions requires caution. Instead try these fun alternatives!

Dandelion Drink

13-ounce package of lime-flavored powdered drink mix
46-ounce can of unsweetened pineapple juice
sugar to taste

Following the package directions, add water to the powdered drink mix. Stir in the pineapple juice; then add sugar to taste.

Dandelion Puff Cookies

12-ounce box of vanilla wafers
16-ounce package of softened cream cheese
or white frosting
14-ounce package of coconut

To make a dandelion puff cookie, spread cream cheese or frosting on a vanilla wafer. Dip the cookie into the coconut.

Giant Dandelions And Puffballs

Make these dandelions and puffballs to use with the outdoor and fingerplay ideas on this page, or as manipulatives during math activities. Cut a 4" square from cardboard. Wrap a length of yellow or white yarn (about 6 1/2 yards long) around the square 100 times. Carefully slide the wrapped yarn off the cardboard; then tie and knot a length of yarn around the center of the looped yarn. Cut the loops; then shape the ball. These fluffy flowers never fade!

Happy Dandelions

Using the directions in "Giant Dandelions And Puffballs," make ten dandelions and ten puffballs. Ask ten volunteers to stand in a line; then give each volunteer one dandelion and one puffball. Ask each child to hold the dandelion in front of him with one hand and the puffball behind his back with the other hand. As you recite each verse of this rhyme, ask one student to switch the position of the dandelion and puffball so that the dandelion is hidden behind his back and the puffball is in front of him.

Pam Crane

Ten happy dandelions
Growing in a line.
One turned to fluff and
Then there were nine.

Nine happy dandelions
Growing by the gate.
One turned to fluff and
Then there were eight.

Eight happy dandelions
Growing toward heaven.
One turned to fluff and
Then there were seven.

Seven happy dandelions
Growing to be picked.
One turned to fluff
And then there were six.

Six happy dandelions
Growing up with pride.
One turned to fluff and
Then there were five.

Five happy dandelions
Growing more and more.
One turned to fluff and
Then there were four.

Four happy dandelions
Growing wild and free.
One turned to fluff and
Then there were three.

Three happy dandelions
Growing just for you.
One turned to fluff and
Then there were two.

Two happy dandelions
Growing in the sun.
One turned to fluff and
Then there was one.

One happy dandelion
Having lots of fun.
It turned to fluff and
Then there were none!

—Deborah Burleson

Puffball Toss

Once you've made a supply of puffballs, go outside for a round of puffball toss. Encourage students to toss the puffballs to partners. Or challenge them to toss the puffballs into baskets. Encourage any student who wishes to play independently to close his eyes, toss the ball into the air, then open his eyes to discover where the ball landed.

Dandelion Growth-Cycle Pattern
Use with "Flower Or Fluff?" on page 74.

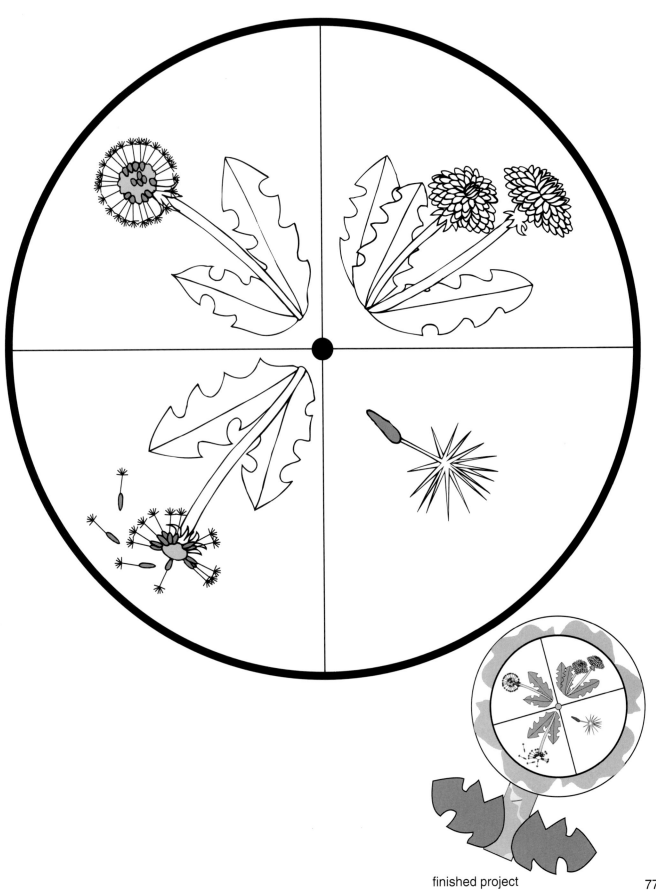

finished project

Bubble Magic

Mix a little soap with water and what do you get? A magical solution for good, clean fun! So take a deep breath and blow into a unit that is positively bubbling over with art, science, language, and movement discoveries!

ideas by Lucia Kemp Henry

The Magic Potion

1/8 cup dishwashing liquid
1 cup water

This simple solution and the bubble-blowing tools suggested below are all you'll need to burst into bubble-blowing mania. Consider mixing a personalized plastic container full of the solution for each child. Or create a laboratory for the serious study of bubbles by multiplying the soap and water amounts as needed to fill a water table full of the solution. Place the water table outside along with these bubble-blowing tools made from inexpensive and easy-to-find household items. Students are sure to be delighted to discover that they can create billions and billions of bubbles!

What is a bubble?
A bubble is air trapped inside a ball of liquid.

Magic Wands And Bubble Blowers

Loop-And-Handle Wand
Twist a pipe cleaner as shown. Dip the loop into the bubble solution and blow through the opening or wave the wand in the air.

Fly Swatters
Dip a plastic fly swatter into the bubble solution; then wave it through the air.

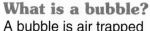

Six-At-A-Time Bubble Wand
Tape a set of plastic, soda-can rings to one end of a dowel. Dip the rings in the bubble solution; then wave them through the air.

Bubble Straws
Cut a drinking straw in half; then cut the tip four times as shown. Dip the cut tip of the straw in the bubble solution. Gently blow through the clean end of the straw.

Spool Blowers
Soak an empty, plastic spool in warm water to remove the label. Dip one end of the spool in the bubble solution; then gently blow through the other end.

Bubble Tubes
Cut cardboard tubes into three-inch lengths. Dip one end of a tube in the bubble solution. Blow gently through the other end.

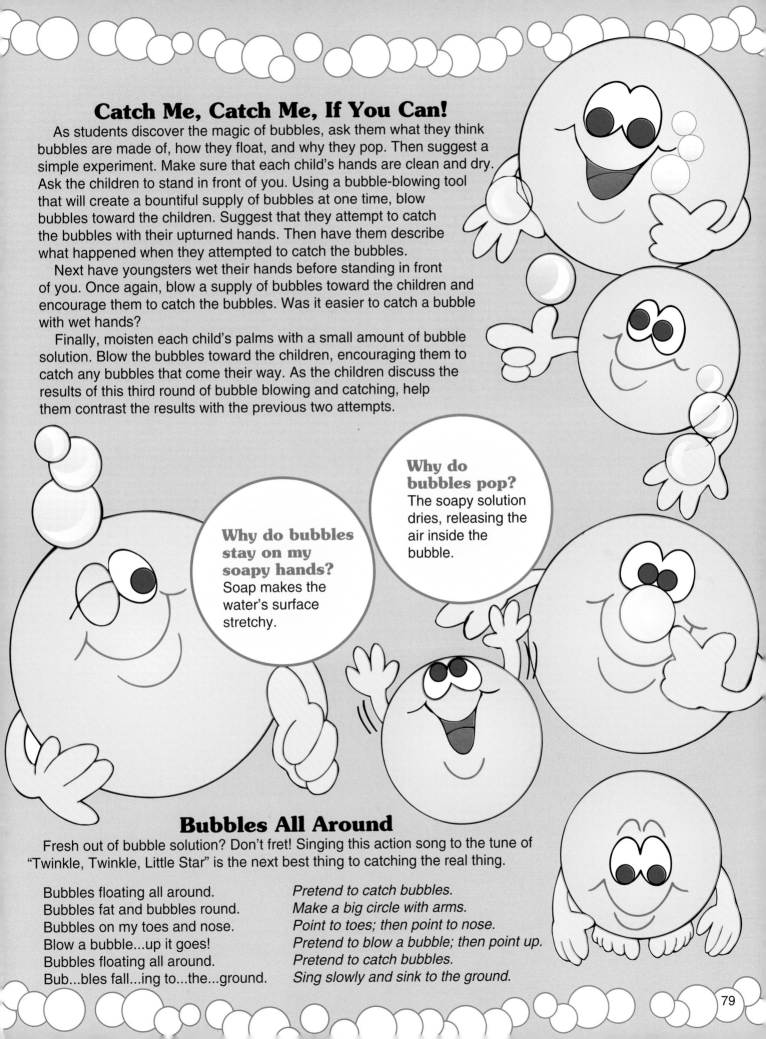

Catch Me, Catch Me, If You Can!

As students discover the magic of bubbles, ask them what they think bubbles are made of, how they float, and why they pop. Then suggest a simple experiment. Make sure that each child's hands are clean and dry. Ask the children to stand in front of you. Using a bubble-blowing tool that will create a bountiful supply of bubbles at one time, blow bubbles toward the children. Suggest that they attempt to catch the bubbles with their upturned hands. Then have them describe what happened when they attempted to catch the bubbles.

Next have youngsters wet their hands before standing in front of you. Once again, blow a supply of bubbles toward the children and encourage them to catch the bubbles. Was it easier to catch a bubble with wet hands?

Finally, moisten each child's palms with a small amount of bubble solution. Blow the bubbles toward the children, encouraging them to catch any bubbles that come their way. As the children discuss the results of this third round of bubble blowing and catching, help them contrast the results with the previous two attempts.

Why do bubbles pop?
The soapy solution dries, releasing the air inside the bubble.

Why do bubbles stay on my soapy hands?
Soap makes the water's surface stretchy.

Bubbles All Around

Fresh out of bubble solution? Don't fret! Singing this action song to the tune of "Twinkle, Twinkle, Little Star" is the next best thing to catching the real thing.

Bubbles floating all around.	*Pretend to catch bubbles.*
Bubbles fat and bubbles round.	*Make a big circle with arms.*
Bubbles on my toes and nose.	*Point to toes; then point to nose.*
Blow a bubble...up it goes!	*Pretend to blow a bubble; then point up.*
Bubbles floating all around.	*Pretend to catch bubbles.*
Bub...bles fall...ing to...the...ground.	*Sing slowly and sink to the ground.*

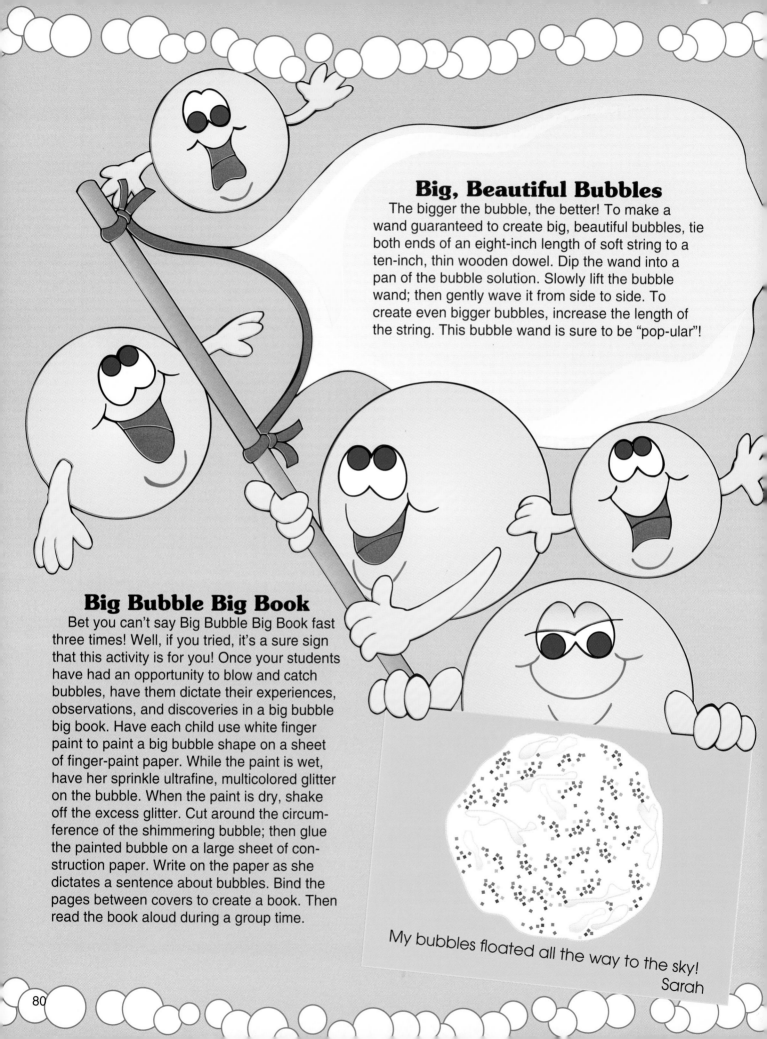

Big, Beautiful Bubbles

The bigger the bubble, the better! To make a wand guaranteed to create big, beautiful bubbles, tie both ends of an eight-inch length of soft string to a ten-inch, thin wooden dowel. Dip the wand into a pan of the bubble solution. Slowly lift the bubble wand; then gently wave it from side to side. To create even bigger bubbles, increase the length of the string. This bubble wand is sure to be "pop-ular"!

Big Bubble Big Book

Bet you can't say Big Bubble Big Book fast three times! Well, if you tried, it's a sure sign that this activity is for you! Once your students have had an opportunity to blow and catch bubbles, have them dictate their experiences, observations, and discoveries in a big bubble big book. Have each child use white finger paint to paint a big bubble shape on a sheet of finger-paint paper. While the paint is wet, have her sprinkle ultrafine, multicolored glitter on the bubble. When the paint is dry, shake off the excess glitter. Cut around the circumference of the shimmering bubble; then glue the painted bubble on a large sheet of construction paper. Write on the paper as she dictates a sentence about bubbles. Bind the pages between covers to create a book. Then read the book aloud during a group time.

My bubbles floated all the way to the sky!
Sarah

80

The Shape Of Bubbles To Come

Yet another bubble discovery awaits your little ones with this simple experiment. Blow some bubbles using a standard bubble-blowing wand with a round opening. Ask your little ones to observe the shape of the bubbles as well as the shape of the wand. Then bend several plastic-coated hangers into different shapes. Ask youngsters to predict how the bubbles blown from these wands will be shaped. Blow the bubbles and discuss the results.

Why are bubbles rounded in shape? The surface tension of the bubble solution pulls it inward. At the same time, the air inside the bubble is pushing out in all directions.

Bubble-Shaped Prints

With this group art activity, it really is circle time! Have your little ones gather around a large, bulletin-board-paper circle. Fill several meat trays with the same color of tempera paint; then set the trays on sheets of newspaper arranged outside the circle. Encourage youngsters to dip circular-shaped sponges and cardboard tubes into the paint, then press them onto the large circle. When the bubble-shaped prints are dry, replace the paint with a different color. Then invite students to gather around again for a second round of printing. Round and round and round we go!

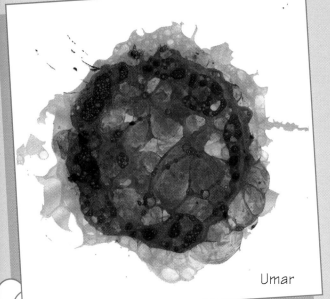

Umar

Pop Art

Capture the beauty of bubbles with this entertaining art project. Fill several plastic cups with water. Add several drops of dishwashing liquid and a spoonful of a different color of dry tempera paint to each cup of water. Stir the mixtures; then place the cups on a tray or towel. Provide each child with a straw and a personalized piece of white construction paper. To make pop art, a child uses his straw to blow air into a cup. When he has blown a fountain of bubbles, have him gently place his paper atop the bubbles. Repeat as desired to capture different colors of bubbles. Your little ones are sure to be blown away by the results!

Bubble Colors

The sky isn't the only place to spy a rainbow! There's a whole spectrum of colors on every bubble your little ones blow. To help children discover the colors on bubbles, invite them to join you in this activity. After seating the children on the floor, turn the lights off so that the lighting in your classroom is dim but not completely dark. Blow bubbles into the room; then ask the children to describe any colors they could see on the bubbles. Then take the class to a sunny area outside. Again blow bubbles and ask the children to describe the colors they could see. Have youngsters discuss the differences in the two rounds of bubble-blowing and give reasons for the appearance of colors on the bubbles when they were blown outside.

Why are there colors on a bubble?

When light shines through a bubble, the water bends the light and splits it into the colors of the rainbow.

A Rainbow In A Bubble

Let's look inside a bubble
To see if there might be
A few bright rainbow colors
For all of us to see.

Can you see red?
Can you see blue?
So many, many colors—
How do they look to you?

Can you see yellow?
Can you see green?
Aren't these pretty colors
The best you've ever seen?

Can you see purple?
Can you see rose?
How did such pretty colors
Get inside one of those?

How do bubbles get their colors?
Do you think you know?
Perhaps a rainbow lives inside
Each bubble that we blow!

—Lucia Kemp Henry

Watercolor Bubbles

After completing the activity described in "Bubble Colors," read the poem "A Rainbow In A Bubble" to your children. Ask volunteers to answer the questions posed in the poem. Then give each child an opportunity to record his discovery by painting watercolor bubbles. Provide each child with a sheet of painting paper on which a large circle has been traced. Have each child paint the circle with watercolor paints. When the paint is dry, cut out each child's circle. Mount all of the watercolor bubbles on a bulletin board along with a copy of the poem "A Rainbow In A Bubble."

Bubbles, Bubbles Everywhere!

Little ones are fascinated by the magic of bubbles floating through the air. Make these simple bubble projects to suspend from your ceiling and you'll add a bubbly touch to your classroom that will never pop or float away! To make a floating bubble, cut a circle from tagboard; then cut out a circle from the center. Squeeze glue along the edge of one side of the circle. Press a sheet of white tissue paper that is slightly larger than the circle onto the glue. Allow the glue to dry, then repeat the process on the other side of the circle. Trim the excess tissue paper from around the circle. Then splatter-paint both sides of the circle with light blue tempera paint. Punch a hole near the edge of the circle; then thread with clear fishing line. Tie a knot in the fishing line and suspend the circle from the ceiling. Bubbles, bubbles everywhere. Floating, floating in the air!

Why do bubbles float up?

Warm air is lighter than cold air. If the air you blow into a bubble is warmer than the air around you, the bubble will float up.

Double The Bubble Fun

The most magical thing about bubbles is that no matter how you blow them, you always end up with lots of fun! As a culminating activity, videotape your youngsters blowing bubbles. Take the class outside on a sunny day and provide them with plenty of the magic potion and the magic wands or bubble blowers described on page 78. Using a portable tape player, play the instrumental music of your choice. Film the class in action, being sure to get a close-up of each child. If desired, interview each child as he blows bubbles.

After watching the video as a class, prepare to send the video home by wrapping it in plastic bubble wrap. Place the wrapped video in a bag along with a loop-and-handle bubble-blowing wand and a copy of the bubble-solution recipe (see page 78). You may wish to send along a copy of *Bubble Bubble* by Mercer Mayer (Rain Bird Products). Also include a note encouraging parents to enjoy the video for several days and to keep the recipe and wand when returning the video, book, and bag to school. Replace the recipe and wand before sending the bag home with another child. Bubbles away!

We captured our bubble magic on video! When you have enjoyed the video and the book, please return them. Keep the recipe and wand for your own bubble fun!

Tutti-Frutti

The time is ripe for seeing, touching, smelling—and certainly tasting—fruit. Here's a unit with sensational fruit activities along with a bumper crop of suggestions for giving your classroom learning centers tutti-frutti appeal.

Bunches Of Fruit

To really sink your teeth into this seasonal topic, you'll want to gather a wide variety of fruits. Compile a list of fruits—including those named in Lois Ehlert's *Eating The Alphabet* (Harcourt Brace Jovanovich, Publishers)—that you would like to include in your fruit exploration. Send a note home requesting that each child visit the grocery store. Suggest that parent and child together scan the selection of fruits available and select two pieces of fruit to bring to school—one piece of the child's choice and one piece of the requested fruit.

When the students arrive at school with their fruit selections, have each child name his fruits and indicate which was his personal choice. Set the requested fruits aside. Then, using a large floor graph, graph the children's chosen fruits and discuss the results.

During another group time, read aloud *Eating The Alphabet*. Encourage students to identify the real fruits that match Ehlert's illustrations.

Jennifer Bouse—Four- And Five-Year-Olds
Laurens Community Preschool
Laurens, IA

A Close-Up Look

If you're focusing on fruit, you won't want to miss the opportunity to visit an apple orchard, walk through an orange grove, and ride through a cranberry bog. And wouldn't it be ideal if your little ones could observe the entire fruit cycle—from planting to picking to eating? It's all possible with a live-action video called *Fruit: Close Up And Very Personal* (available from Stage Fright Productions: 1-800-979-6800). Since this is a no-narration video, be sure to engage youngsters in conversation as you watch. It'll be a very fruitful language experience!

All Sorts Of Fruit

Fruit can be sorted into six families: pomes (apple, pear); citrus fruits (orange, tangerine, lemon, lime, grapefruit); tropical fruits (banana, pineapple, papaya); melons (watermelon, cantaloupe, honeydew); berries (blackberry, blueberry, strawberry, cranberry, kiwi fruit, grape); and drupes (peach, cherry, plum, apricot). But provide youngsters with baskets of fruit and they'll probably come up with some classifications of their own. Working with a small group of children, take the time to carefully look at and feel the fruits you have collected. Invite young- sters to gently thump the fruits to see if they produce different sounds. Encourage the children to sort the fruits by color, size, texture, and weight.

What's Inside?

Isn't it about time to take a peek inside that delicious-looking fruit? Group the fruits according to the six classifications. Then continue your sensory exploration by slicing into each type of fruit. Lead students to observe the differences in the fruits that have seeds, pits, or cores. While you're at it, cut the fruit into small pieces so that each student can feel, smell, and taste each fruit.

Fruit Medley Melody

Encourage each child to personalize this song by naming the fruits she chose to include in her own fruit salad.

(sung to the tune of "Jack And Jill")

[Pears] and [grapes] went in the bowl.
[Bananas] and [cherries] were added.
[Apples] were next and tossed with the rest.
I made my own fruit salad!

—*Nancy Jo Mannix
Orlando, FL*

Fruit Salad By Design

You'll probably have fruit left over when you complete the activity described in "What's Inside?" Cut the remaining fruit pieces into bite-sized chunks or slices and place each different kind of fruit in a sepa- rate bowl. Arrange the fruit on a table along with several types of fruit-flavored yogurt. Provide each child with a small bowl or cup and a spoon; then encourage him to fill his bowl with the different fruits of his choice. Have him top his salad with a spoonful of yogurt. As each child is enjoying his unique fruit salad, have him list the fruits he chose to include. Write his dictation on a sheet of art paper. When he has finished eating, provide him with fruit-scented crayons or markers for illustrating his page. "Fruit-licious!"

Zach's Fruit Salad

bananas   strawberries   blueberries

Strawberry
Blueberry

Sweet And Seedy Centers

Delicious Dramatic Play

Stock your dramatic play center with an assortment of real and artificial fruit. Provide a tub of water and towels for washing and drying the fruit and several small boxes for packing the produce. Collect a supply of canned fruit to place in the center as well. Suggest that youngsters use their imaginations to transform the center into a grocery store, restaurant, fruit stand, or produce warehouse. Whatever the setting, encourage children visiting the center to count and sort the fruit. Would you like some fruit today?

A Basketful Of Books

An artificial tree loaded down with holiday apple ornaments and other artificial fruit (available at craft stores) is sure to entice little ones to visit your classroom library. In the center, place a basketful of preschool-appropriate picture books about fruit. Here are some top picks:

Fruit: A First Discovery Book
Written by Gallimard Jeunesse and Pascale de Bourgoing
Illustrated by P. M. Valet
Published by Scholastic Inc.

What Am I? Looking Through Shapes At Apples And Grapes
Written by N. N. Charles
Illustrated by Leo and Diane Dillon
Published by The Blue Sky Press

Count The Ways

How can youngsters use fruit for math exploration? Let us count the ways! Stock the center with a supply of real, plastic, and canned fruit; fruit baskets; fruit boxes; and a measurement scale. Challenge your little ones to use the fruit to:

- sort and classify
- create patterns
- count as they fill and empty baskets
- create sets of more and less
- compare and seriate according to size

"A-Peel-ing" Art

Students are sure to have a "berry" fun time at your classroom art and painting centers when picking from these art projects.

(Note: Remind little ones that everything that smells good is not intended to be eaten or tasted. While completing these sweet-smelling art projects, keep plenty of fresh fruit on hand for snacking!)

Painting Produce

Add pizzazz to your painting center with paint that smells as good as it looks. Mix 1/2 cup of cold water with a 3-ounce package of fruit-flavored gelatin. Depending on the flavor of gelatin chosen, cut large fruit shapes from appropriate colors of construction paper for each child. Encourage painters at the center to paint a shape using the fruit-smelling paint. Then display the textured fruits on large bulletin-board paper trees. What an orchard!

Fruity Putty

Invite youngsters to sculpt fruit likenesses using different colors of this fruity-smelling dough.

0.3-ounce package of sugar-free, fruit-flavored gelatin
2 cups flour
1 cup salt
4 tablespoons cream of tartar
2 cups boiling water
2 tablespoons cooking oil

Mix the dry ingredients in a pan. Add the boiling water and cooking oil. Stir over medium-high heat until the mixture forms a ball. Place the ball on waxed paper to cool. Store in an airtight container. Cut the fruit picture from the gelatin box and attach it to the lid of the container to label it.

Cynthia Zsittnik—Preschool
Surrey Child Care Center
Hagerstown, MD

Where Does It Grow?

Make this sorting center to add to your science or discovery area. From garden catalogs and magazines, cut pictures of fruit as well as fruit-bearing plants, vines, bushes, and trees. Mount the pictures on tagboard cards; then laminate the cards. Attach the hook side of a piece of self-adhesive Velcro® to the back of each picture card. Next cover a large box with paper. Label each side of the box with the word *plant, vine, bush,* or *tree* and draw a corresponding picture. Attach to each side of the box the loop side of as many Velcro® pieces as you have pictures for that category. As children visit the center, assist them in deciding where each pictured fruit grows. Then have them attach the picture to the appropriate side of the box.

Nancy Jo Mannix
Orlando, FL

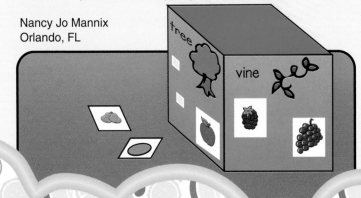

THE WAGON TRAIL

Feel like you're pulling youngsters through the lazy days of summer? If so, then load a day's worth of fun into little red wagons and head outside. A day on the wagon trail is all you'll need to get things rollin'!

WAGONS HO!

Find out which students in your class have wagons. Request that parents bring the wagons to school in advance of wagon day. When you are sure of the number of wagons you'll have, use these ideas to fill each wagon with the materials needed for independent play as well as teacher-directed activities. Consider asking for parent volunteers for your wagon day so that you'll have adult supervision at each station.

Once you've prepared the wagons, take them outside and arrange them in a circle. Based on the number of wagon stations you'll have on your wagon trail, divide the class into groups. Assign each group a station; then rotate the groups throughout the day. Wagons ho!

SPINNING YOUR WHEELS

In advance of wagon day, have each child bring to school toys that have wheels. (Be sure to label each toy with the owner's name.) Place the toys in a wagon. Encourage children at this station to discuss the similarities and differences in the toys. If desired fill the wagon with sand or soil.

Eva Murdock—Preschool
Children's Center, Shenandoah Baptist
  Church
Roanoke, VA

READING ABOUT WHEELS

Fill a wagon full of transportation-related titles. Encourage youngsters to find pictures of vehicles with wheels. Be sure to bring these great titles along for the ride!

Big Wheels
Written & Illustrated by Anne Rockwell
(Check your library.)

Wheels
Written & Illustrated by Byron Barton
(Check your library.)

Wheel Away!
Written by Dayle Ann Dodds
Illustrated by Thacher Hurd
Published by HarperCollins Children's
  Books

The Big Book Of Things That Go
A Dorling Kindersley Book
Published by Dorling Kindersley
  Publishing, Inc.

On The Go
Written by Ann Morris
Photographed by Ken Heyman
Published by Mulberry Books

MEALS ON WHEELS

How about snacks on wheels? Encourage youngsters to roll on over to this station to make edible wagons. For each child you will need one graham cracker broken in half lengthwise; four 1/2" thick, unpeeled banana slices; two toothpicks; several animal crackers; peanut butter; and a plastic knife. To make an edible wagon, spread peanut butter on both halves of the graham cracker. Secure a banana slice on each end of both toothpicks. Place the banana wheels and toothpick axles atop one peanut-butter covered graham cracker. Press the second graham cracker atop the first, so that the peanut butter is facing up. Press animal crackers into the peanut butter. Wow! It's an edible animal wagon!

Eva Murdock—Preschool
Children's Center, Shenandoah Baptist
   Church
Roanoke, VA

WATER WHEELS

Water play will add a cool touch to your outdoor wagon day. Fill a wagon with water and provide water wheels for exploration. Also include toy paddle boats and egg beaters for extra fun. Keep some towels nearby. The fun is sure to be wet and wild!

A WAGON OF MY OWN

To make a toy wagon of her own, each child will need one small shoebox, four wheels cut from black poster board, four large brads, one 12" pipe cleaner, red tempera paint, and a paintbrush. Prepare this station for painting by spreading newspaper inside the real wagon. To make a toy wagon, direct each child to paint her shoebox. When the paint is dry, assist her in attaching the wheels to the box with the brads. Poke two small holes in one end of the box. Thread one end of the pipe cleaner through both holes; then twist the pipe cleaner to secure it. Twist and shape the opposite end of the pipe cleaner so that it resembles a handle. These wagons really roll!

HAVE A BALL

Fill a wagon with a supply of small balls (or beanbags) in a variety of colors. Encourage the children to throw the balls into the wagon, count as they fill the wagon with balls, and sort the balls by color.

JOIN THE BANDWAGON

Stock a wagon station with rhythm instruments, a battery-operated tape player, and audiotapes of lively music. Sounds like wagon fun has begun!

IN AND OUT

This interactive station offers practice with locational concepts and opposites while encouraging language development. Place as many teddy bears or stuffed toys in the wagon as you will have children visiting the station at one time. When a group arrives at the station, give each child a toy to hold. Then read aloud *Sam's Wagon* by Barbro Lindgren (William Morrow and Company). As a follow-up, instruct each child in turn to place his toy inside, outside, under, and beside the wagon. Encourage each child to explain where his toy is located in relationship to the wagon. Next have pairs of children demonstrate opposite locations such as in and out, or over and under the wagon. Culminate the activity by inviting each child in turn to get in the wagon with his toy and go for a wagon ride. Wheee!

Kathy Mulvihill—Four-Year-Olds
Wee Care Preschool
Allendale, MI

BUILDING BLOCKS

A wagon makes the perfect foundation for a tower. As each group visits this station, encourage the children to cooperatively build a tower or building. When the group's structure is complete, carefully wheel it around the wagon trail for everyone to admire. Or, if your trail is bumpy, take a picture of each group of children with their structure.

COVERED WAGONS

Isn't it the perfect time of year for a parade? Culminate your day by returning the materials in each wagon to the classroom. Wash and dry any wagons containing sand and water. Then return the wagons to the trail. Provide youngsters with a collection of construction paper, markers, streamers, and cloth scraps. Encourage them to decorate the wagons by taping or tying on materials as desired. Then load everyone into the wagons, provide noisemakers, and head off on a wagon day parade.

Beauie Withrow—Pre-K Special Needs
E. M. Yoder Elementary
Mebane, NC

Crafts For Little Hands

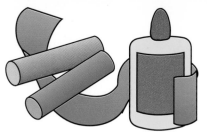

Crafts For Little Hands

Sweltering Sunlight

As the sun beats down with a vengeance, have your students create striking sun projects. To begin, draw a simple sun design on white art paper. Then use any color of glue to trace over the lines. Set the paper aside for a day or two to thoroughly dry. Use chalks to color the sections between the dried glue. Using lots of reds, yellows, and oranges will really turn up the heat!

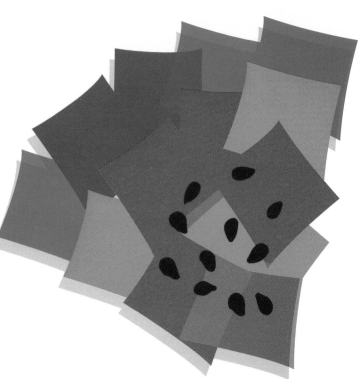

Mouthwatering Watermelon

You're going to want some watermelon seeds for this project, so why not give each student a wedge of real watermelon to get this project off to a tasty start. Ask students to save their watermelon seeds. Wash and dry the seeds before students begin their artwork. For this project, quarter several paper plates to create wedges. Provide two shades of green tissue-paper squares, and ask each student to glue some of these squares along the rim area of her wedge. Then provide two shades of red tissue-paper squares and have her glue them to cover the remaining area. To finish the watermelon wedges, have each student glue on several watermelon seeds. Yum!

Sponge Printing

Printmaking is lots of fun when you use giant sponges. Using tempera paint, paint a design directly onto a jumbo sponge. Pick up the sponge and press it, painted side–down, onto a sheet of paper. Just rinse and wring out the sponge, and it's ready for the next student. Not only is this type of printing much easier for young children, but the sponge also soaks up excess paint, eliminating runs.

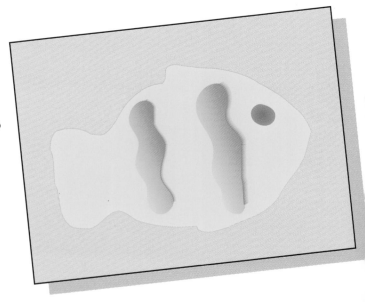

Frames With Flair

Ice-cream sticks or craft sticks can be used to make lovely gifts for National Grandparents Day. In advance, soak the sticks in food coloring and rubbing alcohol to create several colors of sticks. Allow the sticks to dry thoroughly. Have each student glue together four sticks to create a frame. Embellishments—such as ribbon and shaped sequins or tiny, punched-out paper designs—can be glued to the frames. The following day, assist each youngster as she glues a drawing or a photo to the back of the frame. On the back of each child's drawing or photo, attach a ribbon loop for hanging. Won't Grandma be surprised?

Chalk It Up!

Combine your students' artwork, stencils, and paper plates to create these rounded masterpieces. Soak large sticks of colored chalk in liquid starch for a few minutes. (Soaking time will vary depending on how porous your chalk is.) Using the chalk, have each student color in random fashion on heavily textured art paper. Allow the artwork to dry and weight it down to flatten it. Trace a stencil or template of each student's choice onto a thin paper plate. Use an X-acto® knife to cut on the resulting outline for each child. Have each student put glue on the rim of his paper plate, before turning it upside down onto the dried chalk artwork. When the glue is dry, have each student cut the excess paper from around the rim of his plate. If desired, have each student use colored glue to decorate his plate.

Apples, Apples Everywhere

Read aloud *Johnny Appleseed* by Steven Kellogg (Scholastic Inc.). Then provide students with sponges that have been cut into apple shapes. Clip a spring-type clothespin to each sponge for a handle. Pour tempera paint into pie tins. Have each student dip a sponge into paint and repeatedly press it onto white art paper. To finish the apple designs, have him paint stems and leaves on the apple prints.

Crafts For Little Hands

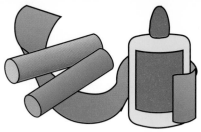

Fall Foliage Mobile

Your little ones will love the colorful effect of this work of art. To make a leaf mobile, arrange a fresh leaf on a sheet of waxed paper; then add a sprinkling of crayon shavings. Place a second sheet of waxed paper on top of the crayon shavings; then place the sheets between layers of newspaper. Press the sheets together with an iron set on low heat. Remove the waxed paper sheets from the newspaper and let them cool. Next cut loosely around the leaf and punch a hole in the top of the cutout. Personalize each cutout and tie it to a leafless tree branch with a length of monofilament line. Suspend this mobile from the ceiling for a colorful fall display.

Halloween Windsocks

These windsocks will add an attractive seasonal flair to any classroom. To make a windsock, dip a Halloween or seasonal cookie cutter into a thin layer of paint, colored glue, or glitter glue; then repeatedly press the design onto a 12" x 18" sheet of orange, white, or black construction paper. Continue in this manner using different cookie cutters. When dry, roll the paper into a loose tubelike shape; then staple it. Punch a hole on each side of the top of the windsock tube. Tie a length of string in each of the holes; then bring the two pieces of string together and knot their ends. Attach tissue-paper streamers to the bottom of the windsock.

Betsy Ruggiano—Three-Year-Olds
Featherbed Lane School
Clark, NJ

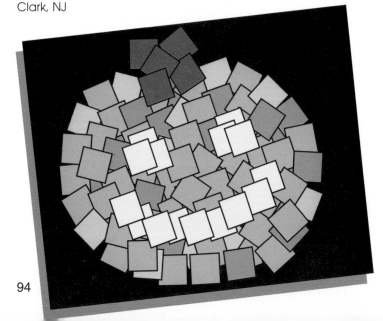

Torn Up About Jack-O'-Lanterns

Here's a Halloween idea your youngsters will love to get torn up about. Play some Halloween music or a story tape as you have youngsters tear orange, yellow, and green tissue paper into small pieces. To create this illuminating masterpiece, draw a circle on black construction paper and spread glue to fill the circle. Press enough orange paper pieces on the glue to cover it; then glue the yellow paper atop the orange paper to create a jack-o'-lantern's face. Add a green paper stem in the same manner. How's that for haunting results?

Indian Corn

As a tribute to the fall season, fill your room with these decorative works of art that resemble Indian corn. To make an ear of corn, trace a corncob shape onto construction paper; then cut on the resulting outline. Crumple small pieces of brown, orange, yellow, red, and black tissue paper. Glue the tissue paper to the corncob cutout to resemble corn kernels. When the glue dries, complete the activity by wrapping a large piece of tissue paper around the cutout to represent cornhusks. Mount these harvest projects on a wall or bulletin board, arranging them in columns among tissue-paper leaves and stems to resemble cornstalks.

Betsy Ruggiano—Three-Year-Olds
Featherbed Lane School
Clark, NJ

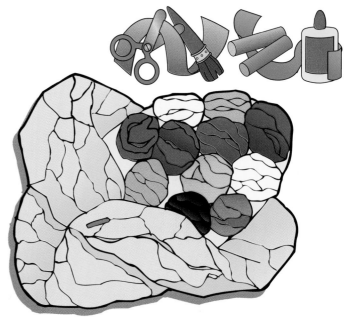

A Real "Corn-ucopia"

With a little shucking and painting, this "corn-ucopia" is bound to be a big hit. In advance, purchase Indian corn and fresh corn still in the husks. Shuck the corn. If you're using Indian corn, have youngsters shell it and use just the cob for this project. To make a cornucopia, dip either the ear of corn or the corncob into a shallow pan of brown tempera paint. On a sheet of construction paper, press and roll or drag the corn or cob to make a cornucopia-shaped design. Then roll several of the cornhusks into ball shapes and secure the ends with rubber bands. Dip a husk ball in a shallow pan of tempera paint; then repeatedly press it onto the paper near the cornucopia to resemble fruits and vegetables. Continue in this manner several times, using a different color of paint for each cornhusk ball. It's harvesttime!

Donna Selling and Brenda vonSeldeneck—Pre-Kindergarten
First Presbyterian Preschool, Waynesboro, VA

A Decorative Gobbler Centerpiece

Now these turkeys are worth gobbling about! To make a turkey, use pinking shears to cut a large half-circle from orange construction paper and a slightly smaller half-circle from brown construction paper. Then cut a turkey body, a square for the beak, and turkey feet from construction paper. Use a hole puncher to punch two circles for eyes. Glue the eyes and the turkey feet to the turkey's body. Fold the square to create a triangular-shaped beak; then glue the beak to the body. Attach a length of red curling ribbon to the beak to represent a wattle. Then glue the body to the smaller half-circle and the smaller half-circle to the larger half-circle. Staple a tagboard strip to the back of the turkey pattern. Next wrap the strip around a small pumpkin or vase filled with fresh flowers, sizing it accordingly. Then staple the ends of the tagboard strip. Display the completed projects in your classroom; then have each child take his turkey home for the Thanksgiving holiday. Gobble, gobble!

Ruth Meryweather—Three- and Four-Year-Olds
Uncasville, CT

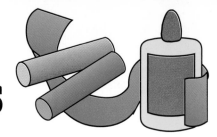

Crafts For Little Hands

compiled by Marie Iannetti

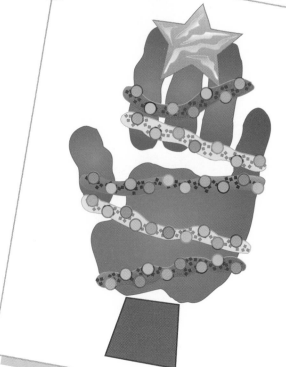

"Hand-y" Christmas Trees

Deck the halls with these terrific Christmas trees. To make a tree, press a hand into green tempera paint. Keeping the fingers and thumb close together, press the hand onto a sheet of white construction paper to represent tree leaves and branches. Cut a tree trunk from brown paper and glue it under the tree leaves. Then glue a gold or silver foil star to the top of the tree. To complete the project, use glitter glue, paint, or small candies to decorate the tree.

Tammy Bruhn—Pre-K, Ann Arbor, MI

Snowballs

Displaying these snowballs will create a spectacular winter sight. To make a snowball, place a Styrofoam ball in the bottom part of an egg carton to prevent the ball from rolling. Brush the upper half of the ball with thinned white glue; then place white and blue tissue-paper squares on the glue. Brush glue on the tissue paper and add additional squares so that they overlap the others. Sprinkle silver or clear glitter sparingly over the wet surface. Allow the glue to dry and repeat the process to complete the other half of the ball. It's a snowball to keep!

Wreath Ornaments

Spruce up any Christmas tree with these wreath ornaments. To make one, use green tempera paint to paint seven 2 1/2-inch-wide pieces of paper-towel or toilet-tissue cardboard tubes. When the paint is dry, thread a pipe cleaner through each of the pieces and twist the ends to secure it. Glue a red paper bow to the wreath. Thread a length of red ribbon through one of the cardboard pieces and suspend the wreath ornament on a tree for a festive display.

Martha Berry—Two-Year-Olds, Main Street Methodist Preschool Kernersville, NC

Angel Ornaments

These adorable angels make a heavenly display! To make an angel, use white tempera paint to paint a toilet-tissue tube. Allow the paint to dry. On foil wrapping paper, trace your hands; then cut on the resulting outlines. Laminate the cutouts if desired. On a two-inch circle cutout, draw a face. Staple the hand cutouts to the back of the toilet-tissue tube to resemble wings; then glue the face to the front of the tube. Use a hole puncher to punch a hole in the back of the tube; then attach a length of gold cord for suspending the angel. Hang these sweet cherubs on a tree or on your classroom door.

Martha Berry—Two-Year-Olds
Main Street Methodist Preschool
Kernersville, NC

Antique Photos

Here's a great project that little ones can give as gifts. In advance use black-and-white film to photograph each child wearing clothing such as floppy hats, boas, jewelry, oversized coats, vests, dresses, and sweaters. Have the film developed. Glue each photo to a piece of black poster board. Have each of your students glue items such as lace, ribbon, pearls, sequins, buttons, old jewelry, and doilies to the poster board. There you have it! An antique-looking memento that is sure to be a treasure.

Carol Hargett—Four-Year-Olds, Kinderhaus III, Fairborn, OH

A Sweet Gift

Have little ones make these sweet treats for holiday gift giving. For each child, supply a clean, plastic container from a beverage mix or frosting. Spray paint the lids with nontoxic paint, if desired. Have each child select from recent artwork, a small drawing, a section of a painting, or a finger-painting sample. Trim it to fit the side of the container. Assist each student in painting Mod Podge® on the exterior of the container, excluding the rim and bottom. Help each child place the artwork on the Mod Podge®. Brush over the artwork with a coat of Mod Podge®. Then have each student sprinkle the entire container with clear or frosted glitter. When the containers are dry, have each of your little ones fill his container with assorted wrapped candy for gift giving.

97

Crafts For Little Hands

compiled by Marie Iannetti

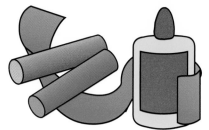

A Valentine Gift

These valentine keepsakes will surely help youngsters win the hearts of those they love. In advance copy the poem onto white paper; then photocopy a classroom supply onto construction paper. Assist each child in cutting an 8" x 11" piece of lace (or sheer netting). Have each child lay the lace (right side down) on a flat surface and place a handful of potpourri in the center of the lace. Help each child wrap the lace around the potpourri and gather the excess lace. Secure it with a rubber band. As a finishing touch, have each youngster cut a length of ribbon to tie around the sachet. Attach the poem to the sachet.

This pretty bag of potpourri
Was made for you by little me.
In it there are leaves and flowers
That will smell sweet for many hours.
I helped cut the ribbon and lace,
And tied it in a special place.
So keep it somewhere it can stay
To remind you of this Valentine's Day!

Tina Summers, North Little Rock, AR

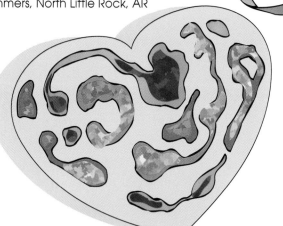

Sweetheart Art

Now, these hearts have lots of sparkle! In advance pour corn syrup into several containers (squeeze bottles work well). Add several drops of food coloring to tint each portion a different color; then stir well. Supply each child with a large red, pink, purple, or white heart cutout. Have each child squeeze the tinted corn syrup onto the cutout in the design of his choice. Then have him sprinkle glitter atop the wet syrup. Let the syrup dry for several days. Display these pretty-as-can-be hearts on a wall or bulletin board.

Sunflower Wind Dancers

Watch students' excitement bloom when they make these sunflower wind dancers. Supply each child with a yellow paper plate. Instruct each child to cut out triangles around the rim of the plate to resemble a sunflower. Punch two holes near the top of each flower. Thread a length of yarn through the holes and tie the ends. Then supply each child with three strips of 2" x 20" green crepe-paper streamers and a handful of sunflower seeds. Have each child glue the streamers to the back of the plate. Then have him turn the plate over and glue the sunflower seeds to the center of the plate. Suspend these wind dancers from your ceiling. Spring's right around the corner!

Gail Moody—Preschool
Atascadero Parent Education Preschool
Atascadero, CA

Shimmering Shamrocks

These shimmering shamrocks are sure to dazzle everyone who catches a glimpse of them. Have each child
place a dab of blue and a dab of yellow finger paint atop
a sheet of finger-paint paper. Then have him use his fingers
to blend the colors together and paint the paper. While
the paint is still wet, have each child sprinkle green glitter
(and foil pieces if desired) atop the paint. When the paint
dries, cut out a shamrock shape from each paper. These
sparklers will add a festive touch to any classroom!

Tammy Bruhn—Pre-K
Temperance, MI

Love That Rainbow!

This cooperative art project will add a splash of
color to your room. Using tape create arches on a
half-round table to create separate sections of a
rainbow. Then fill several pie pans with different colors of washable paint. Have your students finger-
paint inside each arch with a different color of paint.
When each arch has been painted, place a large
sheet of white bulletin-board paper (slightly larger
than the table) over the table. Gently press the paper onto the table. Carefully lift the paper; then let
the paint dry. Trim the excess paper from around the
rainbow. There you have it—a ravishing rainbow!

Joan Grossman
Bet Yeladim School
Columbia, MA

Suncatchers

Look out! These suncatchers are really hot! Tape a long sheet of clear
Con-Tact® covering (sticky side up) onto a tabletop. Provide students with
craft materials such as foil pieces, glitter, sequins, confetti, tissue paper, and
shaped hole punchers. Have each child use the punchers to create shapes
from various types of paper. Have each child choose from the items and
sprinkle the selected ones atop the Con-Tact® covering, decorating as
much of the covering as possible. Then place another sheet of clear Con-
Tact® covering, identical in size and shape, atop the first sheet. Gently press
the pieces together.

To display this cooperative project, suspend the sheet from a window for
a sparkling presentation. To make individual suncatchers, cut out desired
shapes from the decorated sheet of Con-Tact® covering. Punch a hole at
the top of each suncatcher. Thread a length of ribbon or yarn through the
hole; then suspend each suncatcher from a window.

Paula M. Piraino—Four-Year-Olds
Trinity Pre-School
Topsfield, MA

Crafts For Little Hands

Hens And Chicks

These hens and chicks are so adorable, even Old MacDonald would be proud! To make a hen, partially stuff a lunch-size paper bag with newspaper. Twist the remainder of the bag to create the hen's neck; then tie it with yarn. Staple the opening of the bag; then add crayon eyes and a construction-paper beak. Glue a supply of colorful feathers onto the paper-bag chicken.

To make a chick, purchase yellow cotton balls or tint cotton balls yellow by shaking them in a bag of yellow paint powder. To the cotton-ball chick, glue an orange construction-paper beak and black eyes that have been hole-punched from construction paper. Squirt a drop of glue in the bottom of a plastic Easter egg; then set the chick inside. Display the hens and chicks using the bulletin-board idea on page 287. Cluck, cluck!

Audrey Englehardt—Preschool Hearing Impaired
South Roxana School
South Roxana, IL

Easter Bonnets And Top Hats

After your little ones make these bonnets and top hats, you'll want to plan to have an Easter parade! To make a bonnet, trace the top of a small, paper bowl onto the center of a paper plate. Cut a circle from the center of the plate that is slightly smaller than the resulting outline. Insert the bottom of the bowl through the hole; then staple the rim of the bowl to the plate. Paint the bonnet. When the paint is dry, embellish the bonnet with ribbon, lace, artificial flowers, netting, feathers, or small, decorative animals. Punch two holes opposite each other on the rim of the hat; then tie a length of curling ribbon through each hole.

To make a top hat, paint a small popcorn tub black. Cut a brim from black poster board; then staple it to the rim of the tub. Add pizzazz to the top hat by adding wide ribbon, large feathers, or small, decorative animals. Hats on, everyone? It's time for an Easter parade!

Cindi Zsittnik—Pre-K, Wesley Grove Pre-K, Hanover, MD

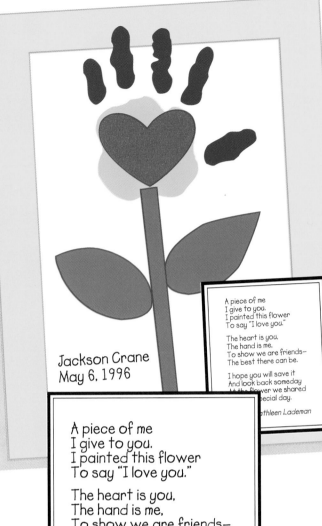

Jackson Crane
May 6, 1996

A piece of me
I give to you.
I painted this flower
To say "I love you."

The heart is you,
The hand is me,
To show we are friends—
The best there can be.

I hope you will save it
And look back someday
At the flower we shared
On your special day.

–Kathleen Lademan

Mother's Day Flower

Mothers will cherish these special flowers for years to come! In fact, you may want to suggest that these posy prints are perfect for framing. To make one, mount a sheet of white paper on a larger sheet of construction paper. Paint a child's palm a color chosen by the child, and his fingers a different chosen color. Have him press his hand onto the paper. When the paint is dry, glue a construction-paper stem and leaf cutouts below the flower. Glue a heart-shaped cutout to the center of the flower. Enlarge and duplicate the poem; then mount it below the print. Write, or have the child write, his name and the date. If desired make a card from the print by folding the paper in half and asking the child to write "Happy Mother's Day" on the outside of his card.

Kathleen Lademan—Pre-K, Noah's Ark Child Care Center
Portland, ME

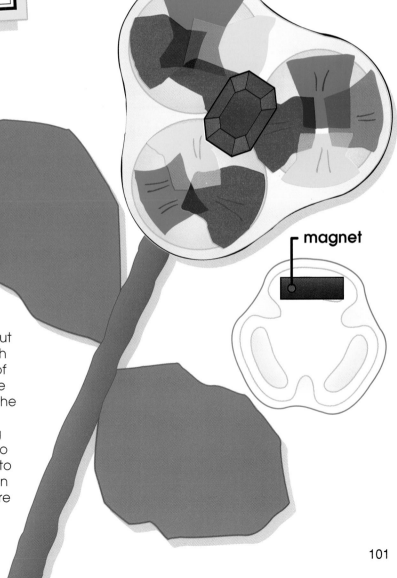

magnet

Pretty Plastic Posies

These fabulous flowers didn't come from the earth—but making them can help take care of it! Recycle plastic soda bottles (any size) by making them into pretty plastic posies. To make a flower, cut the bottom off a plastic soda bottle about one inch from the bottom. Paint thinned glue on the inside of the flower; then press tissue-paper squares atop the glue. When the glue is dry, mount a fake jewel on the center of the flower. Attach a piece of magnetic tape to the back of the posy to create a blooming magnet. Or tape construction-paper leaf cutouts to a green pipe cleaner; then tape the pipe cleaner to the back of the posy. Mount the posies on a bulletin board for a springtime display. It must be May! There are flowers everywhere!

Debbie Rowland—Two-Year-Olds
Valley View Christian Church Preschool, Dallas, TX

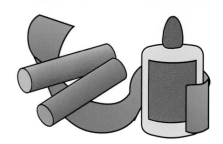

Crafts For Little Hands

Preschool Pals Pillowcase

Saying good-bye at the end of a year spent with friends can be difficult. Cheer up your little ones by having each child make a preschool pals pillowcase. Provide a white, prewashed pillowcase for each student, or ask each child to bring one. Inside each child's pillowcase, place a personalized sheet of paper that is the length and width of the pillowcase. On one side of each pillowcase, use a permanent fabric marker to write the poem shown, replacing the school name with your school's name. Then have each child use fabric paint to make a handprint on each pal's pillowcase. Label each handprint with the fabric marker. To permanently set the prints before washing, follow the paint manufacturer's instructions. When sleeping on these keepsakes, youngsters are sure to have sweet dreams of their preschool pals.

Cathy Schmidt—Preschool
DePere Co-op Nursery School, Green Bay, WI

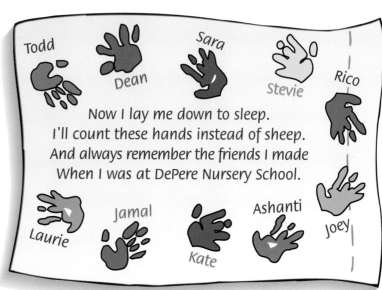

Todd
Dean
Sara
Stevie
Rico

Now I lay me down to sleep.
I'll count these hands instead of sheep.
And always remember the friends I made
When I was at DePere Nursery School.

Laurie
Jamal
Kate
Ashanti
Joey

Picture This, Dad!

Here's a frame Dad will be proud to display. To make a frame, glue eight craft sticks together in pairs; then set the sticks on waxed paper to dry. Glue the pairs together to form a frame. When the glue is dry, glue various types of pasta onto the frame. Again set the frame aside to dry. Brush on tempera paint or spray-paint the frame. When the paint is dry, spray the frame with acrylic finish. Attach a strip of self-adhesive magnetic tape to the back of the frame and it's ready for a pasta-perfect picture. Happy Father's Day!

Betsy Ruggiano—Three-Year-Olds
Featherbed Lane School
Clark, NJ

Fantastic Fruit Basket

Here's a fresh art idea—weave a paper basket; then use real fruit to make tasty prints! To make the basket, fold a 9" x 12" sheet of construction paper in half. Cut a basket shape. Then cut slits in the basket one inch apart, stopping one inch from the outer rim of the basket. Weave one-inch-wide construction-paper strips through the slits. Trim, adjust, and glue the strips. Glue the basket to a 12" x 18" piece of construction paper. Cut an assortment of fresh fruit in half. Then dip the fruit in appropriate colors of paint and press the fruit onto the paper. Fruit, anyone?

Carmen Carpenter—Pre-K
Highland Preschool
Raleigh, NC

Flashy Fish

Splish, splash! These flashy fish will swim by just in time to create a fantastic display. To create a one-of-a-kind fish, glue oval-shaped tissue paper and foil pieces onto a white construction-paper fish shape. Attach a black dot sticker to resemble an eye. Punch a hole near the mouth of the fish. To display, suspend a length of rope from your ceiling; then attach the fish to the rope by sliding one end of an opened paper clip through the rope and the other end through the fish's mouth. Wow—what a catch!

Gail Moody—Preschool
Atascadero Parent Education Preschool
Atascadero, CA

Handprint Octopus

Journey to the depths of the ocean and you'll find these awesome octopi. Using fluorescent, liquid tempera paint, paint a child's palm one color and his fingers (excluding his thumb) four different colors. With his hand slightly tilted to one side, have him press his hand on a sheet of black construction paper. Then have him press just his fingers under the palm print to resemble the remaining four arms of the octopus. When the paint is dry, glue two wiggle eyes to the octopus and add facial features with a marker. If desired add ocean-related stickers to the paper to create an underwater scene.

Jan Stremel—Four-Year-Olds
St. Paul Preschool
Dallas, TX

Sweet Starfish

Students will create star-quality starfish with this sweet painting technique. Combine sugar and several drops of food coloring with enough water to create a thick but paintable mixture. Use crayons to add features to a construction-paper starfish. Then paint the sugar mixture onto the starfish or spread the mixture on with your fingers. When the sugar mixture is dry, add these sweet starfish to a sand-and-surf display.

Joannie Netzler—Three-Year-Olds
A Special Place
San Jose, CA

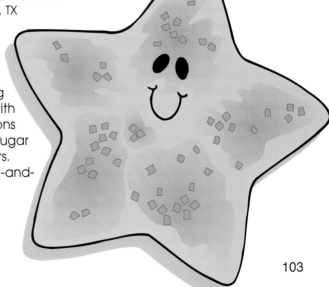

Super Suncatchers

Catch some rays with these super suncatchers. Before beginning this project, prepare a sun-shaped template. Using a permanent marker, trace the template onto a sheet of waxed paper. Paint slightly watered-down glue over the resulting sun shape; then cover the entire area with yellow and orange tissue-paper squares. Carefully apply additional glue over the tissue paper. Press another sheet of waxed paper atop the glue-covered tissue paper. When the glue is completely dry, cut a sun shape by cutting through all thicknesses along the marker outline. Give the suncatcher personality by adding marker and foam-piece facial features. Punch a hole near the top of the suncatcher and thread with a length of yarn; then suspend it near a window. Let the sun shine!

Pamela Vance—Preschool
Lake Geneva Cooperative Preschool
Lake Geneva, WI

Firecracker, Firecracker!

Boom, boom, boom! These dazzling fireworks explode with color and sparkle! To create a fireworks display, prepare several colors of tempera paint so that the paint is of a thick consistency. Add ultrafine glitter to the paint. Randomly put several drops of each different color of paint on a sheet of black construction paper. Using cotton swabs, spread the paint away from the drops so that they resemble fireworks. As a finishing touch, sprinkle multicolored glitter over the wet paint. Display these fantastic works together and you're sure to set off a big bang of compliments!

Gayle Simoneaux, Linda Powell, and Ellen Knight—Four-Year-Olds
Pineville Park WEE
Pineville, LA

Top-Notch Dinosaur

These decorative dinosaurs are sure to razzle-dazzle even the youngest of dinoenthusiasts! Cut the outline shape of a triceratops dinosaur from half a sheet of white poster board. Using two different colors of paint, sponge-paint the dinosaur shape. Set the painted shape aside to dry. Cut a coffee filter in half. Using a piece of colored chalk that matches one of the colors of paint, gently rub the flat side of the chalk over the ridges of the coffee-filter half. To adhere the chalk to the filter, spray it with hairspray. Glue the filter half to the neck, a wiggle eye to the head, and spiral-shaped pasta to each of the dinosaur's horns. These triceratops really are tops!

Janine Nordland—Preschool
Owatonna, MN

The Art Cart

The Art Cart

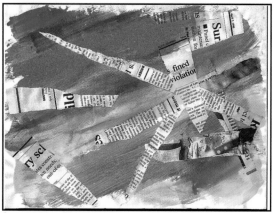

On art paper, torn newspaper and bold, wide strokes of brushed-on colored glue may be combined.

Newspaper, neon paper, and white and tinted glues have a striking impact on black construction paper.

Cuttings from painted or finger-painted papers mesh with tissue-paper pieces for this unusual look.

Welcome to "The Art Cart," where the creative process is in full bloom! Decorate a table in your classroom to resemble a cart. Stock the cart or adjacent shelving with the three types of materials mentioned (right). Then invite your youngsters to visit the art cart to create, using any variety of the available materials. While students are at the art cart, be supportive and encourage them to enjoy the creative process. So that their creations will be truly theirs, make a concerted effort not to guide the children's work or to advise them toward the achievement of a certain end product. Amazing things will soon be happening at your art cart!

Let the creativity begin!

Pam Crane

Stock your art cart with three types of things:

Any kind of paper—tissue paper, crepe paper, newspaper, finger-painted or painted papers, gift-wrapping paper, wallpaper, notebook paper, confetti, construction paper, tagboard, paper bags, corrugated paper, etc. Paper of any kind can be used for a background. Scraps or cuttings from any paper sheets can be glued onto the selected background.

Any color of glue—White school glue can be tinted by mixing in tempera paint or food coloring. Or pretinted glues can be purchased. A good variety of colors would include white (untinted) glue, black (or dark gray) glue, and several bright colors. To encourage varying uses of the glue, put some of each color into squeeze bottles and some of each color in margarine tubs. For each tub of paint, provide a wide brush like those that are used to apply house paint.

Any safe pair of scissors—There used to be just two types of scissors: plain ones and pinking shears. There's a lot more variety than that now. If you have scissors that make interesting cuts, such as scallops and waves, include them along with regular school scissors in the art cart. Thoroughly consider the safety implications before placing any scissors at the art cart.

A sculptured three-dimensional effect takes form with creative gluing.

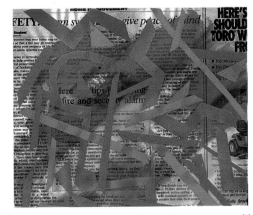

Torn or cut pieces of paper attached to newspaper with brushed-on colored glues entice the eye.

Thick streams of black glue attach bright papers to newspaper. Drizzled-on tinted glues add festive appeal.

The Art Cart

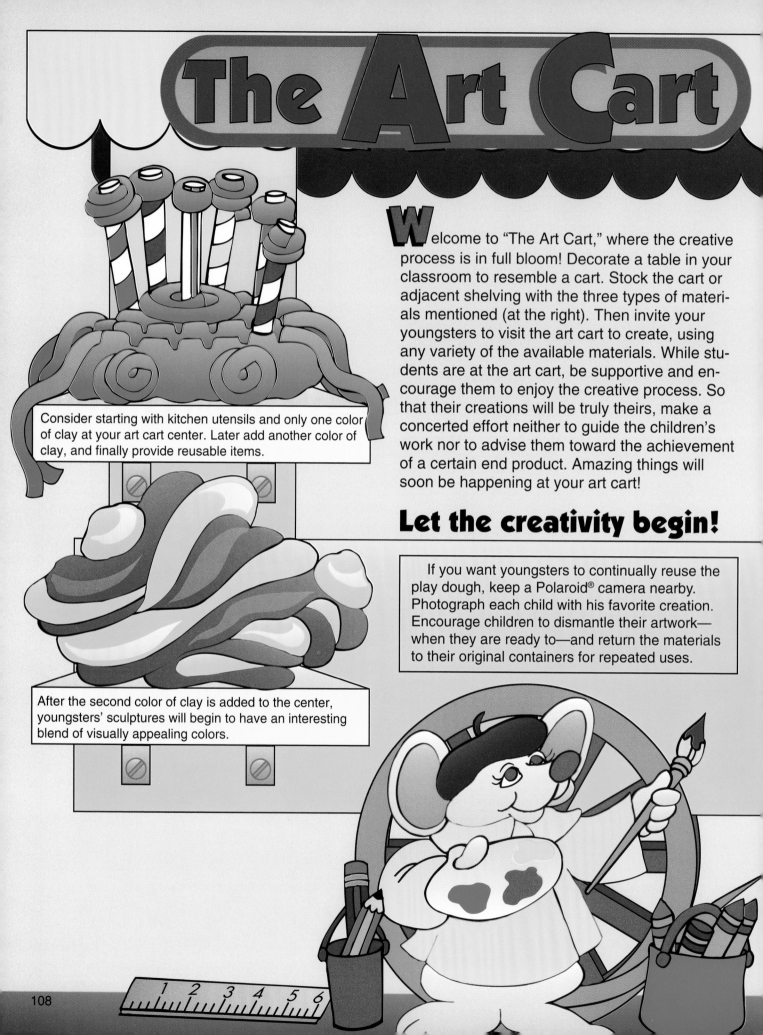

Welcome to "The Art Cart," where the creative process is in full bloom! Decorate a table in your classroom to resemble a cart. Stock the cart or adjacent shelving with the three types of materials mentioned (at the right). Then invite your youngsters to visit the art cart to create, using any variety of the available materials. While students are at the art cart, be supportive and encourage them to enjoy the creative process. So that their creations will be truly theirs, make a concerted effort neither to guide the children's work nor to advise them toward the achievement of a certain end product. Amazing things will soon be happening at your art cart!

Let the creativity begin!

If you want youngsters to continually reuse the play dough, keep a Polaroid® camera nearby. Photograph each child with his favorite creation. Encourage children to dismantle their artwork—when they are ready to—and return the materials to their original containers for repeated uses.

Consider starting with kitchen utensils and only one color of clay at your art cart center. Later add another color of clay, and finally provide reusable items.

After the second color of clay is added to the center, youngsters' sculptures will begin to have an interesting blend of visually appealing colors.

Stock your art cart with three types of things:

Soft, pliable dough—Prepare large batches of two primary colors of your favorite play dough or the recipe below. Although you may want to start with only one color of dough available for student use, later you may want to introduce a second color. Eventually, as students mix the two doughs together, a third color will be formed. Store the dough in airtight containers.

A variety of kitchen utensils—Rolling pins, garlic presses, cookie cutters, potato mashers, plastic knives, and other kitchen utensils come in handy when preschoolers are creating with dough. Store the utensils in a basket.

Reusable items—Collect jug lids, metal juice lids, Styrofoam packing pieces, straws, meat trays, and other reusable items. Prepare them for use by cleaning them if necessary. Cut the straws and meat trays into small pieces. Store each type of reusable item in a different container.

Using a single color of clay and the reusable items of their choice, preschoolers can create eye-catching masterpieces.

Before long youngsters will begin to explore all the possibilities opened up by combining the uses of different colors of clay, utensils, and recyclables.

Play Dough

1 cup flour
1/2 cup salt
2 teaspoons cream of tartar
1 cup water
1 1/2 teaspoons vegetable oil
food coloring

Mix the dry and wet ingredients separately before mixing them together. In a heavy skillet, cook the mixture over low heat until it thickens, stirring frequently. Cool the dough; then knead it until it's soft and smooth.

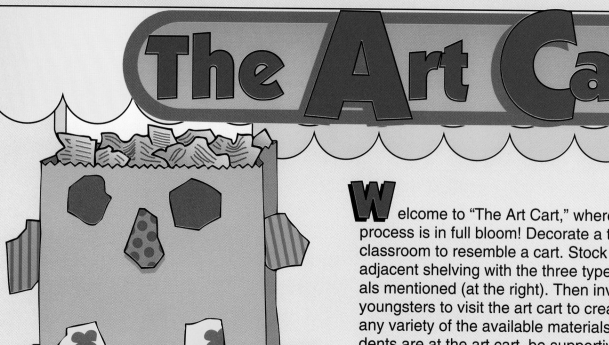

The Art Cart

An awareness of symmetry is apparent in this creature, which was created by cutting and gluing colorful paper to a brown grocery bag to create eyes, a nose, arms, legs, and feet. A piece of paper was also cut and glued to the inside of the bag so that the monster would have a stomach. As a finishing touch, the bag was stuffed with crumpled newspaper.

Welcome to "The Art Cart," where the creative process is in full bloom! Decorate a table in your classroom to resemble a cart. Stock the cart or adjacent shelving with the three types of materials mentioned (at the right). Then invite your youngsters to visit the art cart to create, using any variety of the available materials. While students are at the art cart, be supportive and encourage them to enjoy the creative process. So that their creations will be truly theirs, make a concerted effort neither to guide the children's work nor to advise them toward the achievement of a certain end product. Amazing things will soon be happening at your art cart!

Let the creativity begin!

Tools That May Be Used:
- scissors: pattern-cut-style and regular-cut-style
- hole puncher

This colorful, paper lunch bag was transformed into a hat by cutting the edges of the bag and attaching crepe-paper streamers. Crumpled tissue paper was attached to the hat with colored glue.

Stock your art cart with three types of things:

A variety of paper bags—Various colors and sizes of paper bags can be purchased at a craft store. Also provide brown paper lunch bags and large paper grocery bags.

A variety of papers—Provide newspaper, tissue paper, foil, crepe-paper streamers, finger-painted or painted papers, gift-wrapping paper, wallpaper, confetti, construction paper, tagboard, corrugated paper, etc.

Any color of glue—White school glue can be tinted by mixing in tempera paint or food coloring. Or pretinted glues can be purchased. A good variety of colors would include white (untinted) glue, black (or dark gray) glue, and several bright colors. Several colors of commercially made glitter glue will also add more variety. To encourage various uses of the glue, put some of each color into squeeze bottles and some of each color in margarine tubs.

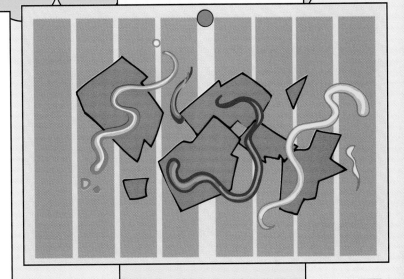

This collage was created by cutting apart a colorful, paper lunch bag. The pieces were glued to a large piece of newspaper. Colored glue was then drizzled over the entire project.

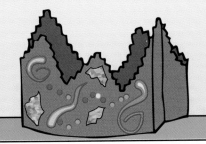

A colorful paper bag was cut using zigzag scissors. The top of the bag was inverted and decorated with foil pieces, confetti, and glitter glue—creating a crown.

The Art Cart

Rolling was a popular painting technique of our preschool testers. In this example, a roller brush was dipped in paint, then rolled onto a large piece of bulletin-board paper. Later a deodorant bottle filled with a different color of paint was rolled across the paper.

A pot scrubber was dipped in paint, then pressed onto a construction-paper flower shape.

The length of the cash-register tape was intriguing to many preschoolers. An empty thread spool was used to create the designs on this strip of paper.

Welcome to "The Art Cart," where the creative process is in full bloom! Decorate a table in your classroom to resemble a cart. Stock the cart or adjacent shelving with the three types of materials mentioned (at the right). Then invite your youngsters to visit the art cart to create, using any variety of the available materials. While students are at the art cart, be supportive and encourage them to enjoy the creative process. So that their creations will be truly theirs, make a concerted effort neither to guide the children's work nor to advise them toward the achievement of a certain end product. Amazing things will soon be happening at your art cart!

Let the creativity begin!

Ideas Contributed By:
Dawn Hurley—Two-Year-Olds, CUMC Child Care Center, Bethel Park, PA
Doris Porter—Preschool, Headstart, Anamosa, IA
Suzanne Fosburgh—Preschool, De Pere Cooperative Nursery School, Green Bay, WI

Stock your art cart with these three types of things:

Various types of paper—Construction paper in a variety of colors, poster board, cardboard, rolls of cash-register tape, tracing paper, newsprint, finger-paint paper, large sections of bulletin-board paper, etc. Cut the paper in a variety of sizes and shapes (some seasonal, if desired).

A variety of unusual painting tools—Potato mashers, empty thread spools, shaped sponges, forks, cotton balls, cotton swabs, combs, toothbrushes, pot scrubbers, feathers, ice scrapers, blocks, eyedroppers, Styrofoam® pieces, an old shoe, plastic cups, stencils, and any other items that will create unique designs. Of course, you'll want to include bristle, foam, and roller brushes in a variety of sizes.

Various colors of paint—To encourage varying uses of the paint, store the paint in containers such as margarine tubs, pie tins, baking pans, plastic ketchup or mustard bottles, roll-on deodorant bottles, refillable bingo bottles, and squirt bottles (such as hairspray bottles or plant misters). If the paint is too thick, thin it with water to produce a consistency suitable for spraying. Consider providing only one or two colors of paint when the painting tools are introduced. After your children have experimented with many of the painting techniques, increase the available colors of paint.

Recycled cardboard packaging was chosen as the background for these prints, which were created with a potato masher.

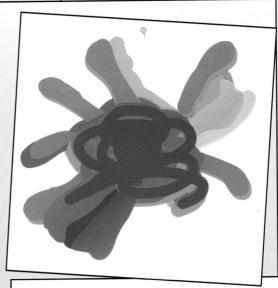

Traditional paintbrushes in several sizes were a favorite among a group of painting participants. A younger preschooler—fascinated by the process of painting and by the results of mixing paint colors—created this example. It may look brown, but, in fact, many colors were used!

The Art Cart

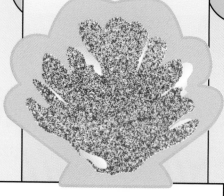

One preschooler used his fingers to rub paste on a construction-paper seashell shape. Yellow sand was then sprinkled over the paste.

Welcome to "The Art Cart," where the creative process is in full bloom! Decorate a table in your classroom to resemble a cart. Stock the cart or adjacent shelving with the three types of materials mentioned (at the right). Then invite your youngsters to visit the art cart to create, using any variety of the available materials. While students are at the art cart, be supportive and encourage them to enjoy the creative process. So that their creations will be truly theirs, make a concerted effort neither to guide the children's work nor to advise them toward the achievement of a certain end product. Amazing things will soon be happening at your art cart!

Let the creativity begin!

Preschoolers love to squirt glue! Working from left to right, a youngster squirted glue across this construction-paper pennant shape. He then covered the glue with sand.

When working with colored sand, consider moving your art cart to a location outdoors. Keep a supply of Handi Wipes and a large container nearby for easy cleanup. Encourage youngsters to shake excess sand into the container. Then, when your art projects are complete, pour the multi-colored sand into your sand table.

This example was made by a child who found the poster-board shape of the letter that begins his name. A glue stick was rubbed over the letter; then the sand was added.

Stock your art cart with these three types of things:

Colored Sand—Prepare several colors of sand using the recipe below. Store the sand in empty Parmesan cheese containers that have tops designed for both shaking and pouring. If the cans are not clear, wrap white paper around them and label them according to the color of the sand within.

Paper—Provide various types of sturdy paper such as construction paper, drawing paper, or poster board. Cut the paper in various sizes and shapes.

Glue—Provide bottles of white glue, glue sticks, bottles of roll-on glue, and bottles of paste with spreaders.

Colored Sand

1 cup of sand
2 teaspoons of dry tempera paint
1 teaspoon of water

Add the dry tempera paint to the sand; then mix well with a fork. Stir in the water. Allow the sand to dry for several hours before using it.

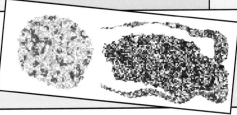

Negative space was explored as one child used a bottle of roll-on glue to cover the perimeter of this poster-board rectangle.

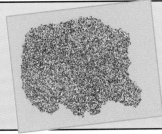

A preschooler worked on this project in stages—repeating the process of adding glue, then sand several times. When asked to describe her work, she explained that it was a mountain with a lake.

As the children glue and add sand, have them pour the extra sand into a large container. The sand on this project is a mixture of the different colors of sand used.

Color Units

Splashes Of Red!

Fun and colorful ideas to help your little ones experience the color red!

Colorful Literature

Introduce your youngsters to the color red by reading red-related literature and dressing for the occasion! Wear articles of red clothing while reading aloud the book *Red Is Best* by Kathy Stinson (Firefly Books, Ltd.). After reading, ask each youngster to look around the classroom for items that are red. Then have your children sit in a circle to play a game similar to Hot Potato. Show them a red apple. As you play a musical recording, have each student in turn pass the apple to the child sitting next to him. Stop the music periodically, and have the child holding the apple stand up and point out an item that is red.

Need some other splashes of red? Try these colorful, red-related books:

> *Mary Wore Her Red Dress & Henry Wore His Green Sneakers* adapted and illustrated by Merle Peek (Clarion Books)
> *Is It Red? Is It Yellow? Is It Blue?* by Tana Hoban (Greenwillow Books)
> *Who Said Red?* written by Mary Serfozo and illustrated by Keiko Narahashi (Macmillan Children's Book Group)
> *Finding Red Finding Yellow* by Betsy Imershein (Harcourt Brace Jovanovich, Publishers)
> *The Red Poppy* by Irmgard Lucht and translated by Frank Jacoby-Nelson (Hyperion Books For Children)

Circle Time

Little ones will love this "color-rific" circle-time idea. While learning about the color red, ask each youngster to bring a small, red item from home in a paper bag. During circle time, have each youngster bring his paper bag to the circle. Ask a student to volunteer to give the rest of the class clues about the object in his bag. Encourage the rest of the students to ask questions about the object; then have them try to guess what it is. Have the student volunteer reveal what's in his bag. Continue in this manner until each child has had a turn.

Really Red Fruit Salad

Stir up some colorful enthusiasm in your room by having youngsters create really red fruit salads. In advance, cut up pieces of red apples, cherries, watermelon, strawberries, and red grapes; then place each of the fruits in a different bowl. Place the bowls on a table. Provide each child with a red plastic spoon and a red cup. Encourage him to spoon the fruits of his choice from the bowls into his cup. Yum!

Red Day

Designate one day of the week to be Red Day. The day before, instruct youngsters to wear as many red articles of clothing as possible on Red Day. Then place a red stick-on dot on the back of each child's hand as a special reminder before he goes home. When this special day arrives, have your little ones discuss their red clothing with the rest of the class.

Centers With A Colorful Flair

● Try these quick-and-easy suggestions to help youngsters recognize the color red. Supply your math center with red poker chips, buttons, blocks, and other manipulatives. Have your little ones sort and classify the items by shape, size, and texture.

● Put a variety of red clothing in the dramatic play area, along with pictures or actual samples of red food items.

● Stock your art center with old magazines, scissors, red crayons, glue, and white construction paper. To use this center, have your students look through the magazines and cut out pictures of things that are red; then have them glue the pictures to the construction paper. A child may also choose to draw objects that are red. Now that's a red picture!

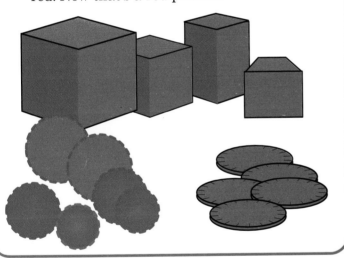

Moving Right Along

Select musical recordings carefully for this activity, and your youngsters will be color dancing in no time. Before starting the music, tape red crepe-paper streamers around each child's wrists. As you start the music, encourage your children to dance and move freely to the rhythm so that their streamers move expressively.

This looks like a flower. Katie

"Red-y" For Art?

● Your students will be caught red-handed with smiles of delight when making these creative collages. Supply each child with red craft items such as glitter, markers, glitter glue, sequins, ribbon, feathers, crayons, yarn, pom-poms, and tissue paper. Have each child glue the craft items of his choice onto a large sheet of white construction paper. After the glue dries, allow time for each child to talk about his special collage.

● On another day, have each child place a dab of red paint inside a folded sheet of white construction paper. Refold the paper. Starting at the fold, have each child push the paint out toward the edges of his paper. Then have him open the folded paper to see his design. Have each child dictate a sentence about his design, as you write the sentence at the bottom of his paper.

● When your little ones do this red art activity, it will not only prove to be lots of fun, but your room will smell fresh and clean too. In advance, cover your tabletops with white bulletin-board paper. Squeeze a dab of shaving cream in front of each child; then add 1/4 teaspoon of red water-based paint or red powdered tempera paint to the shaving cream. Using his fingers, have each child mix the shaving cream and paint. Encourage each child to finger-paint with the red shaving cream, making the designs of his choice.

Judy Jones—Preschool; Get Ready, Set, Grow; Boca Raton, FL

Splashes Of Orange

Colorful ideas to help your little ones experience the color orange!

Color Of Autumn

Roll up your sleeves. Pass out the art smocks. It's time to be up to your elbows in orange paint! To introduce the color orange, scoop large dollops of red and yellow finger paint onto a clean tabletop. Mist the tabletop with water. Encourage several students at a time to take turns smearing the two colors of paint to blend them. Monitor this process to stimulate discussions about what is happening to the paint and to mist the table whenever it becomes too dry. When youngsters have tired of finger-painting, press a giant, white, bulletin-board paper leaf cutout onto the table. Smooth it down; then carefully lift it up and place it where it can dry. Repeat this process several times, if desired, to "colorize" several giant leaf cutouts and to give each youngster an opportunity to mix red and yellow to get orange. Later post the leaves with student-dictated thoughts about things that become orange in autumn.

Orange Floats

A scoop of orange sherbet is the main ingredient in this irresistible drink. Lead into this activity by having students brainstorm foods and beverages that are orange. Ask students to tell what their favorite orange foods are. Slice or peel three or four oranges while the youngsters watch. As you discuss the color, smell, and taste of the fruit, have your preschoolers help you separate the oranges into sections. Put a scoop of orange sherbet in a small cup for each youngster. Then assist as each child pours some orange soda into the cup, garnishes the drink with a section of orange, and inserts a straw. While students are sipping their orange drinks, make it more of a festive occasion by singing the song in "Orange Sillies."

Orange Sillies

While students are sipping their orange floats (described above), lead them in singing a silly orange song. In the first four lines of the song, sing one phrase at a time, pausing for students to echo or repeat the phrase (indicated by italics), before singing the phrase on the next line.

Sippin'
(sung to the tune of "The Silliest Goat I Ever Saw")

The silliest girl (boy); *The silliest girl (boy)*
I ev-er saw; *I ev-er saw*
Was sip-pin' or-; *Was sip-pin' or-*
'Ange through a straw; *'Ange through a straw.*
The silliest girl (boy) I ev-er saw
Was sip-pin' o-range through a straw!

Outside Art

If your playground has a chain-link fence, you've got a great canvas for an orange weaving. To prepare for this activity, cut an orange fabric remnant (or an old sheet that has been dyed orange) into long, three-inch-wide strips. Also provide several similar strips of fabrics of different colors. In your collection, include assorted items that are orange. For example, you may include orange feathers, a string of plastic orange beads, some orange rickrack, or orange clothespins. Store the strips and other orange items in a laundry basket. Take your little ones outside and show them how to weave the strips in and out through the sections of the chain-link fence. Then let the creativity begin! Encourage students' participation in the weaving, but otherwise let the artwork evolve according to the preferences of the children. It's not necessary that the weaving resemble anything in particular. But when it's finally finished, you can step back and admire one thing for sure. That is really orange art!

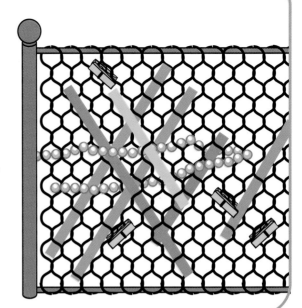

Orange Blossoms

Put out the word. Your class is on the lookout for orange papers and fabrics of all kinds. To get started, show students a few orange things that you have gathered. For example, you might have a remnant of orange cloth, sheets of several orange papers, and a woven orange produce bag. Explain that you are donating these things for a class project; then drop them into a collection bin labeled "orange." Encourage students to contribute to the orange box during the next few days.

When you have an adequate collection, cut the fabrics and papers into one-inch-wide strips. Provide each student with scissors, craft glue, and an 18-inch circle of white poster board. Have the youngster cut and glue strips of her choice to the circle to make a bright orange flower. Display each of the flowers along a classroom wall with paper leaves and stems of varying heights. What an amazing fall flower bed!

Orange Memories

Culminate your celebration of the color orange by setting aside a day to be Orange Day. Ask that on this day, each of the children wears something that is orange. (Have on hand a box of orange accessories—such as badges, hats, and shoestrings—for youngsters who forget about Orange Day.) Once everyone is all decked out in orange, invite them to look in a full-length mirror, then draw their likenesses on art paper. Help each student complete a fill-in-the-blank sentence about the orange clothing he is wearing. Then use masking tape to bind the artwork into a booklet with an orange-embellished cover.

M. Lynne Sypher, Brook Avenue School, Bay Shore, NY

Splashes Of Green

Colorful ideas to help your little ones experience the color green!

by Jayne Gammons

Green From Tip To Tail

Watch out! With this art project, you'll have a slithery, sneaky snake that changes colors. To make a giant snake, you'll need a large piece of finger-painting paper for each child. Tape the papers together, end to end, to create one long strip. Trim along the top and bottom of the strip in a wavy manner, so that it resembles a snake. Using permanent markers, create features and attach a red construction-paper tongue. Spread the snake shape out in a long, uncarpeted hallway or on a long strip of plastic. On each child's section of paper, drop a dollop of blue and yellow finger paint. Then invite several children at a time to put on art smocks and finger-paint their sections of the paper snake. When all sections have been painted and have dried, mount the snake on the wall.

It's A Jungle In There!

Surround your youngsters with the color green by transforming your classroom into a growing green room. Set the mood by draping your cabinets, shelves, and windows with artificial greenery. During a group time, ask your little ones to brainstorm a list of things that can be green. Write each child's suggestion on a large, light green paper leaf shape. Then ask each child to illustrate his suggestion on his leaf with crayons or paints. Mount the illustrated leaf shapes onto slightly larger, dark green paper leaf shapes. Attach each leaf to a green, crepe-paper streamer and suspend it from the ceiling. Now you're growing wild with green!

Grapes are green. Samuel

Dip And Nibble

By now your youngsters have been surrounded with green for viewing and have been up to their elbows in green for touching. What's next in experiencing the color green? Tasting, of course! On your next trip to the grocery store, shop for an assortment of green vegetables such as broccoli, celery, green peppers, zucchini, and cucumbers. (Or ask parents to contribute these vegetables.) Cut the green veggies into portions just right for preschoolers to dip and nibble on. (Save some of the vegetables for "Tossed-Salad Art.") Add green food coloring to ranch dressing; then pour the dressing into small cups or bowls. Provide each child with a cup of the dressing for dipping the vegetables of his choice.

Tossed-Salad Art

Using the green vegetables suggested in "Dip And Nibble," have students make vegetable prints. In an art center, place the cut vegetables and a pie tin of green paint. Provide each child in the center with a white paper plate. Encourage her to dip one of the vegetables in the paint and press it onto the plate. Have her repeat this process using the various vegetables. To create a display, cover a table with a green paper tablecloth. Tape the dry vegetable prints to the tablecloth along with a sign titled "Tossed-Salad Art."

Adapted from an idea by
Suzanne Costner
Maryville, TN

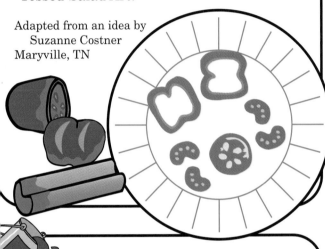

Green Giggles And Jiggles

Make a batch of lime-flavored Jell-O® Jigglers™ gelatin snacks, and you are sure to hear lots of giggles from your little ones. To make the gelatin snacks, follow the directions on a package of lime-flavored Jell-O® brand gelatin. Then provide youngsters with cookie cutters in the shapes of Christmas trees, dinosaurs, and other things that can be green. Assist each child in using the cutter of his choice to cut out a gelatin snack. If desired, provide whipped topping that has been tinted green and green sprinkles for topping the treats. Watch them wiggle! See them jiggle!

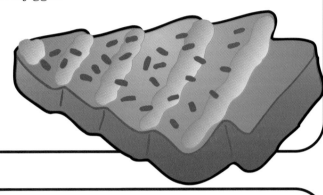

The Grass Is Greener

The ground might be covered with snow outside, but in your class the grass is green and growing. Collect a class supply of half-pint milk cartons. Clean the cartons and cut off their tops. Provide each child with a strip of paper cut to match the height of the carton and long enough to wrap around it. Have each child paint his strip green. While the paint is wet, have him sprinkle the strip with green glitter. When it's dry, tape or glue the strip around a carton. Assist each child in filling his carton with soil. Have him gently press a spoonful of birdseed into the dirt. Place the cartons by a window and watch the green grass grow.

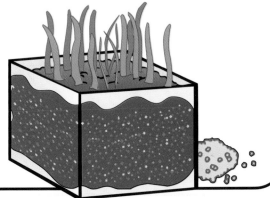

"It's Not Easy Being Green"

Bring your celebration of the color green to a close by listening to everyone's favorite frog sing "Bein' Green." A video-recording of the song can be found on *Sesame Street's 25th Birthday: A Musical Celebration!* (available from Music For Little People at 1-800-727-2233). If possible, manipulate a frog puppet while playing the song.

Splashes Of Purple
Colorful ideas to help your little ones experience the color purple!

compiled by Marie Iannetti

Welcome To Purpleville

Introduce your youngsters to the color purple by transforming your classroom into Purpleville. Before students arrive, embellish your classroom cabinets, windows, and shelves with purple streamers, curling ribbon, and inflated balloons. Cover each table or desk with purple bulletin-board paper. Place a vase filled with artificial purple flowers and a purple paper plate with purple grapes on each desk or table. On the front of your classroom door, tape a sign that reads "Welcome To Purpleville." As your little ones enter, lead them in singing the following song. Have youngsters substitute a different action each time the verse is sung.

WELCOME
TO
PURPLEVILLE

The Land Of Purpleville

(sung to the tune of "Here We Go Round The Mulberry Bush")

In the land of Purpleville,
The children there wear purple still.
They love to dance and they love to sing,
And they love to [clap their hands].

Jean Harrison
Palm Bay, FL

124

Purple Pizzazz

These purple foods have lots of pizzazz. Begin by having your youngsters brainstorm purple foods. Have a few food items such as an eggplant, purple grapes, beets, and red cabbage on hand to display and discuss. After the discussion, ask youngsters to name beverages that are purple. Then show them a bottle of grape soda. For each child, put a scoop of vanilla ice cream in a purple cup. Then assist as each child pours some grape soda into the cup and garnishes the ice cream with purple cake sprinkles. "Purple-licious!"

Color Me A Cookie

Try this sweet idea for some colorful fun. Bake sugar cookies from refrigerated dough according to the package directions. When the cookies have cooled, provide each group of children with cookies, plastic knives, and a small bowl of purple icing (use icing in a tube or add purple concentrated paste to vanilla icing). Encourage each child to cover his cookie with the purple icing. Then have each child top off his cookie with a dab of grape jelly, if desired, and enjoy it!

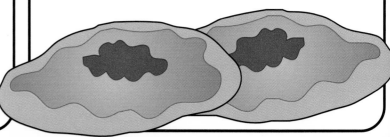

A Royal Show-And-Tell

Your students will feel like kings and queens with this royal idea. In advance paint a medium-size box and its lid purple. When the paint is dry, stock a center with the box, scissors, glue, and purple craft items such as yarn, ribbon, pom-poms, fake jewels, sequins, lace, feathers, felt pieces, and tissue-paper pieces. Then let the decorating begin! Encourage youngsters to embellish the box with the provided items so that it resembles a royal treasure chest.

Later designate one day to be Royal Show-And-Tell Day. On the day before, encourage each child to wear something that is purple and to bring in a purple object from home. As each child enters the classroom on this special day, have him place his purple object in the decorated treasure chest. During show-and-tell, seat your youngsters in a circle on the floor and place the chest in the middle of the circle. In turn, crown each child with a purple construction-paper crown and place a piece of purple cloth around his shoulders to represent a royal cloak. Then have each child describe his purple object without naming it. Have the rest of the class try to guess what the object is before it is revealed.

Jean Harrison
Palm Bay, FL

Ready To Make Purple?

Your little artists will love letting their creative juices flow with this fun idea. On a clean table in front of each child, place dabs of red and blue washable paint. Ask him what he thinks will happen when the two colors are mixed. Using his hands, have each student mix the two colors together. Encourage each child to use his fingers to make the design of his choice in the paint. When each child is satisfied with his creation, gently place a sheet of white construction paper atop his design. Rub your hand lightly over the entire paper. Lift the paper and let the paint dry.

After having each of your youngsters share their prints, have them sing the following song, substituting a different action each time the verse is sung:

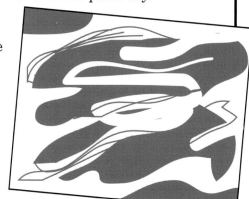

If You Like The Color Purple
(sung to the tune of "If You're Happy And You Know It")

If you like the color purple, [clap your hands].
   Clap twice.
If you like the color purple, [clap your hands].
   Clap twice.
You can make the color true,
By mixing red and blue;
If you like the color purple, [clap your hands].
   Clap twice.

Jean Harrison

How Now, Purple Cow?

Here's a "moo-velous" idea for reviewing the color purple. In advance, use a purple marker or chalk to copy Gelette Burgess's "The Purple Cow" (from memory or a poetry book such as *Favorite Poems Old And New* edited by Helen Ferris) on a chalkboard or piece of chart paper. Ask your students if they have ever seen a purple cow. Graph the results and discuss what the graph reveals. Read the poem aloud; then let students volunteer to share their reactions to the poem. Read the poem several more times, having youngsters join in as they are able. Then give each child a cow-shaped cutout and have him decorate it using art supplies such as purple construction-paper scraps, crayons, glitter, tissue-paper pieces, and buttons.

Splashes Of Yellow

Colorful ideas to help your little ones experience the color yellow!

Yellow, Yellow, Everywhere!

Brainstorm a list of yellow things with your youngsters. Then sing this bright and cheery song to the tune of "Twinkle, Twinkle, Little Star."

Yellow, yellow, bright and fair;
Yellow, yellow, everywhere.
Lemonade and apples, too;
Golden yellow hair on you.
Yellow, yellow, bright and fair;
Yellow, yellow, everywhere.

Tracy Lynn Troup—Pre-K

When Life Gives You Lemons

Make lemon prints and lemonade! In advance cut a quantity of lemons in half lengthwise. Set several of the lemon halves aside to dry slightly. Store the remaining halves in a refrigerator. Then, in an art center, place the lemon halves, white construction paper, newspaper, and a pan of yellow tempera paint. Encourage each child to dip a lemon half in the paint, press it onto the newspaper, and then press it onto a sheet of construction paper. Have him continue in this manner until he has several prints on his paper. As a nifty follow-up activity, make lemonade with the leftover lemons!

Tracy Lynn Troup—Pre-K

Tasty Graphing

Stir up some excitement in your room when graphing youngsters' favorite yellow foods. Using yellow paper, create a graph with the name and picture of each yellow food that will be tasted. Place a variety of yellow foods—such as bananas, cheese, corn, scrambled eggs, macaroni and cheese, and corn bread—on a table. Provide each child with a yellow plate and a plastic spoon. Have each child place a portion of each food on his plate, and encourage him to taste each food. Supply each child with a personalized, yellow happy-face cutout. Have each student indicate his favorite yellow food by placing his happy face in the appropriate place on the graph. Ask questions such as "How many children like cheese the best?" and "Do more people like bananas or cheese?"

Tracy Lynn Troup—Pre-K
Family Day Care/Preschool
Lebanon, PA

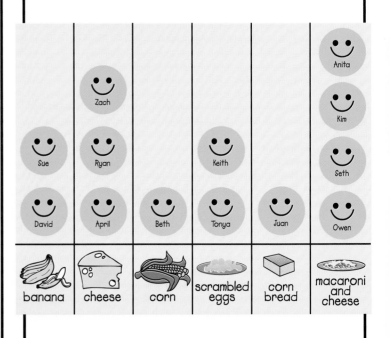

Yellow Mellow Butter

Read aloud *Brown Cow, Green Grass, Yellow Mellow Sun* by Ellen Jackson (Hyperion Books for Children). Spread out the fun of the story by having your youngsters make yellow mellow butter. To make butter, provide each child with a small, plastic jar half filled with room-temperature whipping cream. Secure the lid on each jar. Have each child shake, shake, shake, until the cream is yellow mellow butter. Provide each child with a plastic knife and a slice of bread, and have him spread some of his homemade butter atop the bread. Yum!

Yellow, Yellow, Friendly Fellow

Keep a small, round, yellow pillow in a prominent place for your students to hold when they are feeling gloomy. When a child needs a little extra attention, encourage him to hold the yellow, yellow, friendly fellow pillow. Remind the class to give that student some tender loving care for the day.

Kathy Mulvihill—Four-Year-Olds
Wee Care Preschool
Allendale, MI

You Are My Sunshine

These suns will make you happy when skies are gray. Provide each child with a tagboard circle cutout and yellow tissue-paper pieces. Have each student glue the tissue paper onto the tagboard so that the pieces overlap to cover the circle. Then have each youngster drizzle yellow or gold glitter glue atop the tissue paper. When the glue is dry, glue several yellow streamers to the edge of the circle to resemble a sun. Encourage each of your little ones to hold his sun cutout above his head while singing "You Are My Sunshine" or while listening to Raffi's "One Light, One Sun."

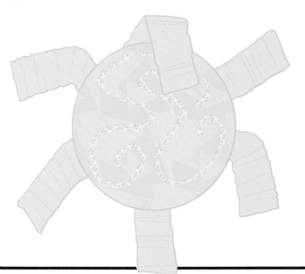

The Yellow Pages

Need a unique art technique? Look in the yellow pages! Reuse old telephone books by removing the yellow pages. Encourage youngsters to tear or cut the pages, then glue them to black construction paper. You'll be able to call these collages one-of-a-kind!

Literature Links

Yellow Ball
Written & Illustrated by Molly Bang
Published by Morrow Junior Books

Little Blue And Little Yellow
Written & Illustrated by Leo Lionni
Published by Mulberry Books

Splashes Of Blue

Fun and colorful ideas to help your little ones experience the color blue!

Blueberries For You

Introduce the color blue with this "berry" nice idea. On a designated day, ask youngsters to wear as many articles of blue clothing as possible. Ask them to bring a toy bear to school on the same day. Upon students' arrival, seat them in a group and read aloud *Blueberries For Sal* by Robert McCloskey (Puffin Books). Explain that since everyone has a bear, it must be time for berry picking. All you need are berry buckets.

To make a bucket for each child, fold down several inches of a closed, white paper bag. Cut a half-circle shape through all thicknesses; then unfold and open the bag. Program each bag with the phrase "Blueberry Bucket." Have each child paint a green bush on his bag. Next have him dip a pencil eraser in blue paint, then press it onto the bag to resemble blueberries. While the students are decorating their blueberry buckets, ask an adult volunteer to hide blueberry snacks, such as blueberries in plastic bags that have been tied with blue ribbons, blueberry cereal bars, blueberry muffins, or blueberry tarts. When the paint dries, let the hunting begin! Have each child hold his blueberry bucket and his bear, and hunt for a blueberry snack. Enjoy another reading of *Blueberries For Sal* while your little ones snack, snack, snack!

Linda Ludlow
Bethesda Christian Schools
Brownsburg, IN

Blueberry Bucket

BLUEBERRY BAR

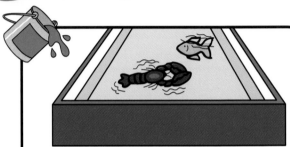

The Deep Blue Sea

Give your water table a feel of the deep blue sea with these exciting additions. Add several drops of blue food coloring to the water. Then add plastic or sponge undersea creatures such as sea horses, starfish, fish, jellyfish, crabs, and lobsters. Play a recording of ocean sounds while little ones dive into some serious play.

Dalia Behr—Preschool
The Little Dolphin School
Ozone Park, NY

Blue Jigglers™

Mixing up these colorful treats in your classroom will no doubt cure the blues. Prepare a pan of blue Jell-O® Jigglers™ following the package directions. Then cut the gelatin into small squares to make individual Jigglers™. Provide each child with several Jigglers™ on a blue paper plate; then allow your little ones to sample these yummy treats while listening to Sesame Street's Grover sing "I Am Blue."

Dalia Behr—Preschool

Blue-Jean Collage

It's all in the jeans—at least in this crafty collage. Provide each child with a blue construction-paper pant shape and scraps of old denim blue jeans. Have each student glue the denim scraps to the pant shape in the design of his choice. Now that's some casual creativity!

Theresa Anderson—Two- And Three-Year-Olds
Children's World Learning Center
Rochester, MN

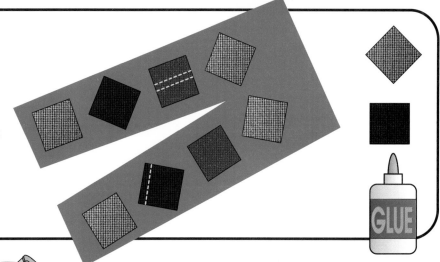

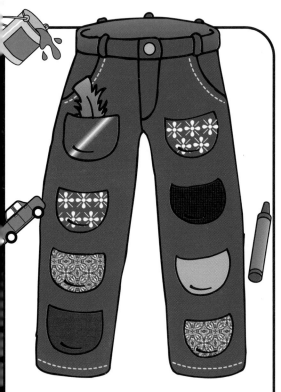

Pockets Full Of Blue

This fun-filled activity will be pockets full of fun. On a pair of old blue jeans, sew or hot-glue blue fabric to create pockets. Place a supply of different-colored small objects in a basket, making certain that there are enough blue objects for each pocket on the jeans. Place the jeans and the basket in a center. To use this center, a child chooses an object from the basket and identifies the color of the object. If the object is blue, he places it in one of the pockets on the pair of jeans. If the object is a different color, he places it back in the basket.

Deborah Ladd
Mustang, OK

I Spy Something Blue

All eyes are searching for something blue with this investigative idea. Provide each child with a cardboard tube that has been painted blue. Have each youngster hold his tube to his eye to represent a spyglass and look for blue objects around the classroom. Have a student volunteer name a blue object that he spies. Continue in this manner until each child has had a turn. Then take youngsters outside to search for other blue items. I spy a blue sky!

Kathy Mulvihill—Four-Year-Olds, Wee Care Preschool, Allendale, MI

A Blue Suncatcher

Put those old, blue crayons to good use by making colorful suncatchers. To make a suncatcher, grate various shades of blue crayons. Provide each child with two 3 1/2" squares of waxed paper. Have her sprinkle some of the crayon shavings on one piece of the waxed paper. Have her place the other waxed-paper square on top of the shavings. Place both sheets of paper on a towel; then place a cloth over the waxed paper. Gently press a warm iron atop the cloth until the crayon shavings in the center of the waxed paper have melted. When the paper has cooled, have each child glue four craft sticks over the edges of the paper square to make a frame. Glue a piece of blue yarn to the back to suspend the suncatcher. Now that's "blue-tiful"!

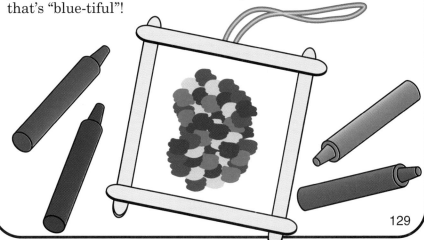

129

Head, Shoulders, Knees, & Toes

Head, Shoulders,

Wiggle-Worm Walk

Wiggle this movement idea into your worm unit (see pages 14–19). Demonstrate for your youngsters how to do the wiggle-worm walk. Stand with your feet together, bend, and touch your hands to the floor just in front of your feet. Walk your hands forward—without moving your feet—until you can't go any farther. Then walk your feet up to your hands. After a round of giggles from your youngsters, ask each child to move around an open space in this wormlike manner. If youngsters have difficulty with this activity, encourage them to lie on the floor and wiggle like a worm in their own way. Once everyone is in the wiggle, play an instrumental recording to add to the fun of the exercise.

Clap Your Hands

Movement is a natural extension to *Clap Your Hands* by Lorinda Bryan Cauley (published by G. P. Putnam's Sons). Read the book aloud; then reread it and have the class move appropriately to each phrase. Next give each child the opportunity to recall a movement (or point to a movement shown in the book) and lead his classmates in that movement. "Fly like an airplane high in the sky. It's time to go now, so wave bye-bye…." Bye-bye!

Statues

This body-awareness activity will help your little ones learn to focus and attend as they copy specific body movements. Begin by having children sit on the floor. Make sure there is enough space between children for each child to extend his arms to the sides without touching another child. Sitting on the floor and facing the group, extend your arms in a specific position. Encourage students to copy your pose. Use simple movements (both arms up or both arms on your waist); then move to more complex movements (one arm on your waist and one arm up). Consider repeating the same movement several times in a row to allow time for every child to duplicate the pose successfully. As children become familiar with the game, create standing statue poses for the children to copy. Then provide opportunities for youngsters to take turns being the leader. For an added language opportunity, discuss the leader's statue pose as a class before copying it. Or describe a pose verbally ("Make a tall statue.") without a visual example. Then have each child create a statue to match the description. Strike a pose!

Knees, & Toes

Wake Up!

Rise and shine! This activity will help wake up the ability in your youngsters to stop and start on cue. Ask youngsters to pretend that they are sleepy; then practice stretching all the parts of the body that can be stretched—from the fingers to the toes. Have your little ones lie down on the floor. Explain that when the lights are off, it will be night and everyone should be very still. When the lights come back on, it will be morning and everyone should slowly begin stretching. Turn the lights off and on again for appropriate lengths of time. Aahhhh. Was that a yawn?

Nest Sweet Nest

Watch motor skills take flight when using this idea. Give each youngster a length of brown yarn or rope. Ask her to lay her string down on the floor with the two ends touching, forming a circle. This will be her nest. Announce a series of directions such as "Run around your nest," and "Hop inside your nest." At the conclusion of the activity, have your little birds settle down in their nests. Provide each little chirper with a surprise Gummy bug or worm snack. Tweet! Tweet!

Sneaky Snake

You'll hear squeals of delight as sneaky snake slips and slides over, under, around, and between a group of little bodies. Ask a group of three children to hold hands in a line. Provide a fourth child with a lengthy piece of green crepe-paper streamer. Direct this child to hold onto one end of the streamer snake and to weave the snake around the bodies of the children holding hands. Encourage him to move between the legs and under the arms of the children in line as he weaves. Remind the children holding hands to be very still so they don't scare or step on the snake. When the child has finished weaving the snake, give a cue for the three children to drop hands and slowly sneak away. Continue in this manner until each child has had an opportunity to weave a snake. Sssss!

Flying Saucers

Your little crew members will zoom into spatial awareness when they participate in this out-of-this-world activity. Begin by assisting each youngster in making a flying saucer by stapling together two aluminum pie pans. Encourage each child to embellish his spacecraft with stickers, markers, or streamers. Once every child has his own decorated saucer to hold, play a selection of slow, celestial-sounding music. The album *Music of Cosmos* (available from Collector's Choice Music Catalog at 1-800-923-1122) has several selections suitable for this activity. Direct each child to "fly" his saucer around the room, avoiding other saucers that are also flying in space. Stop the music. Ask each child to land his spacecraft on the floor. Continue starting and stopping the music as long as the children are enjoying the space adventure.

Today's Weather Report

The forecast is clear for self-expression and creativity when you dramatize the daily weather report. Begin each day's weather discussion with the sunrise. Students may wish to rise slowly, spreading their arms out to the sides or raising their hands above their heads to form circles. Next encourage children to act out the weather condition for the day. For example, if it is raining, students may wish to open up pretend umbrellas and dodge puddles around the room. Or if it is storming, students might make jerky movements like lightning or loud noises like thunder. Conclude the activity with each child's interpretation of a sunset.

A Carousel Ride

The horses are waiting. The music is playing. So hop on for a carousel ride into fun with this idea. Read aloud *Carousel* by Donald Crews (published by Greenwillow Books) or *Up And Down On The Merry-Go-Round* by Bill Martin, Jr. and John Archambault (published by Henry Holt And Company). Play a selection of music similar to music that might be heard from a carousel. Encourage children to move up and down while standing in place, as they would if they were on a carousel. Next have a small group of children form a circle with one child in the center of the circle. Ask the child in the center to hold above his head one crepe-paper streamer for each child in the circle. Then give each of the children the end of a streamer to hold. As the music plays again, have the children walk in a circle while the child in the center turns slowly, adding up-and-down movements as they are able. Boom, toot, toot! What an amusing carousel ride!

Knees, & Toes

Snow Pals

Just can't wait for that first snowfall to build a snow pal? Let students pretend to build snow pals using their real pals! Group youngsters in pairs. Explain that one child should pretend to be a lump of snow while the other child molds his partner into a snowman. The finished snow pal will need to hold her pose while the builder describes his creation. As the snow pals remain frozen, use the discussion time to help children label body parts and analyze the different poses. Then have the partners switch roles. Consider showing the video of Raymond Briggs's *The Snowman* as a culmination to this winter movement activity.

Dr. Grace Morris, Southwest Texas State University, San Marcos, TX

Whirling, Twirling Snowflakes

Every snowflake is unique in the way it looks and in the way it moves. Give your youngsters the opportunity to explore in their own unique ways how snowflakes whirl and twirl. Have children move first like soft, fluffy snowflakes that float to the ground; then like hard, icy snowflakes that move swiftly in a blizzard. As they flurry about, sing "Dance Like Snowflakes" (page 148 together or listen to "The Dance Of The Sugar Plum Fairies" from *The Nutcracker* by Tchaikovsky.

Add these perfectly designed snowflakes to your creative-movement activity and you'll soon have a swirling, twirling snowstorm right in your classroom. Cut out a pair of tagboard snowflakes—slightly larger than a child's hand—for each student in your class. Attach strips of white, plastic garbage bags to the bottom of the snowflake cutouts. Staple both ends of a tagboard strip to the back of each snowflake cutout to create a place for the child to place his hand. As the children move about, their snowflakes will whirl and twirl through the air.

Dr. Grace Morris

Freeze! Melt!

Increase your youngsters' muscle control with this wintry, stop-and-go game. In advance, prepare a large sun design and a large snowflake design. Explain to youngsters that when the air is cold, water in the air can freeze and turn into snow. Continue to explain that the sun's heat makes the air warm so that the snow melts. Show youngsters the sun and snowflake designs. Demonstrate how to freeze when the snowflake is displayed and how to begin moving slowly when the sun is displayed. To increase youngsters' abilities to focus on visual cues, play the game using the snowflake and sun designs without giving verbal cues. Or try this variation using sound cues. Using a set of bells, establish one tone to indicate "freeze" and a different tone to indicate "melt." The children should move or stand still based on the tone that they hear. Either way, little ones are sure to enjoy this game all winter long.

135

Head, Shoulders,

Bouncing Bear

Your little ones will learn to work together with this group movement activity. Space your children evenly around a parachute or a large sheet. Instruct each child to hold the parachute tightly with both hands. Next place a teddy bear in the center of the parachute and challenge the children to move their hands so that the bear bounces and flips in the air, rolls from one side of the parachute to the other side, and rolls in a circle around the parachute. Hurrah for teamwork!

Susan Burbridge—Four-Year-Olds
Trinity Weekday School
San Antonio, TX

Bubbles, Bubbles Everywhere

Follow up the bubble-blowing activity in "Out And About" (page 272) with this poem and movement idea. Teach children the poem. Then encourage them to "float" around the room like bubbles as they chant the poem together. At the end of the poem, have the children clap their hands—to simulate the sound of bubbles popping—and then sit down quickly.

Bubbles, bubbles everywhere,
Floating gently through the air.
Let's all count now: 1, 2, 3.
Pop your bubbles now with me!

Deborah Garmon—Preschool
Foursquare Christian Daycare
Groton, CT

Musical Hearts

There won't be any broken hearts with this Valentine's Day version of musical chairs. In advance cut as many red, poster-board heart shapes as there are children in your class. To play, arrange the heart shapes in a circle on the floor. Play music as the children walk around the circle of hearts. When the music stops, direct each child to find a heart to stand on. Remove one heart after each round. Each time the music stops, ask the child who does not have a heart to stand on to share a heart with another child. Encourage the children sharing hearts to hug. Continue play until everyone is hugging and sharing hearts.

Maria Cuellar Munson—Preschool
Garland, TX

Knees & Toes

Movement Ideas For Preschoolers

Rainbow Movement Wands

Perk up those gray March skies with this colorful movement activity. To make a rainbow movement wand, paint a paper-towel tube with white tempera paint. When the paint is dry, attach 12-inch lengths of colorful paper streamers to one end of the tube. Provide each child with a wand and play the movement song of your choice. As the children listen to the music, encourage them to think of a rainbow in the sky and to move their wands above their heads.

Linda Anne Lopienski
Asheboro, NC

From Caterpillar To Butterfly

If you're going to read aloud *The Very Hungry Caterpillar* by Eric Carle (Scholastic Inc.), consider this movement activity as a follow-up. To each child's arms, tie several brightly colored paper streamers. One at a time, have each child pretend to be a caterpillar and roll himself up in a blanket cocoon. After waiting for a few moments, have the child roll out, stretch his arms, and "fly" away.

Cathie Pesa—Pre-K
Youngstown City Schools
Youngstown, OH

Ring Around The Shamrock

Shimmering shamrocks! Here's the St. Patrick's Day game you've been wishing for! Before playing the game, cut a large shamrock shape from green paper. Add green glitter if desired. Direct the children to hold hands in a circle; then place the shamrock on the floor inside the circle. As a class, circle around the shamrock and sing the shamrock poem to the tune of "Ring Around The Rosie." Between each repetition of the poem, select a child to make a wish.

Ring around the shamrock,
Lucky, lucky shamrock,
Shamrock, shamrock,
Let's make a wish!

Betty Silkunas
Lansdale, PA

Head, Shoulders

C-r-a-c-k!

Encourage your little ones to pretend to be chicks hatching from eggs as you read this action rhyme.

I am a tiny, little chick
In my egg so white.
I tap, tap, tap, tap with
   my beak.
I tap with all my might!

I make a tiny, little crack
In my white eggshell.
I tap, tap, tap, tap with
   my beak
Until I've cracked it well.

I make a bigger, wider crack.
I know just what to do!
I tap, tap, tap, tap on my
   shell
Until it cracks in two!

I make a push with both my
   feet.
I know what I'm about!
I push, push, push, push on
   my shell,
And now at last I'm out!

—Lucia Kemp Henry

Flight Of The Bumblebees

Keep your busy bees busy while developing spatial awareness, the ability to stop and start on cue, cooperation, and decision-making skills. To prepare for a game of musical bees, cut large flower shapes from colorful vinyl or different colors of laminated construction paper. Randomly place the flower shapes on the ground in an open space. As you play a recording of "The Flight Of The Bumblebee," encourage youngsters to buzz around in the open space. When the music stops, have each child find a flower to land on. For a variation, ask children to land on a different flower each time or to land only on specific colors of flowers. Buzzz!

Quack! Quack! Quack! Quack!

All of your little ducks will surely come back when you add this movement suggestion to the favorite song "Five Little Ducks." Invite a different group of six children to participate each time you sing and act out the song. From the group, have a volunteer pretend to be the mother or father duck. As you sing the song together, encourage the baby ducks to waddle around. Ask one baby duck to sit down after each consecutive verse is sung. When singing the final verse, have the mother or father duck loudly announce, "Quack, quack, quack, quack!" All of the baby ducks then come waddling back!

Beth Beecy—Preschool
"Quality Time" For Children
Salem, NH

138

Knees, & Toes

Funny Bunny Hop

Make bunny-ear headbands for your little ones to wear; then get ready to do the bunny hop, hop, hop! To make a headband, staple two white, poster-board bunny-ear shapes to a colorful strip of construction paper. Staple the ends of the strip together. Give each child a headband to wear. Get ready to wiggle!

Funny, little bunny goes hop, hop, hop!
Funny, little bunny, please stop, stop, stop!
Wiggle your ears and crinkle your nose.
Then wiggle, wiggle, wiggle right down to your toes.

Dr. Grace Morris, Southwest Texas State University
San Marcos, TX

Colorful Movement

Looking for a fun way to reinforce color recognition, develop thinking skills, and promote fitness? If so, try this colorful movement game. Ask each child to find his own space in an open area. Depending on children's interest levels and abilities, announce movement directions such as, "If you are wearing blue, hop on one foot," or "If you are *not* wearing yellow, shake your arms." Be sure to adapt your directions to match students' physical abilities as well. Get moving!

Linda Anne Lopienski
Asheboro, NC

Make Way!

Follow up a reading of Robert McCloskey's classic *Make Way For Ducklings* (Viking Children's Books) with this "quacked-up" version of Follow The Leader. As a group, practice moving in different ducky movements such as waddling, wing-flapping, swimming, splashing, and bug-catching. Then ask students to form a line. Ask the child at the front of the line to demonstrate the ducky movement of his choice while the other children copy the movement and follow along. After an appropriate length of time, ask the leader to go to the end of the line, and have the next child choose and demonstrate a new ducky movement.

139

Head, Shoulders,

A Colorful Dance

Chances are you know what happens when you mix blue and yellow. Do you know what happens when you mix a reading aloud of *Color Dance* by Ann Jonas (Greenwillow Books) with a supply of colorful scarves? Play a selection of instrumental music, give each child scarves (or lengths of sheer fabric), and you'll soon find out! Encourage your little ones to move their scarves freely to the music and a color dance as beautiful as the one in the book will surely be the result. "Spectrum-tacular!"

The "Dino-Pokey"

What has claws, sharp teeth, big feet, and a long tail? A preschooler pretending to be a dinosaur! Ask all of your prehistoric preschoolers to form a group circle. Then encourage them to sing this song (to the tune of "The Hokey Pokey") and move along!

Put your claws in. Put your claws out.
Put your claws in and scratch them all about.
Do the "dino-pokey" and turn yourself around.
That's what it's all about!

Put your teeth in…chomp them all about.

Put your feet in…stomp them all about.

Put your tail in…wag it all about.

Diane DiMarco—Three- And
    Four-Year-Olds
Country Kids Preschool
Groton, MA

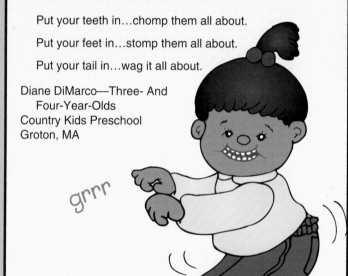

grrr

Let's Do The Twist

Come on, baby! Let's do the twist—the shapes twist, that is! In advance prepare a giant Twister® gameboard. Using a different color of construction paper for each different shape, cut out one 2" and two 5" circles, squares, triangles, ovals, rectangles, and diamonds. In random fashion, adhere the larger shapes to one side of a clear, vinyl tablecloth using clear Con-Tact® covering. To make a spinner, visually divide a tagboard circle into six sections; then glue one of the smaller shapes in each section. Laminate and attach a spinner. To play the game with a small group of children, place the gameboard on the floor with the smooth side facing upward. Ask each child in turn to spin the spinner and to identify the designated shape. Have him place either a foot or a hand on a matching shape on the gameboard. Continue play until each child has had several turns. Now your youngsters will really be in shape!

Karen Eiben—Pre-K
The Kid's Place
La Salle, IL

Knees & Toes

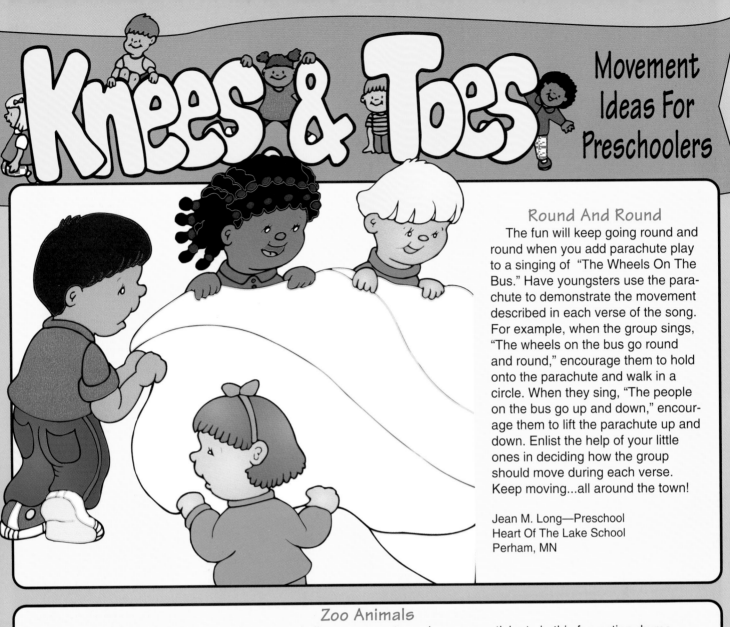

Round And Round

The fun will keep going round and round when you add parachute play to a singing of "The Wheels On The Bus." Have youngsters use the parachute to demonstrate the movement described in each verse of the song. For example, when the group sings, "The wheels on the bus go round and round," encourage them to hold onto the parachute and walk in a circle. When they sing, "The people on the bus go up and down," encourage them to lift the parachute up and down. Enlist the help of your little ones in deciding how the group should move during each verse. Keep moving...all around the town!

Jean M. Long—Preschool
Heart Of The Lake School
Perham, MN

Zoo Animals

There's plenty of room at the zoo for you and all your youngsters when you participate in this fun action rhyme. During a zoo unit, discuss the way that different types of animals found in a zoo might move. As a group, recite the rhyme and tap a steady beat (as indicated) on your legs. At the conclusion of the rhyme, point to one child. Encourage that child to move like the animal named in the rhyme. Naming a different animal each time, repeat the rhyme until each child has had a turn.

```
  *       *   *    *
This is the way to the zoo.
  *       *   *    *
This is the way to the zoo.
     *        *      *       *
The [monkey] house is almost full,
     *       *      *
But there's plenty of room for you!
```

Dr. Grace Morris
Southwest Texas State University
San Marcos, TX

141

Songs & Such

SONGS & SUCH

School Song

(sung to the tune of "Polly Wolly Doodle All The Day")

Oh, I go to school to learn and play,
Singing polly wolly doodle all the day!
Oh, I go to school to learn and play,
Singing polly wolly doodle all the day!

Fare thee well. Fare thee well.
Fare thee well, dear Mom (Dad) today!
For I go to school to learn and play,
Singing polly wolly doodle all the day!

Betty Silkunas • Lansdale, PA

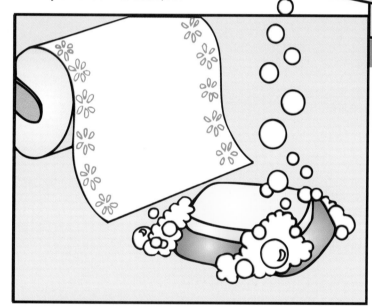

Singing As They Scrub

To encourage little ones to thoroughly wash their hands—rather than just give them a quick rinse—teach your children the following song. Then ask that each child sing the song through twice while he washes his hands.

(sung to the tune of "Clap, Clap, Clap Your Hands")

Wash, wash, wash your hands.
Play this cleanup game.
Rub. Scrub. Scrub and rub.
Germs go down the drain.

Donna Leonard—Preschool • Head Start • Dyersville, IA

The Apple Tree

While singing the first stanza of this song, have students walk in a circle, holding hands. During the second stanza, have the children stop and pretend to climb a tree. During the third stanza, encourage them to pretend to pick apples from a tree.

(sung to the tune of "Here We Go 'Round The Mulberry Bush")

Here we go 'round the apple tree, the apple tree, the apple tree.
Here we go 'round the apple tree on a cool and sunny morning.

This is the way we climb the tree, climb the tree, climb the tree.
This is the way we climb the tree on a cool and sunny morning.

This is the way we pick the fruit, pick the fruit, pick the fruit.
This is the way we pick the fruit on a cool and sunny morning!

Deborah Garmon—Preschool & Daycare
Pooh Corner Preschool And Daycare • Old Mystic, CT

Leaving The Sand Outside

Want youngsters to leave most of the sand outside in the sand-box? Sing and act out this song with your little sand lovers to ensure that most of the grit stays where it belongs.

(sung to the tune of "Row, Row, Row Your Boat")

Clap, clap, clap your hands.
Clap the sand away.
Clap, clap, clap your hands.
Clap the sand away.

Brush, brush, brush your arms (legs).
Brush the sand away.
Brush, brush, brush your arms (legs).
Brush the sand away.

Stomp, stomp, stomp your feet.
Stomp the sand away.
Stomp, stomp, stomp your feet.
Stomp the sand away.

Shake, shake, shake yourself.
Shake the sand away.
Shake, shake, shake yourself.
Shake the sand away. Hey!

Debbie Berthold—3-year-olds • Emmanuel Day School • Virginia Beach, VA

Car Wash

Turn your waterplay table into a car wash for the day. In-clude sponges, gentle liquid cleanser, and a few toy cars. To give your car wash a musical lift, teach your youngsters the song that follows:

*(sung to the tune of
"The Oscar Mayer® Weiner Theme Song")*

Oh, I really like to give a car a car wash.
Squirting, soaping, scrubbing dirt away!
Oh, I really like to give a car a car wash.
Why, I could sing and scrub away the day!

Betty Silkunas • Lansdale, PA

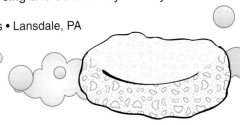

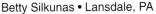

SONGS & SUCH

What's The Weather?

Learning is likely with a good chance for laughter when you sing this weather-report song.

(sung to the tune of "Clementine")

What's the weather?
What's the weather?
What's the weather like today?
Tell us [child's name],
What's the weather?
What's the weather like today?

Is it sunny?   *Hold arms above head in a circle.*
Is it cloudy?   *Cover eyes with hands.*
Is it rainy out today? *Flutter fingers downward.*
Is it snowy?   *Wrap arms around body and shiver.*
Is it windy?   *"Blow children over" with a swoop of your arms.*
What's the weather like today?

Lori Kracoff—Preschool • Lin-wood Community Child Care Center • Lincoln, NH

Pumpkin Pie Song

Encourage youngsters to create their own motions for this tasty treat of a song. If a trip to a pumpkin patch is planned, follow up the outing by cooking pumpkin pie. Be sure to take pictures that correspond to each verse of the song; then use the pictures and the text of the song to create a book.

(sung to the tune of "Paw Paw Patch")

Where, oh, where are all the children?
Where, oh, where are all the children?
Where, oh, where are all the children?
Way down yonder in the pumpkin patch!

Pickin' up a pumpkin. Put it in the wagon…

Take it home and cut it open…

Cut it all up. Mash it and mash it…

Pour it in the piecrust. Put it in the oven…

Bake it and bake it until it's ready…

Put it in my tummy. Yummy! Yummy!…

Dr. Grace Morris • Southwest Texas State University • San Marcos, TX

Falling Leaves

This smooth, soft autumn song gives little ones practice with slow and controlled movement. Before adding motions to the song, discuss the movement of leaves and how leaves might be affected by the wind. As a music extension, use a set of bells or an Autoharp® to help children hear the downward movement of the melody. Encourage them to show this downward movement with their bodies as they dance freely to the song.

Leaves are fal-ling down.
Slow-ly to the ground.
Some are gold. Some are brown.
Nev-er make a sound.

Dr. Grace Morris • Southwest Texas State University • San Marcos, TX

Leaves Are Falling Down

Leaves are fal- ling down.
Slow- ly to the ground.
Some are gold. Some are brown.
Nev- er make a sound.

The Pumpkins Are Here

After introducing the song, give each youngster a pumpkin cutout that has been mounted on a straw or a craft stick. As the song is sung, have each youngster hold his pumpkin as indicated by the words.

(sung to the tune of "The Farmer In The Dell")

The pumpkins are here; the pumpkins are there.
The pumpkins, the pumpkins are everywhere.

The pumpkins are up; the pumpkins are down.
The pumpkins, the pumpkins are all around.

The pumpkins are in; the pumpkins are out.
The pumpkins, the pumpkins are all about.

The pumpkins are low; the pumpkins are high.
The pumpkins, the pumpkins all say, "Good-bye."

Lucia Kemp Henry

Gobbly, Wobbly Turkeys

(sung to the tune of "Ten Little Indians")

One little, two little, three little turkeys,
Gobbly, wobbly, bobbly turkeys,
Hurry, scurry, worry turkeys,
It's Thanksgiving Day!

Betty Silkunas • Lansdale, PA

SONGS & SUCH

The Reindeer Pokey

Round up all of your little reindeer for this holiday version of "The Hokey Pokey."

(sung to the tune of "The Hokey Pokey")

You put your antlers in. You put your antlers out.
You put your antlers in and you shake them all about.
You do the Reindeer Pokey and you turn yourself around.
That's what it's all about!

You put your hooves in….

You put your red nose in….

You put your fluffy tail in….

You put your reindeer body in….

Tara K. Moore
Hightower Elementary
Doraville, GA

Dance Like Snowflakes

For movement suggestions and a craft idea to accompany this song, see "Whirling, Twirling Snowflakes" on page 135.

(sung to the tune of "Frère Jacques")

Dance like snowflakes,
Dance like snowflakes,
In the air.
In the air.
Whirling, twirling snowflakes,
Whirling, twirling snowflakes,
Here and there.
Here and there.

Betty Silkunas
Lansdale, PA

An Instrumental Snowstorm

Explore the concepts of loud, soft, fast, and slow with this blizzard of an idea. You will need instruments that make ringing sounds such as bells, finger cymbals, and triangles, as well as instruments that make swishing sounds such as sand blocks and shakers. Give each child an instrument. After providing an opportunity for free exploration of the instruments, help the children separate into groups based on instruments that sound alike. Create a snowstorm by having the children begin to play their instruments slowly and softly. To create the effect of a building snowstorm, encourage the children to gradually play faster and louder. As the snowstorm peaks, direct children to begin playing slowly and softly again. Whew! What a storm!

Dr. Grace Morris, Southwest Texas State University, San Marcos, TX

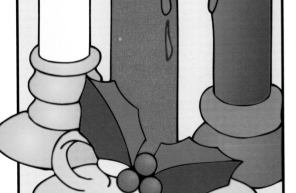

Here's A Little Candle

Many winter holidays share the hope for love and warmth symbolized by light. Whether your little ones will light a Christmas candle, a menorah, or a candle to celebrate Kwanzaa, this is a holiday song that everyone can sing together.

(sung to the tune of "I'm A Little Teapot")

Here's a little candle dressed in white,
Wearing a hat of yellow light.
When the night is dark, then you will see
Just how bright this light can be!

Here's a little candle straight and tall,
Shining its light upon us all.
When the night is dark, then you will see
Just how bright this light can be!

Here's a little candle burning bright,
Keeping us safe all through the night.
When the night is dark, then you will see
Just how bright this light can be!

Lucia Kemp Henry

Friends

Join hands for peace and sing this song to celebrate the birthday of Dr. Martin Luther King, Jr.

(sung to the tune of "Jingle Bells")

Friends hold hands. Friends hold hands.
Friends hold hands and smile.
All our classmates are our friends.
Let's sing with them awhile.

(Repeat verse.)

Betty Silkunas

SONGS & SUCH

Community Helpers' Songs

February is the perfect month to learn about these community helpers. Sing each song to the tune of "Row, Row, Row Your Boat." If desired manipulate hand puppets that depict a dentist, doctor, or mail carrier when singing each song. Or display flannelboard characters of each helper.

The Dentist's Song

February is National Children's Dental Health Month. So brush, brush, brush your teeth!

Brush, brush, brush your teeth.
Keep them clean each day.
Then you'll have a pretty smile,
And healthy teeth all day.

The Doctor's Song

A doctor might sing this song in February. After all, it *is* American Heart Month!

I use a stethoscope
To listen to your heart,
To help you be a healthy child
And heal you when you aren't.

The Mail Carrier's Song

This first-class song makes a perfect addition to the Post Office unit on pages 48-53.

Write, write, write your cards,
And lots of letters, too.
I will bring them to your friends,
And they will write back soon.

Cindy Wunderlich—Preschool
St. Luke's United Methodist Child Development Center
Orlando, FL

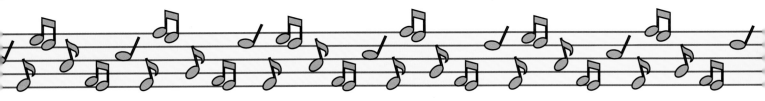

Little Fingers

While singing this song to the tune of "Ten Little Indians," encourage students to make motions associated with each verse. Pause between the stanzas to ask questions or make statements similar to the ones indicated. Once your children are familiar with this song, encourage them to suggest new verses.

One little, two little, three little fingers.
Four little, five little, six little fingers.
Seven little, eight little, nine little fingers.
Ten fingers on my hand.

Spoken: What can they do?

Wiggle, wiggle. Wiggle all around.
Wiggle, wiggle. Wiggle all around.
Wiggle, wiggle. Wiggle all around.
Ten fingers on my hand.

Spoken: What else they can do?

Tickle, tickle. Make me giggle...

Pat, pat. Pat my head...

Scratch, scratch. Scratch my back...

Spoken: These ten fingers have worked hard. Let's put them to rest.

Rest now fingers on my lap.
Rest now fingers on my lap.
Rest now fingers on my lap.
Ten fingers on my hand.

W. L. Harris
St. Petersburg, FL

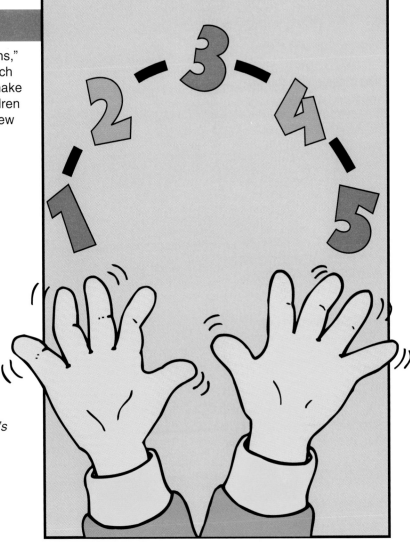

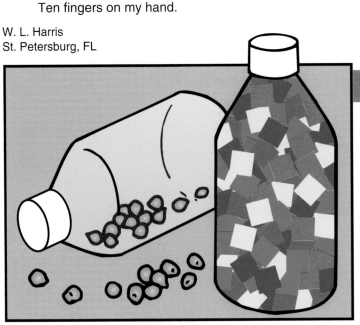

Silly Shakers

Shake! Shake! Shake your sillies out with these easy-to-make instruments. In advance collect an empty, plastic soda bottle (16 or 20 oz.) for each child. Clean the bottles and remove the labels. Have each child pour several spoonfuls of popcorn kernels into his bottle. Hot-glue the lid to the bottle. To decorate the shakers, have each child use a paint-brush and thinned glue to glue various colors of tissue-paper squares to the bottle. When the glue is dry, encourage each child to sing the song "Shake My Sillies Out" (as made popular by Raffi) while shaking his colorful instrument.

Susan Burbridge—Four-Year-Olds
Trinity Weekday School
San Antonio, TX

Mr. Sun

Rise and shine! Singing and moving with this song will wake up any sleepyhead. Begin in a crouched position with your arms outstretched to the right. Slowly rise as the melody ascends, and raise your arms above your head. Beginning with the word "Now," return slowly to the crouched position and shift your arms to your left side as the melody descends. For added fun, provide each child with a large sun-shaped cutout to hold as he moves and sings along.

Dr. Grace Morris
Southwest Texas
State University
San Marcos, TX

Mr. Sun

Mr. Sun is waking up. He's rising from his bed. Telling everyone he see, "Wake up, you sleepyhead!"

Up and up and up and up he climbs up in the sky. Till at noon he finally says, "I think this is too high!

Now it's time for me to rest. I'll just sink in-to the West"

A Song Of Springtime

(sung to the tune of "Did You Ever See A Lassie?")

Come sing a song of springtime,
Of springtime, of springtime.
Come sing a song of springtime.
The warm days are here.

With warm breezes blowing
And flowers all growing.
Come sing a song of springtime.
The warm days are here.

Teresa Thomassen
Shelby, NC

On Mother's Day

(sung to the tune of "Oh, Christmas Tree")

On Mother's Day,
On Mother's Day;
Oh, how I love you, Mom.

On Mother's Day,
On Mother's Day;
Oh, how I love you, Mom.

You give me joy and happiness.
I give you love—a hug and kiss.

On Mother's Day,
On Mother's Day;
Oh, how I love you, Mom.

Carol Lovell • Jacksonville, FL

My Umbrella

You and your little ones will be singing in the rain with this fun song and movement activity. Provide each youngster with a small umbrella. (If you have safety concerns, place masking tape over the ends of the spokes of each umbrella.) Encourage youngsters to stand under, to the left side of, to the right side of, in front of, and behind their open umbrellas. Then sing this rainy-day song to the tune of "I'm A Little Teapot."

Here's my new umbrella,
Wide and high.
It keeps me cozy, warm, and dry.
If the rain starts falling from the sky,
I'll just open it up and I'll stay dry!

Lucia Kemp Henry

Singing About Shapes

Before introducing this song, cut a supply of geometric shapes from construction paper. During a group time, provide each child with a shape. Then sing this song to the tune of "Mary Had A Little Lamb," substituting a different child's name with each verse. To prepare each child to respond successfully at the end of his verse, say, for example, "Let's sing our song to someone holding a triangle."

[Child's name] has a little shape,
Little shape, little shape.
[Child's name] has a little shape.
Please tell us what it is.

Carolyn Bryant—Pre-K • First Baptist Church Powder Springs • Powder Springs, GA

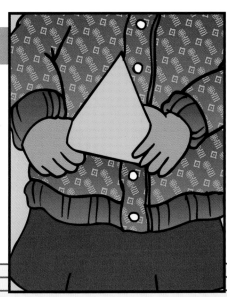

SONGS & SUCH

Kindergarten, Here We Come!

It's time to close the curtain on another year. If you'll be sending your little ones on their way to kindergarten, be sure to celebrate by singing this song to the tune of "I've Been Working On The Railroad."

I've been going to my preschool,
All the whole year long.
I've been going to my preschool,
And I've learned a lot of songs.
I can count and say the letters,
I know my colors, too.
I've been going to my preschool,
All the whole year through.

Graduation day, graduation day,
Graduation day is finally here.
Graduation day, graduation day,
Graduation day is finally here.

Kindergarten, here I come.
Kindergarten, I will be there soon.
Kindergarten, here I come.
I'm so glad it's finally June!

Lori J. Fink
Hamburg, PA

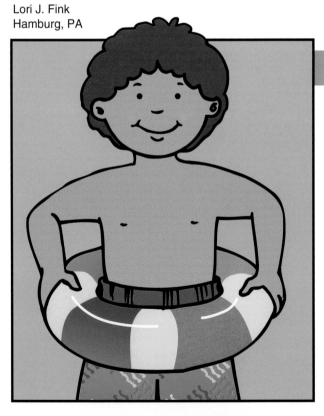

My Really Cute Bathing Suit

Planning a preschool water day? Don't forget to bring your really cute bathing suit. Where is it? Ask your youngsters to help you answer that question by encouraging them to sing the second verse, substituting their own prepositional phrases (such as "in the tub" or "in the drawer") each time the verse is sung.

(sung to the tune of "The Muffin Man")

Have you seen my bathing suit—
My really cute bathing suit?
Have you seen my bathing suit?
I'm going to the pool.

Yes, we've seen your bathing suit—
Your really cute bathing suit.
Yes, we've seen your bathing suit.
We saw it [under the bed].

Betty Silkunas
Lansdale, PA

Fingerplays, Poems, & Rhymes

Fingerplays,

Wiggles

Use this fingerplay when you need a smooth transition from an active time to a quiet time.

 I wiggle my fingers;

 I wiggle my toes.

 I wiggle my shoulders;

 I wiggle my nose.

 Now no more wiggles are left in me,

 So I'm as still as I can be.

–Kay Tidwell, Savoy, TX

Poems, & Rhymes

Little Wiggle Worm

Use this poem when your little worms need to wiggle.

I'm a little wiggle worm,

Watch me go!

I can wiggle fast,

Or very, very slow.

I wiggle all around,

Then back I go.

Down into the ground,

To the home I know.

–Beth Jones, Ontario, Canada

Fingerplays,

This Little Pumpkin

It's time to go pokin' around the pumpkin patch. Use this poem to perk up your little pumpkin pals.

 This little pumpkin was small and round.

 This little pumpkin sat on the ground.

 This little pumpkin was short and fat.

 This little pumpkin wore a silly hat.

 This little pumpkin had a grin so keen.

 This little pumpkin said, "Happy Halloween!"

—Lucia Kemp Henry

Poems, & Rhymes

Turkey's Tail

The talk around town is about turkeys! Here's a poem that will lead your little ones into gaggles of giggles.

 Turkey's tail is big and wide.

 He swings it when he walks.

 His neck is long; his chin is red.

 He gobbles when he talks.

 Turkey is so tall and proud.

 He dances on his feet.

And on each Thanksgiving Day,

 He's something good to eat.

—Author unknown

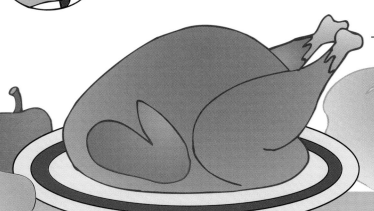

A Gift For You

Encourage your little darlings to recite this poem when giving gifts to loved ones. What could be sweeter?

 Here is a gift that's just for you.

 It didn't cost a penny.

 I checked my pockets for some coins,

 But I could not find any.

 So then I worked to make a gift.

 It wasn't hard to do.

 I made it with my own two hands,

 With love from me to you!

Lucia Kemp Henry

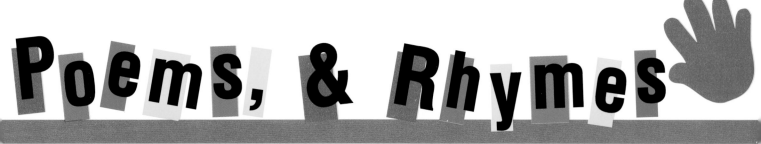

Poems, & Rhymes

Warming Up

What warms me up on a cold, cold day?

Cocoa warms me up in a chocolaty way.

What warms me up on a cold, cold day?

A fire warms me up in a toasty way.

What warms me up on a cold, cold day?

A quilt warms me up in a snugly way.

What warms me up on a cold, cold day?

A hug warms me up in a loving way!

Lucia Kemp Henry

161

A Teddy Bear

What's more lovable and "snuggable" than a teddy bear? Invite your children to bring teddy bears to school; then teach them this teddy-bear rhyme.

Two tiny eyes

And a little, round tummy.

Two furry paws

For scooping up honey.

A soft, "snuggable" snout;

Ears that listen and care;

When you put them all together,

You have a teddy bear.

—Mary Sutula, Orlando, FL

162

Poems, & Rhymes

I'm A Little Sunflower

Watch your little ones bloom with sunny smiles as they say this simple fingerplay. For added fun, make the "Sunflower Wind Dancers" shown on page 98.

I'm a little sunflower.

I'm so small.

Soil,

Sun,

And water

Make me tall.

When I get all grown-up,

You will see,

That I'm as big as I can be!

—*Lucia Kemp Henry*

Fingerplays,

The Flower And The Bee

In springtime bees and flowers are the best of friends!

 Here is a great big flower.

 Here is a tiny bee.

 The bee flies by with a buzz, buzz, buzz.

 The flower says, "Visit me!"

—*Lucia Kemp Henry*

Poems, & Rhymes

Here Is The Nest

 Here is the nest,

 All warm inside.

 Three little birds

 Can safely hide.

 Here is the nest,

 All hidden away.

 Three little birds

 Can flap and play.

 Here is the nest,

 All cozy and deep.

 Three little birds

 Are all fast asleep.

—*Lucia Kemp Henry*

Sailing

Sail into summer with this nifty nautical rhyme.

This is a sail.

This is the boat.

Upon the ocean,

It will float.

And when a big, strong wind does blow,

Around the ocean the boat will go.

—*Marie E. Cecchini*

Poems, & Rhymes

Five Little Fishes

Thinking about teasing Mr. Shark? Be careful!
He eats one more fish with each consecutive verse of this rhyme!

 [Five] little fishes,

 Swimming in the sea.

 Teasing Mr. Shark,

"You can't catch me!"

 Along comes Mr. Shark,

As quiet as can be...

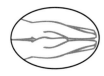 Snap!

 [Four] little fishes,

 Swimming in the sea.

—Andrea Esposito, Brooklyn, NY

It's Circle Time!

Musical Clothing

Children will be dressed for success with this fun game of musical clothing. In advance, fill a gym bag with articles of clothing that cover as many different body parts as possible. Be sure to include at least one item for each child. To play, seat children in a circle on the floor. Ask them to pass the bag from child to child while the music plays. When the music stops, the child holding the bag should close her eyes and pull one item of clothing out of the bag. She then puts the item on and identifies which body part the item is covering. Continue play until each child has had an opportunity to select an article or until the bag is empty.

Sandy DiFilippo—Preschool, Laurel Parks & Recreation, Laurel, MD

Preferred Seating

Help preschoolers find a place to sit during group time with this management tip. From tagboard, cut a large seasonal shape for each child in the class. For example, in October cut large pumpkin shapes from tagboard and in November cut large leaf shapes. Laminate the shapes for durability. Attach the shapes to the floor far enough apart so that each child has his own space and seasonal mat to sit on. Have a seat!

Susan Burbridge—Four-Year-Olds, Trinity Methodist Weekday School, San Antonio, TX

Circle-Time Survey

Make the most of the necessary task of taking attendance by turning it into a time of sharing. Each day, pose a question for the children to answer as the students' names are individually called out. After each child has had an opportunity to respond, use the information for further directions. For example, you might ask, "What did you have for breakfast today?" Then direct all children who answered that they ate cereal to stand in line. Each circle-time survey will lead to an enjoyable way for children to learn more about one another.

Terri Nix, Brauchle Elementary, San Antonio, TX

IT'S CIRCLE TIME!

Circle-Time Music Selection

This circle-time idea will keep your little ones humming to their favorite tunes. To make sure that all students have input on the choice of music selected, take photos or make small pictures that represent some of the students' favorite songs. Insert the photos or pictures in six resealable plastic bags, and glue them to all the sides of a small, square box. Select a child to toss the box. The photo that lands on top indicates the first song to be sung. Choose a different child each time you need to make a selection. Photos or pictures can be changed as the students' favorite songs change.

Hi, Jon! Where would you like to play today?

Pass The Colors

Pass on color recognition with this adaptation of Hot Potato. Have youngsters stand or sit in a circle. Give each child a color card. (If necessary, establish whether youngsters will be passing to the left or the right; then practice a circle pass.) As you begin the music, have youngsters pass their color cards around the circle. When the music stops, have each youngster name the color that he is holding. Now that's a "color-rific" idea!

Hello?

Plan your circle time before youngsters go to centers or interest areas to give this nifty idea a try. Have students sit in a circle. Provide one child with a telephone and ask him what center he chooses to visit by pretending to call that youngster on the telephone. You may say something like, "Hi, Jon. Where would you like to play today?" Encourage the child to respond; then have him give the phone to another child. Continue in this manner until each child has had a chance to talk on the phone with you!

Mary Borreca—Preschool, Martinsville Elementary, Martinsville, TX

IT'S CIRCLE TIME!

compiled by Marie Iannetti

The Groundhog Game

It will be lights out when your little groundhogs play this fun game. Seat youngsters in a circle. Choose three student volunteers to hide under a nearby table to represent groundhogs hiding in their holes. Tell the hiding children that when you turn off the lights, they should pretend that they are sleeping. Provide three of the children seated in the circle with a beanbag (evenly spacing the bags between children). Then turn out the lights. Have each child with a beanbag pass it to the child sitting to his left. Have students continue to pass the beanbags until you turn on the lights. The students pretending to be groundhogs awaken and pop out of their holes. The three children holding beanbags switch places with the groundhogs. Continue the game in the same manner until everyone has had a turn being a groundhog.

Brenda vonSeldeneck and Donna Selling—Preschool
First Presbyterian Church
Waynesboro, VA

Whose Name Is This?

Try this idea to help little ones recognize their names. In advance write each child's name on a different sheet of shaped notepad paper. (Change to a different notepad shape with each season or theme.) Laminate the notepad paper if desired. Each day when your youngsters are seated at group time, hold up one notepad sheet at a time and encourage each youngster to identify his name when he sees it. For variety direct your children to do different actions when their names are shown, saying, for example, "When you see your name, clap your hands," or "When you see your name, raise your hands above your head." If youngsters have difficulty identifying their names, assist them by giving clues such as "This is a boy's name," or "This name begins with the letter *B*."

Samita Arora—Pre-K and Kindergarten
Richmond, IN

Knock, Knock

Who's there? Youngsters are sure to love this guessing game. Seat the class on the floor. Place a chair in front of the group. Select a child to sit in the chair with his eyes closed and his back toward the group. Quietly select a child in the group to tiptoe to the chair and knock on the back of it. Direct the child in the chair to say, "Who's there?" The child who knocked replies, "It's me!" The child in the chair tries to guess who is knocking only by listening to the knocker's voice. If necessary provide the child with clues about the mystery student so that he can guess correctly before returning to the group. The child who knocked then takes his turn in the chair. Play until each child has had a turn sitting in the chair.

Donna Leonard—Preschool
Head Start
Dyersville, IA

IT'S CIRCLE TIME!

Good Morning Song

Each morning, sing this song (to the tune of "Where Is Thumbkin?") to gather your little ones to your meeting place.

Teacher:	Where is [child's name]?
	Where is [child's name]?
Student:	Here I am.
	Here I am.
Teacher:	How are you today, [child's name]?
Student:	Very well, I thank you.
Teacher:	Please sit down. Please sit down.

Janis Woods—Four-Year-Olds, Ridgeland Elementary School, Ridgeland, SC

Circle-Time Shapes

Do you often use cutouts of geometric shapes during your circle-time games and songs? If so, here's a durable and adorable way to make shapes that your little ones can really get a handle on. Cut shapes in a variety of sizes from various colors of foam board. Using a permanent marker, add smiling faces to the shapes. If you emphasize a different shape each month, consider cutting one large shape from foam board and then displaying it on a wall when the month is over.

adapted from an idea by Joan Banker—Three- And Four-Year-Olds
St. Mary's Child Development Center, Garner, NC

Calendar And Weather Friends

If your calendar and weather activities need a new twist, enlist the help of puppets. Choose a special puppet to ask about the weather each day, and another puppet to ask the date, the month of the year, and the day of the week. After youngsters become familiar with the routine, have student volunteers role-play with the puppets during your calendar and weather learning time.

Renée Siegel—Three-Year-Olds, Temple Judea Nursery School, Massapequa, NY

Circle-Time Travels

Take each youngster on a journey in which his imagination is his guide. Have students sit in a circle. Provide each child with a plastic plate. Have him hold the plate and pretend that it's a steering wheel. Then tell students that they will be going on imaginary vacations. Ask a student volunteer to give a vacation destination—such as Grandmother's house or the beach—and a mode of transportation—such as a car or train. As the children steer their vehicles, encourage them to tell about the people, places, and things they see on their trip. After this trip has been completed, ask another volunteer to make the next destination and transportation suggestion. Off we go!

Glenda C. Roddey, An Academe For Children, Inc., Springdale, AR

Color Bear Bags

These nifty color bears will help youngsters review color recognition. In advance, cut out pairs of bear shapes from different colors of construction paper. Glue one bear from each pair onto a white lunch bag. Open the bags and stand them in a row on the floor. Provide each child with a cutout. In turn, have each child identify the color of his bear and place it in the corresponding bag.

Debi Luke—Preschool, Fairmount Nursery School, Syracuse, NY

The Book Circle

Use this idea during circle time and your little ones will have a calm and relaxing way to cozy up with some books. Have each child bring a book to group time. Seat the children in a circle. Play a classical music selection while each youngster looks at his book. Then, at a designated time, instruct each child to pass his book to the person on his right. Continue in this manner for an appropriate length of time or until each child has his original book.

B. Childery—Three-, Four-, And Five-Year-Olds, Walnut Creek Elementary
Azle, TX

Setting The Stage

Setting The Stage:

Reading Area

Reading On A Park Bench

Create a setting for browsing through books that changes with each season, yet keeps the same tranquil appeal. Secure a large tree limb to a wooden base, or purchase a silk tree. Set the tree near a park bench in a quiet corner of your classroom reading center. As each new season approaches, have youngsters provide appropriate decorations for the tree and attach them to the branches. During the fall, students can sit beneath a tree full of apples or colorful leaves. Provide lots of fall and apple-related literature in the reading area along with some soft, fluffy pillows to cozy up with on the bench.

Becky Buttram, Liberty-Eylau Primary School, Texarkana, TX

Housekeeping Area

If The Shoe Fits...

Little ones won't recognize your housekeeping area when you convert it into a shoe store. Stock your center with a supply of shoeboxes—each box filled with a different pair of shoes. Also provide the center with low floor mirrors, a foot-measuring tool, paper bags, and a toy cash register. To the front of the center, tape a sign that reads "The Shoe Shop." To use the center, have little ones take turns being salespeople and customers.

Cathie Pesa, Youngstown City Schools, Boardman, OH

Water Table

Water-Table Fun

Enrich your water table with this cool idea. Halfway fill your empty water table with ice cubes. Place several pairs of rubber gloves near the table. To use this center, a child puts on the rubber gloves and creates the design of his choice with the ice cubes. For example, he may make an ice castle or an ice house—or he may simply wish to slide the cubes on the table.

Betty Silkunas, Lansdale, PA

Interest Areas And Centers

Woodworking Center

"Woodworking" Corner

Imaginations and creativity will soar when your youngsters bang, pound, hammer, and construct woodworking art! In advance, cover a tabletop with carpet squares. Stock the center with items such as Styrofoam, golf tees, rubber mallets, soft wood, a large block of sculpting clay, tongue depressors, screws, screwdrivers, sandpaper, and a manual hand drill. To use this center, a child uses the materials of his choice to build a sculpture. For example, he may hammer the tees and screws into the clay, Styrofoam, or wood; then add tongue depressors to his design. After building his sculpture, each child may paint it, if desired.

Kelley Sharrock—Pre/K, Church Of The Redeemer Preschool, Reynoldsburg, OH

Math Center

A Sweetie Of A Center

Have your little learners try this sweet activity at your math center. Supply your center with small Ziploc® sandwich bags containing one type of candy such as M&M's®, jelly beans, or Skittles®. Create a graph with a column and a colorful stick-on dot for each of the colors found in the candy; then laminate the graph. Assist each child in graphing his assortment of candy. Then have each youngster interpret and explain his graph. Allow your students to eat the candy afterwards.

Carmen Carpenter—Pre/K, Children's Discovery Center, Cary, NC

Block Area

Milking The Cow

Each of your youngsters can pretend to travel to a class-room barnyard and even milk a cow when he tries this fun-filled center. Using cardboard, make a large cow cutout. Mount the cow onto the side of an easel. Then, using a straight pin, gently poke holes in each finger of a rubber glove. Pour milk into the glove until it is two-thirds full; then knot the top of the glove. Mount the glove onto the back of the cow cutout to resemble the cow's udder. Place a pail or bowl directly under the udder and a small stool in front of the cow. Provide the center with various stuffed farm animals and barnyard decorations or props. To use this center, a child sits on the stool and squeezes the fingers of the glove to milk the cow. Encourage him to build a barnyard fence from blocks before leaving the center. As a fun follow-up, take your youngsters on a field trip to a local farm to milk a real cow!

Terry Hyder—3-year-olds, University Park United Methodist Church Weekday School, Dallas, TX

Pam Crane

Setting The Stage:

Block Area

Block Village

Have youngsters build an awesome village in your block area for lots of hands-on fun. In advance, draw streets, roads, and mountains on the back of a sheet of vinyl fabric. Place the fabric, small blocks, plastic toy people, and toy cars and trucks in the block area. Encourage youngsters who visit this center to use the materials provided to make a village.

Sand Table

Fill It Up!

Convert your classroom sand table for other creative uses. By simply placing a bedsheet on top of the sand, you can fill your sand table with another interesting material such as rice, beans, popcorn kernels, birdseed, or cereal. Also stock the table with fun utensils such as strainers, funnels, measuring cups, and large spoons. Using this method, the sand is undisturbed. Your little ones will love the variety.

Reading Area

A Cozy Corner

In this cozy center, you'll create a warm and inviting environment for your little ones to look through books. Provide your reading center with large and small pillows. Also place a cushioned chair or small sofa in the reading area. Position an end table and a table lamp next to the chair or sofa. No doubt your students will enjoy snuggling up with a good book in this comfy reading area.

Interest Areas And Centers

Housekeeping Area

Preschool Pizzeria

One slice or two? Your little ones will have a hard time recognizing your puppet theater when you convert it into the service counter of a pizzeria. Stock your housekeeping area with small-, medium-, and large-size pizza cutouts, pizza boxes, and pans; and empty soft-drink cans. Also provide the center with a freestanding puppet theater, play money, a toy cash register, a writing pad, and pencils. To the front of the puppet theater, tape a sign that reads "The Preschool Pizzeria." Cover a small table with a checkered tablecloth. To use the center, have little ones take turns being the cashier, waitstaff, and customers.

June Moss—Pre-K, Sunbeams And Rainbows Pre-School
Elmhurst, IL

The Preschool Pizzeria

Water Table

Thanksgiving Stew?

Stir up some excitement at your water table with this recipe for fun. Near your water table, place a basket of plastic food items such as meats and vegetables. Also provide large spoons, ladles, plastic bowls, empty salt and pepper shakers, and plastic spoons. Encourage youngsters who visit this center to pretend to prepare Thanksgiving stew.

Betty Silkunas, Lansdale, PA

Science Center

Take A Closer Look!

Encourage hands-on learning and lots of discovery opportunities at this science center. Provide acorns, a variety of leaves, twigs, pinecones, pieces of tree bark, and magnifying glasses at a table. Also supply paper, crayons, and markers. While in this center, a child uses the magnifying glass to carefully examine the objects. He then draws his scientific observations on paper.

Pam Crane

Setting The Stage:

Housekeeping Area

Deck The Halls!

This holiday season provide youngsters with everything they will need to festively decorate your housekeeping area. In a large box, place realistic pine garland, wreaths, bows, stockings, battery-operated candles, and other extra decorating items you might have. Consider setting up a small, artificial tree along with a supply of easy-to-hang, unbreakable ornaments. Encourage youngsters to use the items to decorate the area. When cleanup time arrives, assist them in carefully returning all the decorations to the box.

Games Area

Magnet Mania

Little ones are sure to be attracted to your classroom games area when you stock it with these inexpensive magnet boards. Obtain several countertop protectors from the housewares department of your favorite store. Along with the boards, place a supply of letter- and numeral-shaped magnets in the center. Or attach magnetic tape to the backs of laminated game pieces to use with the boards. Students will get stuck on the fun!

Teresa Hanak—Three-Year-Olds, Fenton Preschool
Fenton, MI

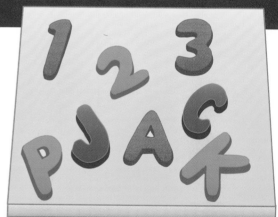

Woodworking Center

Hammers And Nails

Stumped for a way to add variety to your woodworking center? Add an old stump or a large log! Students who visit the center can hammer nails into the stump. If your center is stocked with small pieces of wood, students can also nail these to the stump. And of course, remember to provide safety goggles, establish guidelines, and monitor the center closely when it is in use.

Tanya Rowburrey—Preschool, Milton, FL

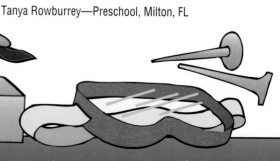

Interest Areas And Centers

Sand Table

An Archeological Dig

Exciting exploration and discoveries await your youngsters when you transform your sand table into the site of an archeological dig. To prepare for the dig, collect pictures from magazines (such as *National Geographic*) of actual archeological digs. Also cut out and mount on tagboard magazine pictures of jewels, coins, pottery, and other artifacts. Laminate and cut around the pictures; then hide them in the sand. Also supply digging tools, plastic baskets for sifting the sand, and brushes for carefully dusting sand from the treasures. Share and discuss with the class the pictures of the actual digs. Then encourage children to visit their archeological site.

Susan Ahlhorn—Pre-K, Wee Wuns Preschool
Cypress, TX

Water Table

Winter Water Wonders

Give your water table the deep freeze with these exciting winter additions. Fill miniature decorator cake pans with colored water and freeze them. Then add the frozen shapes to the water in the table. Add ice cubes and refreezable plastic ice cubes. If icicles are easily found in your area, add several of them as well. For added fun place plastic, Arctic-animal toys in the water. Brrr!

Dramatic Play Area

Peel, Mash, And Stir

Transform your dramatic play area or cooking area into a kitchen that will provide youngsters with delicious fine-motor fun. Stock the center with kitchen objects and real food. Encourage youngsters to peel, mash, or stir such foods as bananas and tangerines. A can opener and canned food are guaranteed to delight. Although this center requires extra supervision, the fine-motor and language development will be well worth the effort!

Cathie Pesa—Preschool Special Needs
Youngstown City Schools, Youngstown, OH

Setting The Stage:

Science Center

Rain Forest

Little ones will think they are actually in the Amazon when you transform an area of your room into a tropical rain forest. To create a rain-forest canopy, drape a large piece of camouflage net (the kind used for hunting) over any furniture in the area. Randomly place plastic or rubber snakes, frogs, crocodiles, and lizards in the netting and around the center. Also place artificial trees, vines, and plants in the center. Play a recording of rain-forest sounds (available from nature stores). Let the adventure begin!

Glenda C. Roddey
An Academe For Children, Inc.
Springdale, AR

Block Center

Creative Block Fun

Give your block center a new twist with this fun idea. Purchase several yards of different-colored, sheer gauzy fabric. Cut the fabric into a variety of sizes. Encourage youngsters who build houses in the center to drape the fabric pieces over the blocks to make doors or windows. Let their imaginations be their guide!

Amy Laubis
Children's Garden Preschool
Kenton, OH

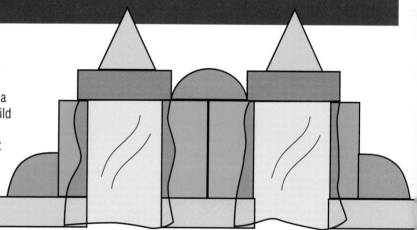

Dramatic Play Area

Preschool Hair-Cuttery

The Preschool Hair-Cuttery

Your students won't recognize the dramatic play area when you convert it into a hair salon. Glue photos of children (preferably your students) with different hair styles to sheets of construction paper. Also mount pictures of blow-dryers, scissors, and hair supplies on separate sheets of construction paper; then laminate the pages. Place the pages between two tagboard covers and bind the pages to make a book. Write the name of the hair salon on the cover of the book. Place the book, chairs, mirrors, empty shampoo bottles, towels, rollers, barrettes, ribbons, combs or brushes, and empty hairspray bottles in the center. Also stock the center with Styrofoam® heads (used by beauticians) and several wigs. To the front of the center, tape a sign that reads "The Preschool Hair-Cuttery." To use the center, have little ones pretend to be barbers or beauticians. Wash and set?

Karen Eiben—Three-Year-Olds
The Kid's Place
La Salle, IL

Interest Areas And Centers

Sand Table

Baskets Full Of Fun!

Enrich your sand table with this hands-on idea. Half-fill your table with colored plastic grass. Place several baskets, small plastic chicks and bunnies, and plastic eggs in the grass. To use this center, have little ones use the materials provided to create nifty spring baskets!

Mary Borreca—Preschool
Martinsville, TX

Water Table

Laundry Table

Set your water table outside and convert it into a laundry table. Half-fill the table with warm water; then add a scoop of mild laundry soap. In a laundry basket near the table, provide clothespins and small cloth items such as old handkerchiefs, doll clothing, and socks. Mount a clothesline between two chairs near the table, or set up a clothes-drying rack. To use this center, a child takes a piece of clothing from the laundry basket and washes it in the laundry table. (If desired, add an additional tub of water for rinsing.) He then wrings the excess water from the piece of clothing and uses a clothespin to clip it to the clothesline. Rub-a-dub-dub!

Reading Center

A Reading Pond

Create a setting in your reading area that your youngsters will dive into—a reading pond! To make a reading pond, place a round blue tablecloth on the floor of a wading pool to resemble water. Randomly place round green pillows in the pond to represent lily pads. Also place turtle and fish puppets in and around the pond. Position live or artificial plants around the pond area. On a table near the pond, provide books about pond life, plus frog headbands or hats. To use this center, allow two children at a time to don frog hats, choose books from the table, and enjoy reading in the reading pond. No doubt this center will make a splash!

Kate Taluga—Preschool
Big Bend Community Coordinated Child Care
Tallahassee, FL

Life In A Small Pond

Setting The Stage:

Dramatic Play Area

Row Your Boat

Ahoy, mateys! Make the most of your ocean theme by creating a boat for use in your dramatic play area. Cut the top or side from a large box; then cut out a few portholes. Use the leftover cardboard to make a sturdy steering wheel and an anchor. Then have little ones help you paint the boat with a bright color of tempera paint. Add some oceangoing props such as a life jacket, a tackle box, and some wooden dowels with strings attached to serve as fishing poles. Then encourage youngsters to set sail into the sea of imagination!

Jennifer Liptak—Three-Year-Olds
Building Blocks Of Learning
Denville, NJ

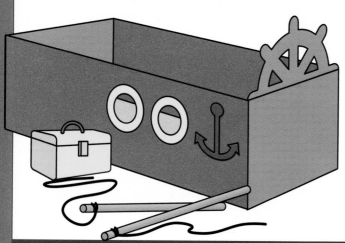

Sand Table

Paper Punches

If you're tired of the same old sand or rice in your sensory table, try something new! Ask a local printing company to save a bag full of paper punches—the small, round paper scraps created when paper is hole-punched for binding. Fill the table with paper punches; then add some hidden treasures such as cookie cutters or poker chips. Invite little ones to "pan" for the treasures using berry baskets. It's a "hole" lot of fun!

Doris Porter—Preschool
Headstart
Anamosa, IA

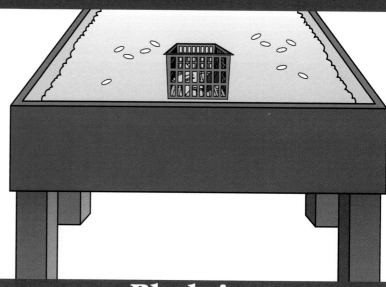

Block Area

Tabletop Town

Enhance your block area with a tabletop town cut from felt. Begin by cutting a large piece of felt to fit on a tabletop. Cut additional colors of felt into strips to create a maze of roads that can be placed on the larger piece of felt. Also cut out felt trees, houses, and other buildings if desired. Decorate the felt pieces with slick or puffy fabric paint. Little ones will love setting up the town and driving toy cars and trucks along its roadways.

Sharon Otto—Preschool
SRI/St. Elizabeth Child Development Center
Lincoln, NE

Interest Areas And Centers

Water Table

Number Float

Make some waves with this number-recognition center! Near your water table, place a plastic pail that contains a set of small, plastic toys or counters. Float a plastic numeral in the water. A youngster looks at the numeral, then places a matching set of toys or counters in the water. It's a splash of counting fun!

Art Center

Festive Flags

Celebrate Flag Day at your art center with some creative red, white, and blue designs. Place large sheets of white paper at your easel, along with large brushes and red, white, and blue tempera paint. Encourage youngsters to paint their own flag designs for a patriotic display in the classroom.

Bernadette Hoyer—Chapter I Pre-K
McGinn and Coles Schools
Scotch Plains, NJ

Games Center

Guess What

Create a bulletin-board game that will please your curious preschoolers— and sharpen their problem-solving and classification skills as well. Collect magazine pictures of familiar objects, animals, or characters. Mount the pictures on a bulletin board. Cover each picture with a piece of construction paper that is identical in size and shape. Cut an opening in the cover sheet to strategically reveal a clue about the picture underneath. Have youngsters take turns guessing what each hidden picture shows. Hmmm…could that be a cat?

Mary E. Maurer
Caddo, OK

Math Matters

Seriation At The Home Of The Three Bears

Provide youngsters with a rich environment for making the types of comparisons that contribute to their ability to seriate, or compare objects according to one attribute and arrange the objects in a logical series. Like Goldilocks, few of your preschoolers will pass up an opportunity to make themselves comfortable in the home of the infamous three bears. Once inside the bears' abode, lots of natural opportunities for comparison—and consequently language development—will arise. Students may choose to seriate the items in and around the house according to weight, texture, firmness, size, thickness, length, height, and sound.

Setting Up And Getting Ready

Do you have a wooden or cardboard house in your classroom? Temporarily convert it into the home of the three bears. If your classroom house is too small to accommodate all the things you'd like for your children to seriate, convert your housekeeping area into the three bears' home for a while. Visually divide the available space into a kitchen area, a living-room area, and a bedroom area.

Stock the house with three different variations of each listed item and any others that are suitable. Improvise whenever necessary to come up with three versions of each item. Once students see what you are placing in the house, they may want to donate items for use. Encourage them to do so. Be sure to read a couple of different versions of *Goldilocks And The Three Bears* to your youngsters when the house is ready for your students to visit.

Outside The House

Place three laminated paper stepping stones of varying sizes so that they lead to the front door.

Partially fill three different-sized flowerpots with sand. In the pots, place identical silk flowers that have been cut to varying heights. Students can compare the weights of the pots and the heights of the flowers.

Invite size comparisons by placing three different sizes of stuffed bears outside the house.

For doorbells, include three bells that produce different sounds.

More ideas: watering hose lengths • watering cans • gardening gloves • rocking or lawn chairs

Barry Slate

Kitchen

The bears' house must have porridge! Stock the kitchen with lidded and sealed oatmeal containers that have been filled with sand for weight comparisons.

Where there's porridge, there must be cooking pots. Put three sizes of cooking pots in the kitchen area of the bears' house.

If you're going to grab a hot pot of porridge, you'll need a potholder. Cut a few imitation potholders from three fabrics that vary from smooth to rough.

Provide porridge bowls, cups, spoons, and placemats suitable for size comparisons.

More ideas: weighted, sealed cereal boxes • milk jugs • aprons • measuring spoons • pitchers

Den

No bear's den would be complete without different sizes of chairs.

Place a few pillows that vary in density in the den area. Students can seriate them according to firmness.

Give the bears' den that homey look with unbreakable framed pictures. Students can compare and seriate the pictures before hanging them on an adjacent wall.

In the den, include three copies of *Goldilocks And The Three Bears* that vary in size and weight.

More ideas: eyeglasses without lenses • comforters • footstools • area rugs

Bedroom

Cots or sleeping bags can be used to replicate the bears' beds, and to encourage size and firmness comparisons.

Pillows of varying firmnesses can be placed on the imitation beds to give students other opportunities to compare density.

On the beds, include blankets that vary in size, thickness, and softness.

In an area set up to represent a dresser, include personal items such as combs, toothbrushes, and T-shirts in varying sizes.

More ideas: teddy bears • shoes • phones • clothes • towels • hats

The three bears' house is *just* right for stimulating the use of seriation in your youngsters' play.

Happy Birthday, EveryONE!

You're Invited To A Birthday Party

Where: The dramatic play area, of course!

Why: To help youngsters learn about a fundamental component of the concept of number—one-to-one correspondence.

To: Derrick

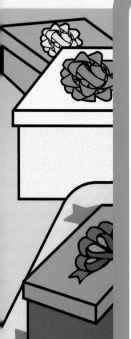

One-to-one correspondence is the understanding that one group has the same number of things as another. Two or more groups of objects can be paired, one for one. For example, at a birthday party, each present has a bow, each slice of cake has a candle, *and* each child has a great time! So why not transform your dramatic play area into a festive center that celebrates learning? Here's how.

Setting Up And Getting Ready

Get youngsters in the mood for a celebration by reading aloud several books about birthdays. Here are a few suggestions:

• *The Secret Birthday Message,* Written & Illustrated by Eric Carle, Published by HarperCollins Children's Books

• *Happy Birthday To You!,* Written & Illustrated by Dr. Seuss, Published by Random House Books For Young Readers

• *A Birthday For Frances,* Written by Russell Hoban, Illustrated by Lillian Hoban, Published by HarperCollins Children's Books

• *Hello, Amigos!,* Written by Tricia Brown, Photographs by Fran Ortiz, Published by Henry Holt And Company

Before you can have a party, you need to decorate! Hang brightly colored streamers above your dramatic play or housekeeping area. Tie helium-filled balloons to the furniture in the area. For longer-lasting balloons, stuff deflated Mylar® balloons with plastic grocery bags; then attach the balloons to a wall or bulletin board near the area. Drape a festive tablecloth over a table and hang a "Happy Birthday" banner nearby.

If you have a classroom mail center, request the honor of each child's presence at the party by sending each one an invitation. Or place an invitation in each child's cubby. Little ones will be delighted to know that they are all invited to the celebration.

Opportunities For Learning About One-To-One Correspondence

Young children are more likely to arrange items in one-to-one correspondence if the items go together in some way. Here are suggestions for encouraging youngsters' exploration of this concept while at the birthday-party center.

For every chair around the table, provide a stuffed toy or doll so that children can seat one toy in each chair.

Provide a party hat for each toy guest at the party.

No birthday party is complete without presents! For each toy guest, separately gift wrap a box and its lid. Encourage children at the birthday-party center to place one small gift item in each box, then top the box with the matching lid. The children can then tape one bow to each gift box before presenting one present to each guest seated at the table.

Birthday parties always have plenty of food (or pretend food!). Make sure the center is stocked with one decorative plate, cup, napkin, and fork for each toy guest seated at the table. Novelty straws and party favors add to the possibilities. Encourage the children at the center to set the table and "serve" each guest at the party.

Prepare a batch of play dough to place in the center. Encourage the children at the center to make a cupcake for each guest by rolling the dough into balls. Youngsters can then place each ball in a foil cupcake liner. Birthday candles, of course, are a must! Encourage children to place one candle in each dough cupcake before serving it to a guest.

Supply a birthday card and envelope for each guest. Encourage children to place one card in each envelope and give one envelope to each guest.

Everyone loves party favors! Encourage youngsters to prepare a bag of goodies for each toy guest. Provide one decorative gift bag for each guest at the party. Supply the same number of each different party favor as there are bags so that the children can drop one of each novelty item in each bag. Don't forget the gift tags!

Wrap It Up

The enjoyment your youngsters get from this celebration station is sure to last a while. However, when it's time for a change, why not wrap it all up with a *real* party? Gather together for food, games, and maybe even presents. Don't forget to conclude the celebration with a round of "Happy Birthday To You!"

MATH MATTERS

Under Construction

The framework for a child's understanding of advanced math concepts is under construction during the preschool years. Build the foundation for problem solving and an understanding of geometry with these ideas that involve awareness of spatial relations. As youngsters build, rearrange, and reshape materials in your classroom blocks center, support their efforts with truckloads of praise, encouraging suggestions, and descriptive observations. These ideas are bound to hit the nail right on the head—so hammer away!

Building Supplies

To help children distinguish between shapes, provide them with plenty of shaped materials to build with and talk about. In addition to building blocks, add many of the following materials to your blocks center construction site:

- Cut large, cardboard shapes for children to incorporate into their buildings. A cardboard shape can be used as a base for a structure, as a floor between the blocks of a high-rise building, or as a roof.
- Place several carpet squares in the center. Cut carpet scraps into circles, triangles, and rectangles.
- Cover boxes of various sizes and shapes with Con-Tact® covering.
- Using masking tape, tape the outlines of various shapes to the floor. Students can build structures and roads along the lines, or they can push toy cars along the shape outlines.
- Place a set of mini traffic signs in the center.
- Place a supply of attribute or pattern blocks in the center to give students smaller shapes to manipulate and add to their structures.

Barry
Slate

Construction Materials

To give children more opportunities to explore geometric and spatial relations, include in your construction site some of the following materials that can be re-shaped and rearranged:

- toy cars and trucks
- paper tubes
- large nuts and bolts
- miniature furniture
- large pegs and pegboards
- Styrofoam pieces
- other commercial products that can be used for building such as Lincoln Logs, Slinky Triangles®, Wee Waffle® Blocks, and letter wood blocks

To help kids get in the mood for building, don't forget to place several hard hats and play tools in the center!

Here's The Plan

Use these teaching suggestions as a blue-print for building youngsters' understanding of geometry and spatial relations:

- Assist children in describing their structures. Ask them to describe the shapes of the building materials they used.
- Ask children to tell you how they used the materials to build their structures.
- Encourage the children to look at their creations from different viewpoints. Have them stand on chairs, lie on the floor, or sit inside their structures.
- Provide paper and crayons so that children can draw their creations from different viewpoints.
- Encourage children to use paper and crayons to trace the shapes of the different materials used.
- Ask a child to build a simple structure; then challenge a partner in the center to copy the structure.

Sandy

MATH MATTERS

A Store (Of Sorts)

Transforming your dramatic play area into a grocery store will provide youngsters with a fantastic environment for classifying, or sorting, objects according to attributes such as color, shape, size, and so on. As youngsters play in the store, ask them to describe how the materials are the same or how they are different. Assist students in describing the objects in different ways. And as the children begin to sort and classify on their own, ask them to talk about what they are doing and to explain why. Learning about classification in a store can be all sorts of fun!

by Jayne Gammons

Setting Up Shop

If your dramatic play area is organized as a housekeeping center, remove the furniture or turn it around so that it faces the outside of the center. Or cover the furniture with bulletin-board paper to change its appearance.

• Prepare and hang a banner that displays the name of your supermarket.

• Hang an authentic open/closed sign on a piece of furniture near the entrance to the area.

• Obtain a toy grocery cart or provide baskets with handles for your youngsters to use as they shop.

• Create a checkout counter by covering a rectangular table with paper. Place a toy cash register full of play, paper money and real coins near the end of the table.

• Stock the center with a supply of small and large paper grocery bags. Obtain grocery bags from several different stores so that the outsides of the bags display different designs. (Note: The National Health and Safety Performance Standards state that all plastic bags should be stored out of reach of children.)

• Collect duplicates of several different types of canned food. Also collect cans that vary in size but have identical labels. Arrange your supply of unopened cans on a bookshelf or on plastic, stacking shelves. On a different bookshelf, arrange food boxes and household products containers that have been emptied and taped closed. Provide both duplicates and varying sizes of each product.

• Collect real and/or plastic fruits and vegetables, and display each different type in a basket on a table.

• Clean several different sizes and types of milk and orange juice cartons. Store them in milk crates.

• Obtain two large, clear plastic storage boxes. Label one "Refrigerator" and the other "Freezer." Place emptied and cleaned plastic and paper containers in the refrigerator box. Place frozen-food boxes that have been emptied and cleaned in the freezer box.

• Obtain several, identical coupon sections from newspapers. Cut out the coupons and glue them to one color of construction paper before laminating them and cutting them out. Store the coupons in a container in the center.

Open For Business

As the children pretend to shop for and sell the items in the store, use the suggestions that follow to encourage them to group the objects based on the items' similarities and differences. Encourage youngsters to develop their own categories for classifying the objects as well.

To the child pretending to be the *cashier,* suggest sorting the coins from the paper money or sorting the coins by color or size.

To the child pretending to be a *shopper,* suggest matching the coupons that are identical.

Encourage children to sort the paper grocery bags by size or to group together the bags that have the same printed design.

Youngsters can arrange the cans on one set of shelves and the boxes on a separate set of shelves. (Suggest, for example, that all of the canned tomatoes be grouped together. Later the small tomato cans can be separated from the larger tomato cans.) Boxes of food can be separated from boxes of household products.

Encourage the children to sort the fruits and vegetables in the baskets by type, color, and size.

Have the children sort the milk cartons by type, such as white or chocolate. The small chocolate-milk cartons can then be separated from the larger chocolate-milk cartons.

Suggest that the children put the boxes of food that might melt or thaw—such as ice cream—in the box labeled "Freezer." From the box labeled "Refrigerator," children can sort the food containers that are plastic from the containers that are paper.

MATH MATTERS

Flower Power

Every patient gardener knows that if she plants flower seeds and cares for them as they grow, they will one day blossom. Every patient preschool teacher—like a gardener—knows that if she plants seeds of learning, they will take root and grow into understanding and knowledge.

Since children in the preoperational stage of development do not yet fully understand the concepts of number, care should be taken to present counting activities in a developmentally appropriate way. Weeds of drill and practice can easily grow and stifle a child's natural curiosity about numbers and counting. Be sure to provide opportunities for counting practice to occur in play activities by supplying plenty of real objects for counting and by introducing numerals as labels for groups of objects rather than as isolated symbols.

Use these ideas to transform your dramatic play area into a floral shop where you can cultivate counting skills in your children. As the children play, observe their actions and listen carefully to their conversations—asking questions, making suggestions, and giving encouragement as needed. In time, counting skills will burst into bloom!

by Jayne Gammons

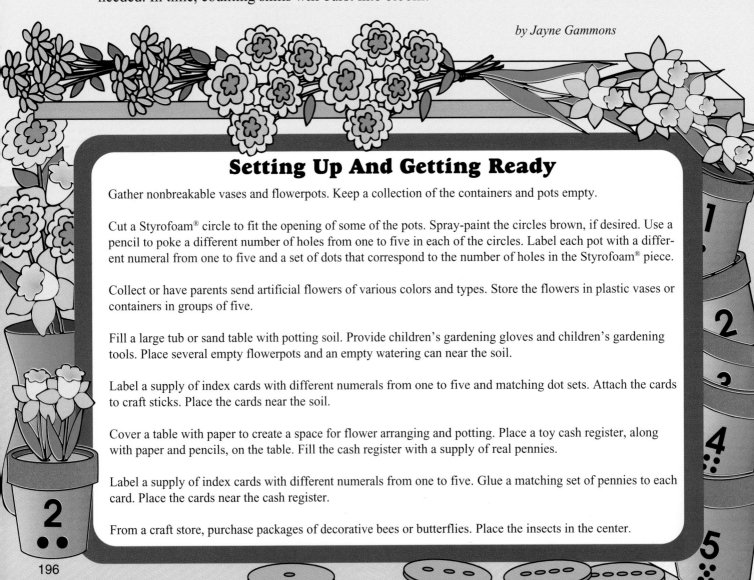

Setting Up And Getting Ready

Gather nonbreakable vases and flowerpots. Keep a collection of the containers and pots empty.

Cut a Styrofoam® circle to fit the opening of some of the pots. Spray-paint the circles brown, if desired. Use a pencil to poke a different number of holes from one to five in each of the circles. Label each pot with a different numeral from one to five and a set of dots that correspond to the number of holes in the Styrofoam® piece.

Collect or have parents send artificial flowers of various colors and types. Store the flowers in plastic vases or containers in groups of five.

Fill a large tub or sand table with potting soil. Provide children's gardening gloves and children's gardening tools. Place several empty flowerpots and an empty watering can near the soil.

Label a supply of index cards with different numerals from one to five and matching dot sets. Attach the cards to craft sticks. Place the cards near the soil.

Cover a table with paper to create a space for flower arranging and potting. Place a toy cash register, along with paper and pencils, on the table. Fill the cash register with a supply of real pennies.

Label a supply of index cards with different numerals from one to five. Glue a matching set of pennies to each card. Place the cards near the cash register.

From a craft store, purchase packages of decorative bees or butterflies. Place the insects in the center.

Learning Opportunities You Can Count On

Encourage youngsters to use the flowers and empty containers to create flower arrangements. Assist them in describing their arrangements by counting the number of flowers or the number of flowers of the same color that are in the arrangement.

Challenge your young florists to place the correct number of flowers in each of the numbered pots.

With youngsters count aloud the number of petals on a flower.

Place a numeral card in the potting soil. Encourage youngsters to "plant" the number of flowers indicated on the card.

While working with the soil, encourage youngsters to count scoops of dirt used to fill containers.

Encourage children to count as many decorative bees or butterflies as there are flowers in the soil, matching one insect to each flower.

Encourage youngsters to tag their arrangements with the numeral cards to which pennies were attached. A child pretending to be a shopper can count and give the corresponding number of pennies to a child pretending to be the florist.

When cleaning up the center, ask children to return five flowers to each container.

All Washed Up!

Ready for some good, clean fun? If so, organize a laundry center either outdoors or in your dramatic play area. While visiting the center, little ones will have an opportunity to wash and dry their way into pattern exploration.

Here's The Dirt (About Patterns)

Did you know that mathematics can be defined as the study of pattern? A child's future understanding of our number system, her ability to problem-solve, and her ability to think abstractly begins with the recognition of patterns in everyday life. For example, when she recognizes the cycle of day and night or the repetition of a daily preschool schedule, she is recognizing pattern. When young children begin to explore pattern, they should use objects, motions, and sounds to copy, create, and extend patterns. Use these suggestions to create a fun-filled center designed for the discovery of pattern.

Setting Up And Getting Ready

Create a washing machine and a dryer for the center by turning two boxes upside down. Cut the boxes as shown; then paint them if desired.

Set up a clothes-drying rack or a retractable clothesline. (Provide adequate supervision.)

You'll want to stock the center with groups of items that can clearly be identified as alike or different. Here are some suggestions:

- wooden clothespins and plastic clothespins of various colors
- regular-size and miniature clothes baskets
- empty detergent boxes and bottles
- detergent scoops of various colors
- white and colored socks
- doll clothes or felt, clothing-shaped cutouts
- pennies and nickels

The Scoop On Pattern Exploration

As your little ones play in the laundry center, encourage their exploration of pattern. Here's how:

Ask a student to alternately put items in the washer and the dryer.

Challenge a youngster to create a pattern of clothespins on the clothesline by alternating wooden and plastic clothespins or by alternating colors of plastic clothespins.

Ask a student to alternately place clothes in a large and a small basket. Or have her line up the baskets, alternating between large and small.

Hang a pattern of white and colored socks on the clothesline. Encourage a child to extend the pattern.

Pair students and ask pairs to line up detergent bottles and boxes to create a pattern. Direct them to thump the bottles and boxes so that they can also hear the pattern they created.

Line up different colors of plastic laundry scoops. Ask a child to copy the pattern.

Assist a student in repeatedly putting a nickel in the washer, then a penny in the dryer.

Create a pattern using any set of objects in the center. Challenge a youngster or youngsters to identify the pattern.

Let's Talk About It!

Children need plenty of opportunities to verbalize their actions and describe their patterns. Encourage youngsters to chant their actions or patterns. For example, while creating a pattern with different-colored clothespins, a child might say, "Pink, blue, pink, blue,…." Or to describe a pattern made with detergent bottles and boxes, he might say, "Bottle, box, bottle, box,…."

The Magic Of Manipulatives

The Magic Of Manipulatives

Your little ones will flip their lids when using these fun activities. And why not? These ideas will promote hands-on learning and will provide limitless discovery opportunities. In preparation for these activities, collect a quantity of jug lids. What next? Get ready to blow the lid off learning and have lots of fun!

- Program a sheet of construction paper with dot sets from one to *five.* Place the paper and 15 lids at a center. To use this center, a child counts each set and then places a lid on each dot.

- Have your youngsters sort various lids by color and size.

- Have each child glue jug lids and craft items of his choice onto a piece of tagboard for a creative collage.

- On pairs of lids, place matching colored stick-on dots. Place the lids in a basket; then place the basket in a center. To use the center, a child chooses a lid, looks at the colored dot, and matches it to the corresponding lid. As a variation, program the lids with matching shapes.

- Place a supply of jugs and a bowl of corresponding jug lids in a center. To use this center, a child twists or snaps the lids on and takes them off.

- Challenge your little ones to see how many jug lids they can stack without making the lids fall. Careful!

- Glue lids on tagboard strips in different-colored patterns. For example, glue two blue lids, two red lids, two blue lids, and two red lids onto the tagboard. Using corresponding-colored lids, have your youngsters make the same pattern.

• Fill a small, clear container with lids and have students estimate the number of lids in it. Then, with your class, count the lids in the container.

• Use the lids for color bingo or for other game markers.

• Have each youngster use a supply of lids to measure his foot, crayon, pencil, or tabletop.

• Have little ones dip a lid into tempera paint, then onto a sheet of construction paper to make lid print designs.

• Have your youngsters estimate how many raisins, popcorn kernels, or sunflower seeds will fit in a lid. Fill a lid using one of these items; then have your class count with you to see how many actually fit.

• Have your little ones toss jug lids into baskets, Hula-Hoops®, or boxes from specified distances.

• Give each of two students several lids in a cup. Have each child shake his cup, then toss the lids onto a table. Together have the students count the lids that landed right-side-up and those that landed right-side-down; then graph and discuss the results.

BARRY SLATE

The Magic Of Manipulatives

Boxes, boxes, and more boxes! Your youngsters will enthusiastically take on this assortment of hands-on ideas and activities. In preparation for these activities, collect different sizes, colors, and shapes of boxes; then get ready for some real classroom fun!

- Encourage youngsters to fit smaller boxes into larger boxes.

- On pairs of small boxes, place matching colored stick-on dots. Place the boxes in a center. To use the center, a child chooses a box, looks at the colored dot, and matches it to the corresponding box. As a variation, program the boxes with matching pictures, stickers, or shapes.

- Wrap the tops and bottoms of several boxes with different styles or colors of gift-wrapping paper. Detach the lids from the boxes and place them in a center for youngsters to match.

- Have your little ones sequence a collection of different-size boxes from the smallest to the largest.

- Place spring-close jewelry boxes and old costume jewelry in a center. To use the center, a child places a jewel in each box and carefully closes the lid.

- Cover a supply of earring boxes with different solid colors of Con-Tact® covering. Or paint the boxes with different colors of spray paint. Place the boxes in a center. Encourage your young learners to use them to make different patterns.

- Paint several cereal boxes. Decorate each box with a silly face. Place the boxes in a row or stagger the boxes. Then, using beanbags, have your youngsters try to knock down the boxes from specified distances.

- Challenge your little ones to see how many boxes they can stack without making them fall.

- Place a large assortment of boxes—such as an egg carton, a shoebox, a cassette box, a jewelry box, an empty tissue box, and an index-card box—in a center. Also provide items that belong in the boxes. For example, provide plastic eggs for the egg carton and shoes for the shoebox. To use the center, a child places each item in the corresponding box.

- Have your little ones use soap-bar boxes to measure items in your room such as tabletops, shelves, and books.

- Bear in the box? Provide bears and boxes of several different sizes. Have youngsters place each bear in the box that fits it best.

- Tape or glue sandpaper around pairs of miniature cereal boxes. Encourage your little ones to rub the boxes together in rhythm as they listen to favorite classroom tunes.

- Provide students with a supply of boxes that vary in size and shape, like those that oatmeal, toothpaste, earrings, tissues, and shoes come in. Also supply youngsters with craft items such as paint, foil, glue, wrapping paper, markers, scissors, construction paper, tissue paper, and buttons. Encourage each student to use the boxes and the materials to make the artwork of his choice.

- Wrap the tops and bottoms of several boxes: each with gift wrap of a different theme. Place the boxes and items that correspond with the boxes' themes at a center. For example, if the gift-wrap theme is baseball, you may have a baseball cap or glove for youngsters to match. To use the center, a child places each item inside the corresponding box.

The Magic Of Manipulatives

Cookie Cutters

Because these hands-on ideas involve cookie cutters, we guarantee that they will be a cut above the rest! Purchase a collection of cutters at your local craft store, or ask parents to loan or donate cookie cutters to your class. Then let the cookie-cutter capers begin!

- Cookie cutters are great for blowing bubbles. Just dip a cutter into a container of bubble solution. Blow gently!

- Encourage children to use alphabet-shaped cookie cutters and play dough to spell their names. If desired prepare a name card for each child by tracing the cutters that spell his name. A student can then match the letter cutters or play-dough letters to his name card.

- Trace the shapes of individual cookie cutters onto index cards. Place the cards and the cookie cutters in a center. To use this center, a child matches each cookie cutter to a card.

- Stock an art center with holiday cookie cutters, stamp pads with colorful ink, and art paper. Encourage students to create decorative paper that can be used as gift wrap if desired.

- Assist the children in making simple sandwiches. Have each child cut his sandwich with the cookie cutter of his choice.

- Collect duplicates of simple cutters. Encourage the children to make patterns with the cutters by stringing them on a shoelace.

- Purchase a package of same-shaped cutters in graduated sizes. Challenge youngsters to sequence the cutters.

- Reinforce shape recognition with geometric cookie cutters. Have little ones use the cutters to make different shapes of—what else? Cookies!

- Place a collection of cutters and cookie pans in a dramatic play area. Add bowls and spoons along with chefs' hats and aprons. You'll have a cookie factory in no time!

- Collect a supply of cookie cutters for several different holidays or themes. Place the cutters in corresponding holiday- or theme-related gift bags. Encourage students to empty the bags. Then have them sort the cutters and return them to the corresponding bags.

- Place a set of numeral-shaped cutters and a supply of play dough in a math center. Encourage children to create a dough numeral from each cutter. Assist them in sequencing the numerals.

- Encourage students to trace simple cookie cutters onto construction paper. Have them cut on the outlines. The cutouts can be used for creative collages.

- Place a supply of decorative cutters in a sand table. Make sure the sand is moist for easy shaping.

207

The Magic Of Manipulatives

Socks

Sock some fun your youngsters' way when doing these hands-on ideas. They'll jump feetfirst into these activities that knit together multiple discovery opportunities and lots of classroom fun. In preparation for these activities, collect pairs of old socks of different colors, designs, and textures. Sock it to 'em!

Ideas by Janet Czapla and Immacula A. Rhodes

- Partially fill two unmatched socks with rice, two with marbles, two with pebbles, two with cube blocks, two with buttons, and two with pennies. Knot the top of each sock. Place the socks in a center. To use the center, a child feels the socks and matches the pairs that feel the same.

- Supply each child with a sock and craft items such as glue, scissors, pom-poms, felt pieces, yarn, wiggle eyes, and buttons. Encourage each student to glue the materials of his choice on the sock to make a simple sock puppet.

- On a wall near your water table, mount a clothesline at students' eye level. Place a laundry basket full of socks along with a variety of clothespins near the water table. Squeeze a few drops of mild laundry detergent or bubble bath into the water. Have students visit the water table, wash a pair of socks, and hang the socks on the clothesline to dry.

- Have your little ones make a sensory sock. To make one, place several items of interesting texture or shape in a large plastic cup. Beginning at the bottom of the cup, slip an adult's tube sock over the cup until the bottom of the cup is in the toe of the sock. To use the sensory sock, a child slips her hand through the sock opening and feels the items in the cup. Add lots of variety to this activity by asking youngsters to describe what they feel, guess what they are touching, or retrieve a specific item without using their eyes.

- Place several socks at your sand table. Have your little ones practice filling the socks with sand and emptying them. Or bury several socks in the sand and have students try to locate them.

- Roll several socks into ball shapes and have your youngsters toss them into laundry baskets or boxes from specified distances.

- Place an assortment of socks in a center. Have your youngsters sort the socks by size, color, design, type, and texture.

- Have your little ones sequence a collection of different-size socks from smallest to largest.

- Have your students estimate how many socks will fit in a small laundry basket. Fill the basket with socks; then have your class count with you to see how many actually fit.

- Provide each small group of students with a pie pan half-filled with red paint, a pan half-filled with blue paint, and a pan half-filled with yellow paint. Squeeze a few drops of cherry extract in the red paint, lemon extract in the yellow paint, and vanilla extract in the blue paint. Provide a sock cutout and an old sock rolled up in a doughnut shape for each child in a group. Encourage each student to dip the sock into the paint(s) of his choice, then onto the sock cutout for "scent-sational" designs!

- Place pairs of socks of different colors, sizes, and patterns in a laundry basket and place the basket and a bag of spring-type clothespins in a center. To use the center, a child matches the pairs of socks in the basket and clips a clothes-pin to each pair.

- Place a small laundry basket filled with socks on the floor. Have small groups of students lay the socks on the floor to make shapes such as circles, squares, triangles, rectangles, and ovals—or have them create the design of their choice.

Barry Slate

209

The Magic Of Manipulatives

Jelly Beans

Lots and lots of jelly beans will be the focus with these sweet hands-on activities. In preparation for these activities, purchase a quantity of assorted jelly beans; then let the fun begin!

by Marie Iannetti

- Ask each child to estimate how many jelly beans he can hold in one hand. Then have each child take a handful of jelly beans from a bowl. Have him count his jelly beans and compare that number with his prediction.

- Use jelly beans for color bingo or other game markers.

- Supply each youngster with a handful of gourmet-flavored jelly beans. Inform youngsters of the different flavors. Have each child examine the color of a jelly bean, eat it, and guess its flavor. When each child has tasted several jelly beans, tell the flavor that each color represents.

- Spray-paint one strawberry basket to match each of the colors found in a bag of jelly beans. Place a bowl of jelly beans and the baskets in a center. To use the center, a child places each jelly bean in the corresponding basket.

- Give each small group of youngsters a cup of jelly beans. Have them cooperatively sort the candy by color.

- Fill a small, a medium, and a large jar with jelly beans. Encourage each child to estimate how many jelly beans are in each jar. Then provide an opportunity for each child to explore the different amounts by allowing him to empty and refill the jars.

- Purchase a quantity of plastic eggs. For each number you would like to include, use a permanent marker to program half of each egg with a dot set and the other half with a corresponding numeral. Place the disassembled eggs in a basket. Place the basket and a bowl of jelly beans in a center. To use the center, a child matches the corresponding egg halves; then he fills each egg with the correct number of jelly beans.

- Have your youngsters estimate how many jelly beans will fill a teaspoon, a tablespoon, and a cup. Then have your class count with you to see how many actually fill each item.

- Have each child pour a spoonful of jelly beans in a plastic soda bottle. Secure each bottle with its lid. Have youngsters shake these bottles to the beat of favorite musical selections.

- Have youngsters use jelly beans for math counters when exploring the concepts of more and less.

- Glue jelly beans on tagboard strips in different-colored patterns. Using corresponding-colored jelly beans, have your youngsters duplicate the same patterns. Then encourage your students to make patterns of their own.

- Have each child close his eyes and select a jelly bean from a bag. Direct each child to open his eyes and find the other students with the same color of jelly bean.

- For each child, cut a slice from a roll of sugar-cookie dough. Encourage each child to use jelly beans to make a design in his slice of cookie dough. Bake the cookies as directed on the package. When the cookies are cool, youngsters will have a sweet treat to sample.

Barry Slate

211

The Magic Of Manipulatives

Seashells

Shell out the fun and learning opportunities with these hands-on activities using—what else? Seashells! Gather a collection of different colors, shapes, and sizes of seashells (available at most school and craft supply stores). Then hang on tight for the wave of enthusiasm to hit your class. Even your shyest students will come out of their shells to join in the fun!

by Mackie Rhodes

- Hide a small object under one in a set of three large shells. Challenge a child to guess under which shell the item is hidden.

- Place an assortment of shells in a center. Have youngsters sort the shells by type, color, shape, and size.

- Play a shell seriation game. Have your little ones sequence a collection of shells from smallest to largest.

- Have children estimate how many small shells will fit in a large clamshell. Fill the clamshell; then count to see how many fit.

- Using a variety of shells, challenge students to place them end-to-end to make shapes, designs, and letters on the table or floor.

- Provide clamshells, solid-colored paper towels, paintbrushes, and a tray of paint. Have a child paint the top of a shell. Then have her place the towel over the shell and gently press. When the towel is removed, it will have an interesting print created by the shell.

- Using seashells with holes formed or drilled in them, encourage youngsters to lace them together for use as necklaces, wind chimes, or room decorations.

212

- Have each youngster paint a seashell with tempera paint. After it dries, encourage him to use craft items such as glue, pipe cleaners, pom-poms, wiggle eyes, and tissue paper to create a sea creature from his shell.

- Invite students to create a rhythm instrument using toilet-paper tubes, glue, crayons, streamers, and a supply of small shells. Have each child color a tube. Staple one end of the tube closed. Direct the child to put a specific number of shells into the open end of the tube; then staple that end. Encourage the child to glue streamers to his instrument. After it dries, have him play the instrument during a music activity.

- Press small shells into play dough to create faces, shapes, and other designs.

- Provide a collection of small shells, glue, and strips of tagboard. Have students glue shells to the tagboard to create a pattern.

- Place a supply of shells in the sand table. Encourage students to use the shells for scooping, pouring, hiding, finding, and counting.

- Use large shells as part of an obstacle course in the classroom. Encourage little ones to crab-crawl around the course.

- Provide a collection of shells to be used as markers in a game of bingo.

- Nest clamshells together. Have students fit the smaller shells into the larger ones.

Explorations

Explorations

Crazy About Caterpillars

Woolly or smooth. Green or spotted. Caterpillars of all varieties are fascinating to children. Follow these directions to make a caterpillar cage. Find your own caterpillar to temporarily inhabit the cage, or order caterpillars (see "In Search Of Caterpillars"). The opportunity to observe firsthand the metamorphosis of a butterfly (or a moth) is an experience your preschoolers will not soon forget.

STEP 1

Before you begin, contact a local entomology expert for information about common caterpillars in your area. Mention that you are hoping to find a caterpillar with a short pupal stage.

Cut one or more windows in the carton. Place the twig and some leaves inside.

STEP 2

Slide the carton very carefully into the hosiery leg. Pull the hose nearly all the way up the carton.

STEP 5

In about two weeks,* your caterpillar may spin a cocoon, if it's a moth...

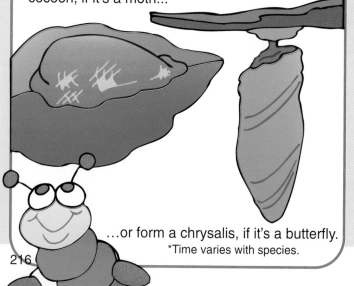

...or form a chrysalis, if it's a butterfly.
*Time varies with species.

STEP 6

About two weeks later,* a moth or butterfly will emerge.

Keep the butterfly (or moth) for only a day. Then release it.
*Time varies with species.

Science You Can Do
by Ann Flagg

To make a caterpillar cage, you will need:
— a clean, empty half-gallon carton
— scissors
— one leg of nylon hosiery
— a twig
— some leaves (preferably the kind of leaves you find your caterpillar on)
— a journal (optional)

In Search Of Caterpillars

Live caterpillars may be ordered from Insect Lore by calling 1-800-LIVE-BUG. Transfer these caterpillars into your caterpillar cage after they have formed their chrysalises. About seven to 10 days later, beautiful painted lady butterflies will emerge.

STEP 3

Find a caterpillar and put it in your caterpillar cage. (See "In Search Of Caterpillars," if you have no luck finding one near your school.)

Stretch the hose up over the top of the carton and knot it to close the cage.

STEP 4

Make regular entries in a journal to document what happens to the caterpillar.

Every day remove the old leaves and waste; then provide fresh leaves for your caterpillar. It will get the water it needs from the fresh leaves.

Did You Know?

- Butterflies lay eggs that are so tiny we do not usually see them.
- After a caterpillar hatches from one of these eggs, it begins to eat many times its own body weight daily.
- Because a caterpillar eats so much, it grows rapidly. It sheds its skin to accommodate the growth.
- A caterpillar lives for at least two weeks before becoming a pupa. It will attach itself to a sheltered spot and form a hard shell, called a *chrysalis.* This stage may last from just a few days to more than a year.
- The chrysalis cracks when the adult butterfly has formed. The butterfly then frees itself.
- One or two weeks is the length of time most butterflies live. But some live up to 18 months.

What Now?

- Read *The Very Hungry Caterpillar* by Eric Carle (G. P. Putnam's Sons). Talk about what is real and what is make-believe in this story.

- Clean out your caterpillar cage. Replace the twig and leaves. Then find a different creature to inhabit the cage for a day. Now where did that ladybug go?

Explorations

Bulbs: A Well-Kept Secret

You know that a flower bulb holds the promise of a springtime bloom. But your preschoolers may not yet know this joyous secret. Can you keep a secret? Keep the role and identity of flower bulbs to yourself for a while. Then have your youngsters plant a few bulbs on school property. How pleased they will be to watch nature at work next spring!

STEP 1

Give each child a bulb.

Ask some questions. Encourage all ideas, but do not volunteer any information about the bulb.

- What are you holding in your hand?
- Is it dead or alive?
- Does it do anything? If so, what?
- If we planted it in the earth, would it grow?

STEP 2

Give each child a paper bulb cutout and drawing paper. Explain that something will come out of the bulb. Have each child glue his bulb on the paper.

Encourage each child to draw a picture of what he thinks might come out of the bulb. Then, as the child dictates, write about his picture. Bind these pages into a class book.

STEP 5

Show students a small onion. Slice the onion in half vertically. Ask students how onions are similar to and different from flower bulbs.

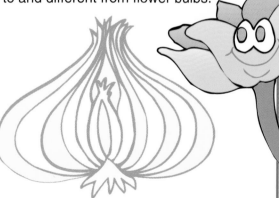

Onions are bulbs we can eat. Heat and serve some frozen onion rings for a tasty bulb snack.

STEP 6

Find an empty flower bed or a corner of the playground and let each child plant a bulb.

Each month have the students check on the progress of the bulbs and make drawings and notes in a bulb-shaped journal. Prolong students' curiosity about what is happening to the bulbs by asking questions such as:

- What are the bulbs doing underground?
- How will weather and temperature affect the bulbs?
- How are other plants responding to the fall (winter, spring) weather?

Science You Can Do
by Ann Flagg

To explore bulbs you will need:
— an assortment of springtime flowering bulbs, 2 or 3 per child
— one brown construction-paper bulb cutout per child
— white drawing paper
— glue   — a small onion
— pencils and crayons
— assorted bookmaking supplies
— pictures of the flowers that your bulbs will produce
— a knife
— magnifying glasses
— frozen onion rings
— an oven or toaster oven
— gardening tools and bulb booster
— a small, bulb-shaped journal

In Search Of Perfect Bulbs

Consult an expert at your local garden center to determine which spring bulbs bloom well in your area. Choose bulbs that are smooth, firm, and heavy for their size. A lightweight bulb may be dried out and a mushy bulb may be rotten. Avoid bulbs with green tips. Instead choose bulbs that are fully dormant.

STEP 3

Show students your entire collection of bulbs. Ask them how the bulbs are alike and how they are different.

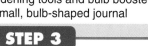

Have the children sort the bulbs according to several attributes such as size and shape. Provide the guidance necessary for students to sort the bulbs by the kinds of flower they will produce.

STEP 4

Display pictures of flowers grown from bulbs. Explain that a flower will grow from each bulb. Slice a bulb in half vertically. Have students use magnifying glasses to look for baby leaves and buds.

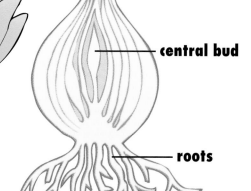

central bud

roots

Explain that the onionlike layers contain stored food that will feed the bulb and give it energy to grow. Roots can sometimes be seen on the bottom of the bulb.

Did You Know?

- A true bulb is a type of bud.
- Bulbs are alive, self-contained, underground storehouses for plants.
- During the time that they have green leaves above the ground, bulbs manufacture all the energy they will need for the long winter and a rapid springtime bloom. Because of this, trimming a bulb's green leaves before they wilt and die can damage the bulb.
- Bulbs develop new bulbs each season. These new bulbs can be dug up and separated from the original bulb, then replanted to produce new plants.
- Most bulb-forming plants also produce seeds in their flowers.
- Onions and garlic are both bulbs that can be eaten.

What Now?

- Grow some bulbs indoors during the winter. This method, calling *forcing,* is easy to do. Ask your local garden center for directions and recommendations on the types of bulbs to use. Involve the children in each step, and send the blooming bulbs home as holiday gifts.

- Take nature walks during the fall and winter. How do other plants behave during the winter? Read aloud *This Year's Garden* by Cynthia Rylant (Aladdin Books).

Pam Crane

Explorations

Sound

With just a few simple materials, you can help your children make a multitude of discoveries about sound. Sounds like fun, doesn't it?

STEP 1

Assist each youngster in stretching a rubber band over a toilet-tissue tube.

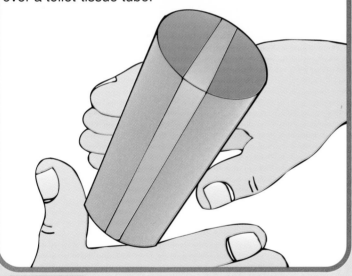

STEP 2

Ask students to predict what they will hear if the bands on the tubes are plucked.
Have each student hold his tube at waist height, pluck the band at one of the tube's ends, and listen.

Find out what each child heard. How do students think the sounds were made?

STEP 5

Holding his arms outstretched, have that student in each pair suspend the hanger in front of and away from his body. Then ask that the remaining student in each pair use a spoon to tap the hanger.

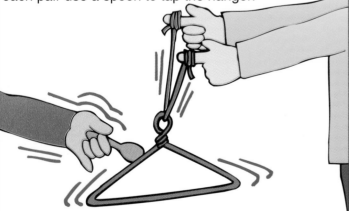

Have students listen to the sounds made. Encourage them to describe the sounds.

STEP 6

Now ask that the student holding the hanger place his index fingers in his ears and lean forward so that the hanger does not touch his body. Ask the remaining student in each pair to use a spoon to tap the hanger. Find out how youngsters would describe the sounds made this time. What is different about these sounds as compared to the sounds made before?

Have students reverse their roles and repeat the last three sets of directions.

Science You Can Do
by Ann Flagg

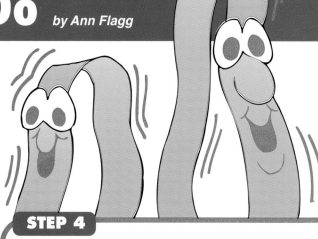

To explore sound you will need:
— one toilet-tissue tube per student
— one rubber band per student
— one 30" length of string for every two students
— one metal clothes hanger (with the hook bent into a loop) for every two students
— one metal spoon for every two children

STEP 3

Show students how to hold tubes close to—but not touching—their ears. Then ask each youngster to hold his tube near his ear and pluck the rubber band at the other end of the tube.

Find out what each child heard. How was this sound different from the sound heard when the tube was at waist height?

STEP 4

Have youngsters work in pairs. Assist each pair in threading a string through the clothes-hanger loop. Then help one student in each pair wind the string's ends around his index fingers.

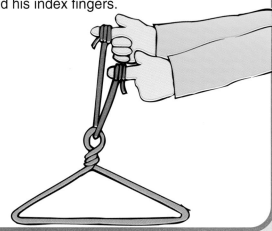

This Is Why

As a child plucked the rubber band and had his partner tap the hanger with the items away from his body, the resulting vibrations made sounds. The sound waves traveled through the air in all directions, but only a small percentage of them reached the child's ears.

When the tube was held close to the child's ear and the string-wrapped fingers were inserted in the child's ears, these materials channeled the sounds directly into the youngster's ears. This made the sounds seem louder.

Did You Know?

- Sound is caused by vibrations.
- Vibrations cause a disturbance in the air that's in the form of a wave, called a *sound wave*.
- Most sound waves that are dispersed throughout the air do not reach our ears.
- Sound travels much better through a solid (such as string) than through air.

What Now?

- Try the first activity, replacing the toilet-tissue tube with other types of tubes, such as a paper-towel tube, a plastic pipe, or a metal pipe. Does the size or material affect the sound of the vibrating rubber band?

- Make some ear extenders. Cut away the bottom of a plastic milk jug. Make a cone from paper. Remove the bottom of a plastic or Styrofoam cup. Place objects of this type in a center. Then encourage children to hold each of these ear extenders up to their ears to capture sound waves. How does the sound change when you use an ear extender?

Pam Crane

Explorations

From The Heart

Participate in American Heart Month with these activities designed to get your preschoolers all pumped up about the human heart.

STEP 1

Give each child a white, heart-shaped cutout reproduced from the pattern below. Ask the children to discuss the shape.

Show the children a picture of the human heart and explain that the cutout is shaped like a real heart. Have each child color his cutout red. Tape it to his shirt over the center of his chest so that the bottom is tipping toward the child's left side.

STEP 2

Lead the children in this action rhyme.

I am your heart and I go beat, beat.
Clap a series of doubles to represent a heartbeat.

I pump blood while you are asleep.
Rest head on hands as if sleeping.

I pump blood when you jump up and down.
Jump up and down.

I pump blood when you run around.
Run in a small circle.

I pump blood when you move your feet.
March in place.

I pump blood as you sneak to your seat…
Sneak to your seat….sneak to your seat….
Sneak to seat.

Have each child put his hand over the paper heart. Ask, "What do you feel?"

The Pumping Station

Set up a pumping station near the water table in your classroom. Using these hands-on experiences, children will begin to understand pumping and how the heart works as a pump in the body. Add red food coloring to the water in the water table if desired. In the center include a turkey baster, an eyedropper, a pipette, a picture of a gas pump, and pictures or books containing pictures of the human heart.

Have A Heart

A three- or four-year-old's heart is about the size of his fist. Use this pattern for the activity described in steps 1 and 2.

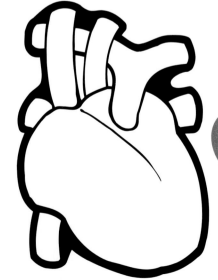

Science You Can Do *by Ann Flagg*

To learn that the human heart is a pump, you will need:
— the provided heart pattern, duplicated on white paper and cut out for each child
— pictures or books containing pictures of the human heart
— red crayons
— tape
— water table
— red food coloring (optional)
— turkey baster
— long, red balloon
— eyedropper
— pipette
— picture of a gas pump

STEP 3

Explain that the human heart is a pump inside the body that pumps blood. The heart pumps with a squeezing action that pushes blood out into the body.

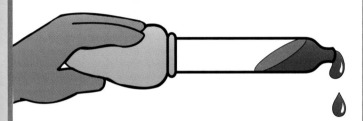

Demonstrate this by filling a turkey baster with water. (If desired, tint the water with red food coloring.) Have a child push the water out of the baster. Repeat this until each child has had a turn.

STEP 4

Partially inflate a long, red balloon and tie the end. Let each child squeeze one end of the balloon to push all of the air into the opposite end of the balloon.

Explain that a heart has two sides. Each side is a *pump.* When the walls of the heart muscle squeeze together, they push—or pump—out blood. Moving the air from one end of the balloon to the other end is similar to the way the heart pumps blood.

Did You Know?
- The heart is a pump that powers the human body.
- With each heartbeat, oxygen-rich blood is delivered to the cells of the body.
- The heart is a hollow muscle that is divided into two sides or pumps. The pump on the left side of the heart is the more powerful because it must push blood through the entire body.
- Because the left pump is the stronger, children may believe that their entire heart lies on the left side of their body. In reality, the heart is positioned in the center of the chest, between the lungs.
- A baby's heart begins to beat eight months before the baby is born. In a 70-year lifetime, an average heart will pump 51 million gallons of blood.
- The "lub-dub" sound heard through a doctor's stethoscope is the sound of the heart valves closing shut, regulating the blood flow in and out of the heart.

What Now?
- Just like all of the muscles in the body, the human heart needs exercise, too. Help your children understand the importance of exercise by having them feel their heart rates increase as they run or do exercises.

- Borrow a stethoscope from a healthcare professional so that the children can listen to heartbeats. If a stethoscope is not available, use a cardboard tube. To use the tube, have one child run in place for one minute to increase the frequency of his heartbeat. Then have another child hold one end of the tube over the first child's heart and listen through the opposite end of the tube.

Explorations

Seed Secrets: Seeing Is Believing!

Just what really happens when a seed gets tucked under a blanket of dirt? Help your young botanists make the connection between seed and sprout with these hands-on activities using lima bean seeds. "Oh! So *that's* what they've 'bean' doing!"

STEP 1

Have each child fill a personalized cup with soil. Then have him plant two lima bean seeds in the soil. Water the soil and place each cup in a warm environment—perhaps by a window—so that the seeds will germinate quickly.

STEP 2

As a class, observe and record the progress of the seeds each day. While waiting for the seeds to sprout, cultivate youngsters' curiosity by asking questions such as, "What is happening to the seeds under the soil?" List the children's ideas—but keep the scientific answer a secret for a while longer.

Our Ideas

The seeds are sleeping under the dirt.   Shanika

My seeds are going to push leaves out.   Taro

The seeds are getting dirty so they can grow.   Maurice

Soon after the planted seeds germinate, explain that you know a way to take a peek to see what growing seeds look like under the soil.

STEP 5

Water the seeds by pouring 1/4 cup of water into each bag. The water level should be below the staples so that the seeds do not rot. The paper towel will absorb the water and deliver it to the seeds. Partially seal the bag to allow the seeds to take in oxygen.

STEP 6

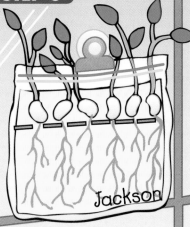

Secure the window gardens to a window using tape or suction-cup clips. (Or staple the gardens to a bulletin board.) Post the children's previously recorded ideas about the activity of the seeds near the window.

Help children develop the ability to infer, or make conclusions from observations, by recording their daily comments about the growth of the window-garden seeds. When the sprouts have grown several inches tall, remove the window gardens from the window and send them home.

Science You Can Do by Ann Flagg

To take a closer look at seeds, you will need:
—one plastic cup per child
—permanent marker
—eight lima bean seeds per child
—potting soil
—chart paper
—one resealable plastic bag per child
—one paper towel per child
—stapler
—tape or suction-cup clips
—a window or bulletin board
—a 1/4-cup measure

STEP 3

Assist each child in making a *window garden.*

To make one, fold a paper towel so that it fits inside a personalized, resealable plastic bag. Staple the layers together two inches below the top of the bag.

STEP 4

Remind the children of the seeds that they planted in cups. Explain that they can "plant" the same kind of seeds in the window gardens. Give each child six lima bean seeds to place above the staples in his window garden.

What Now?

• Read aloud your favorite version of *Jack And The Beanstalk;* then plant lima bean sprouts outdoors. Transplant the bean sprouts from the cups to a prepared outdoor location. Watch your lima bean plants grow! Note: Lima beans grow to maturity in 65 to 80 days. Check your seed packets for regional planting recommendations.

• Soak lima bean seeds in water overnight. Have students compare the seeds with dry lima bean seeds. How does water change a seed? Demonstrate how to peel off the seed coat and open the seed. Can you find the baby plant inside? Use a hand magnifier to take a closer look!

• Try planting other seeds in a window garden. Birdseed will sprout and grow into a colorful selection of plants. Popcorn kernels will sprout as well, much to youngsters' amazement!

Did You Know?

• A seed is the part of a plant that produces a new plant.
• A bean seed consists of the embryo, the food storage tissue, and the seed coat.
• The sprouting process is called *germination.*
• To germinate, seeds need water, oxygen, and the proper temperature. Some seeds must also have light to germinate.
• Water produces chemical changes inside a seed. Water softens the seed coat and causes the seed's internal parts to swell and break through the seed coat.
• Seeds produce the energy needed for growth by taking in oxygen and giving off carbon dioxide.
• After the seed coat breaks and germination begins, a primary root will grow downward and a bud with its first leaves will push upward.

Explorations

I Have A Little Shadow

Do your little ones know where shadows come from and where they go? Help them find out with these shadow escapades.

STEP 1

Position a slide or film projector on a low table so that the light will project onto the wall. Ask several children to stand between the light source and the wall. Dim the lights in the room; then turn on the projector.

As each child moves creatively to make shadows, ask some questions:
• Which shadow is made by your body?
• In what way does it look like you? How is it different?
• Can you make your shadow bigger? Smaller? Can you make it disappear?

STEP 2

Encourage the youngsters to continue to make shadows; then turn off the projector. Lead the children to identify the cause-and-effect relationship between the light and the shadows. Ask them to describe what happened when the projector was turned off. What is needed to make a shadow?

STEP 5

While outside use these suggestions to play a game of following directions similar to Simon Says.

The shadow says:
"Wiggle your shadow's fingers."
"Make your shadow jump."
"Make your shadow small (tall, fat)."
"Touch a friend's shadow."
"Put your shadow behind you."

STEP 6

Ask the children to find out if the moon's light can make shadows. Then send home a note similar to the one shown.

Dear Parent,

We have been learning that a shadow is made when an object prevents light from shining on a surface. At school we explored our shadows with a projector and the sun. Will you help us find shadows made at night? On a brightly moonlit night, go on a shadow hunt with your child.

Happy shadow hunting!

Science You Can Do *by Ann Flagg*

To learn about shadows you will need:
— a light source such as a slide or film projector
— a plain, white wall (If you do not have a white wall, create a screen by securing a white sheet or several sheets of white bulletin-board paper to a wall.)
— a sunny day
— a parent letter for each child

STEP 3

Ask one child to stand behind the projector, one child to stand beside the projector, and one child to stand between the projector and the wall. Ask the children to identify which child's body creates a shadow. Lead them to conclude that to make a shadow, someone must block the light source.

Challenge the remaining children to find somewhere to stand in the room so that their bodies do not cast shadows on the wall.

STEP 4

Take your class outside on a sunny day. Direct students' attention to their shadows.

To help them discover that a shadow is made when a person's body blocks the sun's light, ask some questions:
• What gives us light outside?
• What is blocking the sun's light and creating a shadow?
• Where can you move so that your body does not cast a shadow?

Did You Know?

• A shadow is the shaded area that an object makes when it prevents light from shining on a surface.
• Many types of light can cause shadows—flashlights, lamps, the sun, and even the moon.
• Shadows fall on the opposite side of the light source.
• On bright days when the sun is strong and direct, shadows are dark and crisp. On cloudy days when the the light comes from all directions, shadows are faint or absent.
• The angle of light affects the size and direction of the shadow. In the early morning and late afternoon when the sun is low in the sky, shadows are long. At noon when the sun is directly overhead, shadows cannot be seen.

What Now?

Try this experiment to help children understand that shadows change during the day. Early one sunny morning, have each child stand on a sidewalk. Trace around each child's feet with chalk; then trace around his shadow. Later the same day, have each child stand in the outline of his feet. Is his shadow in the same place? Read aloud *Bear Shadow* by Frank Asch (Scholastic Inc.). As the children look at the pictures, have them describe how the position of the sun changes the bear's shadow.

227

Once Upon
A Story...

Once Upon A Story...

Jamberry

Bruce Degen's luscious pictures with humorous details make this book a feast for the eyes and ears. Reveal one amazing berry episode after another by reading aloud *Jamberry* (Harper & Row, Publishers). Provide blueberries, strawberries, blackberries, and raspberries for students to sample. Then ask each student to decide which of these berries is his favorite and indicate that on a class graph.

Find out if students' fingers were stained by the juices of the berries. What colors are the stains? Provide red and purple paint (excellent berry-related colors), paintbrushes, art paper, and plastic berry baskets (left over from your sampling party). Encourage each youngster to paint a sheet of art paper, then repeatedly press a basket into the wet paint to achieve an unusual imprint. When the paint has dried, display the paintings with the berry baskets attached. Looks like there was a jam jamboree in this classroom!

Jennifer Travis—Preschool • Bright Horizons Childrens Center • Randolph, MA

Clifford, The Small Red Puppy

Emily Elizabeth tells how she came to own Clifford, the big red dog, in this Norman Bridwell book. Before reading aloud *Clifford, The Small Red Puppy* (Scholastic Inc.), talk to students about how they came to have their pets. Find out how many of your youngsters had the opportunity to select their dogs or cats from their litters, and how a decision was made about which one to choose. Then explain that Emily Elizabeth got to choose Clifford, and read aloud the story.

While youngsters are chatting about the story and pets in general, have them help you prepare and eat the following imitation dog-chow recipe.

Dog Chow

9 cups Crispix®
1 cup chocolate chips
1/2 cup peanut butter
1/4 cup margarine
1/4 tsp. vanilla
1 1/2 cups confectioner's sugar

Mix the chocolate chips, peanut butter, and margarine together. Microwave for approximately 1 1/2 minutes. Add the vanilla. Pour the mixture over the cereal and stir to coat. Put the confectioner's sugar in a large, resealable plastic bag. Add the cereal and shake the bag until the cereal is evenly coated with sugar.

Marjorie Martin—Preschool • Charlton Play School Harrisburg, PA

See the corresponding book notes on page 242.

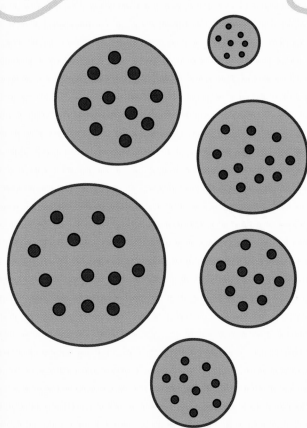

If You Give A Mouse A Cookie

Who would have guessed that indulging a mouse's request could lead to such a fuss? Plan your reading of *If You Give A Mouse A Cookie* by Laura Joffe Numeroff (Harper & Row, Publishers) to coincide with a cookies-and-milk snack. Discuss the story with your youngsters. Then show them several felt cookies in graduated sizes that have been embellished with brown puff paint to resemble chocolate chips. Have the students sequence the cookies from smallest to largest on a flannelboard.

Use the felt cookies to play a subtraction game. Place several cookies on a flannelboard. Count them with your students. Ask your students to close their eyes. Remove one or more of the cookies; then ask students to open their eyes. Explain that while they were not looking, someone took some cookies—maybe it was a mouse! With your youngsters, count the cookies on the flannelboard; then ask them to determine how many cookies are missing. Provide assistance as necessary.

Rosalie Sumsion—Home Day Care/Preschool
Monument Valley, UT

Jack And The Beanstalk

This suggestion is guaranteed to grow on you! Before your little ones arrive one morning, place a few glittered, dried lima beans by a copy of your favorite version of *Jack And The Beanstalk*. Near the beans place a note from Jack asking that your students plant the beans. Place a large flowerpot filled with crumpled pieces of brown paper against a vacant classroom wall. That day, read *Jack And The Beanstalk* to your youngsters; then read Jack's note. Ask your students to help you "plant" the seeds in the flowerpot.

The next morning before students arrive, attach a six-foot, brown, twisted paper vine to the wall near the pot so that the vine appears to be growing out of the pot and up the wall. Prepare a leaf for the vine by writing *Jack And The Beanstalk* and the author's name on a giant, green paper leaf. Draw a sketch on the leaf that shows a scene from the story. Attach the leaf to the wall so that it looks like it's growing from the twisted paper vine. Each time you read aloud another book, have a student or pair of students similarly decorate a paper leaf. When the vine is full of leaves, add another six-foot length of vine. (If you really want to heighten the effect of the vine, use pipe cleaners to attach it to the grid work that supports your ceiling tiles.) Soon people will be crowding into your classroom to see the awesome beanstalk with its magical leaves.

Barbara Meyers
Fort Worth Country Day School
Fort Worth, TX

See the corresponding book notes on page 242.

Once Upon A Story...

It Looked Like Spilt Milk

Sometimes it looks like…and other times it looks like…. You be the judge when reading Charles G. Shaw's *It Looked Like Spilt Milk* (HarperCollins Children's Books). Before reading take your little ones outdoors and have them examine the clouds. Ask them to find clouds that resemble shapes or objects and tell their classmates what they see. If the weather permits, have youngsters sit on a blanket as you read aloud *It Looked Like Spilt Milk*. Then have students reexamine the clouds and tell what shapes or objects the clouds now resemble. Take your students indoors and supply each child with a sheet of folded blue construction paper. Have each student unfold his paper and drop a few splotches of white paint on the fold. Then have him refold the paper and press with his hands to flatten it and spread the paint. Unfold the paper again and allow the paint to dry. Ask each child to complete the sentence "Sometimes it looked like a...." Bind the pages with a front cover to make a class book, or display them on a bulletin board.

Erin M. Hoffman—Four-Year-Olds
Trinity Learning Center
Mt. Penn, PA

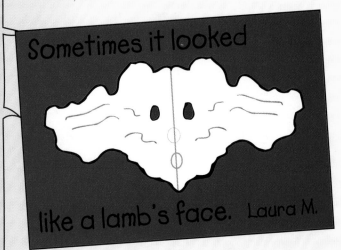

Ten In A Bed

Snuggle up with this story! Borrow a cot from the school nurse and bring a large blanket to school. Slightly dim the lights before reading *Ten In A Bed* by Mary Rees (Little, Brown and Company). Afterward give opportunities for your little ones to dramatize the story. Ask for ten student volunteers to sit on the cot under the blanket. Then, as you reread the story, have youngsters exit in turn to their classmates' right while the rest of your class chorally chants or sings the words on each page. Repeat the activity until each child has had an opportunity to participate. During the story repetitions, pause occasionally to ask the audience to verbalize how many students are beneath the covers, how many have left, and how many remain.

Lisa Vik
Austin Elementary
Vermillion, SD

See the corresponding book notes on page 243.

The Beast In The Bathtub

Rub-a-dub-dub, there's a beast in the tub! Before your little ones arrive, tape brightly colored construction-paper footprints on the floor leading to a bath towel and a bar of soap. This will be a perfect introduction for the story *The Beast In The Bathtub* by Kathleen Stevens (HarperCollins Children's Books). Ask students to predict what the story will be about. Then read the story aloud. As a fun follow-up activity, give each of your youngsters an opportunity to create a bathtub companion of his own. First have each child glue half of a construction-paper oval and two small paper circles to a large sheet of construction paper to make a bathtub. Then have each student draw a bizarre beast as though he is sitting in the tub and color the drawing using watercolor paints or markers. Complete the bathtub scenes by having each student add bubbles "spilling" from his tub and "floating" into the air. To do this, have him print bubbles using assorted sizes of jug lids dipped in light blue paint. Ask each child to think of what a beast might say. Then attach a conversation balloon bearing the child's dictated comment by each beast.

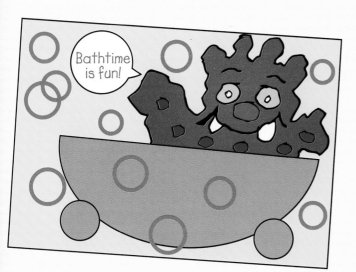

The Little Red Hen

Set the tone for a reading of Byron Barton's *The Little Red Hen* (HarperCollins Publishers) by bringing to school a freshly baked loaf of bread. When your little ones are seated, pass the loaf around and allow them to smell the bread's aroma. Cut the loaf of bread into bite-size pieces and invite the children to sample it. Ask the children what steps were taken to make the bread. Read aloud *The Little Red Hen;* then discuss the story with your little ones. Give each child red construction-paper copies of the patterns on page 244. To create a hen puppet, have each student cut out the patterns and glue them to a lunch bag as shown. To complete his puppet, have the student glue a feather near the top of his hen's head. Now that you've got a whole flock of hen puppets, everyone is going to want to dramatize *The Little Red Hen.*

Melissa L. Mapes—Pre-Kindergarten
Little People Land Preschool
St. Petersburg, FL

See the corresponding book notes on page 243.

Once Upon A Story...

Ira Sleeps Over

This delightful story will reassure any child who may be a little frightened to sleep away from home. Before reading aloud *Ira Sleeps Over* by Bernard Waber (Houghton Mifflin Company), show your students a packed overnight suitcase. Ask them to predict what things might be packed in the suitcase if they were planning to sleep over at a friend's house. Show them some of the items in the bag that a child might typically pack, such as toothpaste, a toothbrush, pajamas, and a teddy bear. Then read the story aloud. Ask youngsters if they were ever in a similar situation and have them share their experiences.

After discussing the story, have youngsters help you prepare the following recipe:

Tah Tah's Teddy Bear Treat

1 box of graham crackers
3 crumbled chocolate bars
1 container of whipped topping
1 box of Teddy Grahams®

Mix the crumbled chocolate with the whipped topping. To make one treat, spread the mixture on a graham cracker section; then place a few Teddy Grahams® in the mixture so that they are standing up. Place the treats on a sheet of waxed paper and freeze for two hours; then enjoy them!

Betty Kobes—Preschool
West Hancock Elementary Kanawha
Kanawha, IA

See the corresponding book notes on page 245.

Elmer

Before reading aloud *Elmer* by David McKee (Lothrop, Lee & Shepard Books), lay several brightly colored blankets or quilts on the floor for your youngsters to examine. Discuss the different patterns and designs in each quilt and how each is unique in its own way. Then have your little ones sit on the quilts while listening to the story. After the story have students cooperatively make a classroom replica of Elmer. Draw a large elephant outline on a piece of white, cotton-blend fabric. Then provide each child with six 4-inch white paper squares. Using fabric crayons, have her color the squares. Starting from the outer lines and working your way in, place the squares facedown inside the elephant outline. Trim any excess paper around the edges of the outline. Then follow the directions on the fabric crayon package to iron the color squares onto the elephant shape. Add facial features and finishing touches if desired. Hang it in the reading area and place a copy of the book *Elmer* nearby.

If you have a flair for sewing, cut a piece of fabric and a piece of quilt batting identical in size to the original fabric. Layer the original fabric with the batting and the other piece of fabric. Pin the three pieces together and sew the edge with binding. Then, using yarn and a large needle, sew the quilt together on each patchwork's corner.

Brenda Hume—Four-Year-Olds
Sangaree Elementary
Summerville, SC

Runaway Mittens

Poor Pica could not keep track of his bright red mittens! After reading aloud *Runaway Mittens* by Jean Rogers (Greenwillow Books), give your little ones the opportunity to search for a pair of disappearing mittens right in the classroom. Cut two pairs of large mittens from red bulletin-board paper. Staple the pairs of mittens together around the edges, and stuff them with paper for a three-dimensional look. Decorate the mittens with "stitches" using Slick® paint or Elmer's® GluColors™. Join the pair together with a length of heavy yarn. Hide the mittens in different locations throughout the day. Then have students take turns searching for them while singing the song below, and when found, have the finder wear the pair around his neck until it's time to hide them again.

(sung to the tune of "Where, Oh, Where Has My Little Dog Gone?")
Where, oh, where did my red mittens go?
Where, oh, where can they be?
I have looked high and I have looked low.
Where, oh, where can they be?

The Gingerbread Man

After reading aloud several versions of *The Gingerbread Man* to your youngsters, compare and contrast the likenesses and differences in the stories. Ask students if there are events and characters contained in some books that were not in others. Then ask students to vote for their favorite version. After the discussion, have your little ones make their own "scent-sational" gingerbread people. From 8" x 10" sheets of sandpaper, cut a gingerbread person for each child. Then have each student rub a cinnamon stick across the rough side of her cutout. Using different colors of Slick® paint, have each youngster decorate her gingerbread person. Attach a bow to complete the cutout. Mount these decorative gingerbread folk on a bulletin board or hang them on a tree to fill your room with the fragrance of cinnamon!

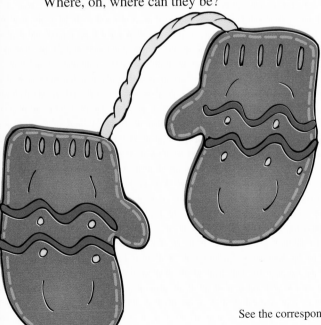

See the corresponding book notes on page 245.

Once Upon A Story...

Goodnight Moon

Make space in your classroom for this bulletin-board display based on the book *Goodnight Moon* by Margaret Wise Brown (HarperCollins Children's Books). After reading the story and discussing what the moon looks like, invite little ones to create their own versions of the moon. Provide each child with a silver paper plate. Leave some of the plates whole, and cut some into half-moon and crescent shapes. Let the children glue a variety of silver art materials—such as tinsel, garland pieces, or wrapping paper—to their moon shapes.

Make a large moon centerpiece by gluing Styrofoam® pieces to a round, cardboard pizza tray. Spray-paint the tray with silver paint. Then cover a bulletin board with a black vinyl tablecloth. Add a white border and blue letters that read "Goodnight Moon." Mount all the moon projects on the board. Complete the display by asking each child to dictate a sentence using the word *moon*. Print the statements and add them to the board.

Nancy Barad—Four-Year-Olds
Bet Yeladim Pre-School
Columbia, MD

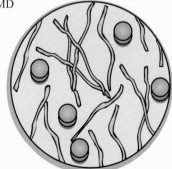

The moon is in the sky at night.

tender green beans,

Lunch

Do your little ones have an endless appetite for good books? Then they'll enjoy *Lunch* by Denise Fleming (Scholastic Inc.). After reading the story, practice color recognition by asking students to think of other foods of the same colors as those eaten by the mouse in the story. Then create a class book titled "Dinnertime." Have students speculate what foods the little mouse might have eaten at dinnertime, naming a food for each color word from the story. Modify the original text by printing the color and name of each food on a separate sheet of construction paper. Have students cut pictures of the foods from magazines, or finger-paint cutouts of the foods, to glue onto the appropriate pages. Bind the pages together and add a cover with a picture of the little mouse.

adapted from an idea by Patt Hall—PreK And Kindergarten
Babson Park Elementary
Lake Wales, FL

See the corresponding book notes on page 246.

If You Give A Moose A Muffin

Are you prepared for muffin mania? Celebrate Muffin Week to follow up a reading of *If You Give A Moose A Muffin* by Laura Joffe Numeroff (Scholastic Inc.). After you read the story, sing "Oh, Do You Know The Muffin Man?" On each of the first four days of the week, serve a different type of muffin. Then put your artistic chefs to work. From light brown construction paper cut four muffin shapes for each child. Have your children paint a different type of muffin each day as follows:

Blueberry Muffins: Dot-paint blueberries with blue tempera paint and a Q-tip®.
Chocolate-Chip Muffins: Glue on semisweet chocolate chips.
Pumpkin Muffins: Finger-paint with canned pumpkin to which pumpkin pie spice has been added.
Lemon-Poppyseed Muffins: Finger-paint with lemon gelatin to which a small amount of water and poppy seeds have been added.

On the last day of the week, bake some muffin cups. Prepare any flavor of packaged muffin mix according to the directions. (One box will make approximately 16 muffins.) For each child, spoon two tablespoons of the batter into a three-ounce paper cup. Place the cups in a preheated electric skillet set at 400 degrees. Cover and bake for 15–20 minutes. (The tops of the muffins will not brown.) Cool, peel off the paper cups, and munch those muffins!

Elizabeth Qualls—Two-Year-Olds
First Baptist Church Weekday School
Greensboro, NC

The Three Billy Goats Gruff

Trip-trap, trip-trap! Who's that reading the story of *The Three Billy Goats Gruff?* Your youngsters will enjoy this classic tale retold by Tim Arnold (Margaret K. McElderry Books) or Harriet Ziefert (Tambourine Books). After reading the story aloud, encourage your little performers to act it out. Provide a wooden plank or fully collapsed table to simulate the bridge from the story. If desired, create headbands for the children to wear. Cut three sizes of horns for the three billy goats' headbands. For the troll headband, glue on a construction-paper circle. Decorate it to resemble the troll's face, with a long nose and colored-yarn hair. Then have youngsters take turns playing the parts of the billy goats Gruff and the troll. Invite students to use appropriate facial and vocal expressions as they reenact the story. Let the show begin!

See the corresponding book notes on page 246.

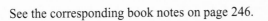

Once Upon A Story...

Feathers For Lunch

All birds on alert! The cat is out and he's looking for lunch! After reading aloud the fun and frolicsome *Feathers For Lunch* by Lois Ehlert (Harcourt Brace Jovanovich), take a closer look at the collage-style illustrations. Encourage the children to describe each different type of bird—as well as give each birdcall a try.

Extend the fun of this spirited story with these suggestions for your activity centers. In your listening center, place a copy of the book, a cassette tape of bird sounds, a jingle bell on a string, artificial flowers, and decorative birds. Encourage students who visit this center to use the storytelling props to retell the story or to make up a new one. Replace the sand from the sand table with birdseed. Stock your art center with paper, paint, glue, and feathers. Invite the children visiting the art center to create interesting feather paintings or feather collages.

As a special treat, stir up a batch of edible bird nests. In a microwave, melt a 12-ounce package of butterscotch chips. Stir in an 18-ounce jar of crunchy peanut butter. Crumble the 12 biscuits in a 10-ounce box of shredded wheat biscuits; then stir them into the mixture. Shape spoonfuls of the mixture into individual nests. Set the nests on waxed paper to harden. With these tasty treats, there'll be more than just feathers for lunch!

Joan Tietz—Preschool/Pre-K
St. James Lutheran
Lafayette, IN

Little Blue And Little Yellow

Any time is the right time for a story about hugging! Introduce youngsters to little blue and little yellow by reading aloud Leo Lionni's colorful story about friendship (Mulberry Books). Afterward give them an opportunity to illustrate a *Little Blue And Little Yellow* book for your class library. On large sheets of white construction paper, write or rephrase the text of the story. Read the story again, allowing each child to choose a page to illustrate. Provide various colors of tissue paper, scissors, and glue. Invite each child to look at Lionni's illustrations, but encourage creativity should a student wish to adapt the illustrations to match the text on his chosen page. When the pages are dry, bind them between construction-paper covers. Share the newly illustrated version of the story with the class; then celebrate your accomplishment with a great big group hug!

Abi Reiffman—Two- And Four-Year-Olds
Yavneh Hebrew Academy
Los Angeles, CA

They hugged each other!

See the corresponding book notes on page 247.

illustration 2

illustration 1

illustration 3

Big Fat Hen

Get ready to count to ten with the big fat hen. After reading this showstopper by Keith Baker (Harcourt Brace & Company), make these cheery chick manipulatives for counting practice. To make a chick, cut a three-inch circle from yellow knit fabric. Using a needle and yellow thread, sew a gathering stitch around the edge of the circle. Pull the thread to slightly gather the fabric; then stuff the circle with fiberfill stuffing or cotton balls. Pull the thread again to gather the fabric into a ball. Sew several additional stitches to ensure that the ball will remain gathered (illustration 1). Twist one-inch lengths of orange pipe cleaners together to make legs. Tack the legs to the back of the chick's body with several stitches. Glue a small circle of yellow felt atop the legs and gathering stitches (illustration 2). Using fabric paint, add eyes and a beak (illustration 3).

Youngsters will enjoy using the chicks with these hen-and-chick counting games. To make counting games, collect pizza boxes. For each number you would like to include, color and cut a large hen shape. Glue the hen shape to the inside lid of a pizza box. Write a different number on each box lid. Glue a corresponding number of plastic egg bottoms to the inside bottom of each box. Encourage youngsters to count chick manipulatives to place in each egg.

Lucia Kemp Henry

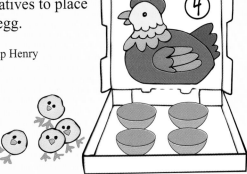

The Ugly Duckling

Remember the classic tale of the ugly duckling? Whether it was told to you by a parent, grandparent, or teacher, you probably remember the story's lessons about being different and yet being beautiful. As Hans Christian Andersen told his stories, he would often cut paper into shapes related to the stories' lessons. Familiarize yourself with a version of this beloved tale. Before you tell the story, trace or duplicate the duck pattern on page 248 on gray construction paper. As you tell the story, hold the paper (with the outline facing you) and slowly cut out the shape. All eyes will be focused on you as all ears listen to the story. At the conclusion of the tale, reveal the shape of the duck. Be sure to allow time for youngsters to share and discuss their feelings about the story. Your storytelling time is sure to have a beautiful and happy ending.

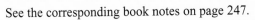
See the corresponding book notes on page 247.

Once Upon A Story...

The Rainbow Fish

Looking for a way to help your little ones understand the value of sharing? Read aloud *The Rainbow Fish* by Marcus Pfister (North-South Books). Then organize this project to help youngsters experience the joy that comes from giving. Send a note home explaining the project and requesting that each parent help his child find one used toy or book—in good condition— that she is willing to give away. Collect the toys and books in a brightly wrapped box. Arrange for the class to deliver the gifts to a local shelter or children's home. If the children are not able to deliver the gifts as a group, obtain permission to take pictures or videotape the recipients enjoying the toys and books. Isn't sharing beautiful?

Sonya Manson—Preschool And Gr. K
Loma Linda, CA

Dinosaurs, Dinosaurs

Here's a book your preschool paleontologists are sure to dig! During storytime share *Dinosaurs, Dinosaurs* by Byron Barton (HarperCollins Children's Books). After carefully viewing the pictures, have youngsters suggest a list of ways that the dinosaurs described in the book are different. As a challenge, have them help you make a list of ways that the dinosaurs are alike.

As a creative story extension, stock an art center with different colors of paint poured into tins, various colors of construction paper, pencils, scissors, and dinosaur-shaped cookie cutters. Encourage each child to dip several different cookie cutters into the paint and press them onto a sheet of paper. Encourage him to describe ways that his dinosaur prints are alike and different. Or suggest that he trace the cutters onto a sheet of paper and cut on the resulting outlines. Later mount the shapes on craft sticks to create puppets.

If making these prehistoric prints or puppets has created big appetites, serve several snacks suitable for plant eaters and meat eaters alike. For the herbivores, prepare plates of lettuce and raw vegetables with a tasty dip. To satisfy the carnivores, serve hot dogs for dipping in chili.

"Dino-mite!"

Diane DiMarco—Three- And Four-Year-Olds
Country Kids Preschool
Groton, MA

Luke

Katie

Ben

See the corresponding book notes on page 249.

The Day Jimmy's Boa Ate The Wash

Yipers! Check out these vipers! Collect a classroom supply of colorful neckties from yard sales and thrift stores. To transform a tie into a snake, tie a knot at the narrow end of the tie. Stuff the tie with fiberfill, stopping about five inches from the open, wide end of the tie. Sew a seam across the width of the tie. Fold the remaining fabric over to form the snake's head. Give each snake its own personality by using pompoms, wiggle eyes, buttons, yarn, ribbon, felt—even plastic soda-can rings—to create features.

Slither into storytime by reading aloud *The Day Jimmy's Boa Ate The Wash* written by Trinka Hakes Noble and humorously illustrated by Steven Kellogg (The Dial Press). Ask volunteers to share the episodes of the story that they thought were the funniest. Then extend the silliness of the story by giving each child her very own boa! Play a recording of "Sally The Swinging Snake" by Hap Palmer and encourage each child to use her snake to demonstrate the motions suggested in the song. Whoa—cool boas!

Susan Burbridge—Four-Year-Olds
Trinity Weekday School
San Antonio, TX

The Tortoise And The Hare

The race is on between the quiet tortoise and the flashy hare. And as you probably know, the true winner is the runner who doesn't give up. Share an adapted version of this Aesop fable by reading aloud *The Tortoise And The Hare* by Janet Stevens (Holiday House, Inc.). Ask youngsters to explain why the tortoise won the race instead of the rabbit. Then share a personal story of a time in which you persevered instead of giving up. Encourage the children to share their own stories as well.

Once your students are familiar with the slow tortoise and the speedy hare, try this music activity to increase youngsters' ability to distinguish between fast and slow, steady beats. For each child, duplicate and cut out the tortoise and hare patterns on page 250. Have each child color his patterns. Invite a small group of children to sit on the floor, placing their patterns in front of them. Clap or use rhythm instruments (such as sticks or a small drum) to demonstrate a fast and then a slow, steady beat. Ask each child to listen to the beat and point to or hold up his tortoise pattern when the tempo is slow or his hare pattern when the tempo is fast. Alternate between a fast and slow tempo for an appropriate number of times. When students show an understanding of the activity, give volunteers the opportunity to demonstrate the tempo as the others listen and respond with their patterns. As a variation, provide each child with the instrument of his choice. As you display either the tortoise or the hare, direct each child to play either fast or slow beats accordingly.

See the corresponding book notes on page 249.

I've been jammin' today!

I listened to

Jamberry,

a book by Bruce Degen.

I could tell you "berry" neat things about *Jamberry.* What would you like to know?

I heard a story about Clifford today. The book was written by Norman Bridwell.

Ask me how big Clifford is.

Maybe we could go to the library sometime. Together we could dig up another book about Clifford, the big red dog. There are lots of Clifford books!

I heard a story about a mouse today. The book was written by Laura Joffe Numeroff. It's called *If You Give A Mouse A Cookie.*

Ask me what happened when the mouse got a cookie.

Wonder what would happen if you gave a moose a muffin? Sniff out the answer at a library. Ask for a copy of *If You Give A Moose A Muffin* by Laura Joffe Numeroff.

I heard the story of *Jack And The Beanstalk* today.

Ask me what was at the top of the beanstalk.

Ask me to pretend I'm a giant and to bellow what the giant sometimes said.

Book Notes

After reading each of the books mentioned below, send home copies of the corresponding note.

I heard the story

It Looked Like Spilt Milk

by Charles G. Shaw.
Let's look at some clouds together.
You can tell me what
things you see
in the clouds
and I'll
tell you
what
I see.

©The Education Center, Inc. • *THE MAILBOX*® • *Preschool* • Oct/Nov 1995

Ten In A Bed

by Mary Rees

is a funny story.

Ask me to tell
you the story.
Let's get a
number book or a
counting book from
the library.

©The Education Center, Inc. • *THE MAILBOX*® • *Preschool* • Oct/Nov 1995

**Rub-a-dub-dub!
I heard the story,**

The Beast In The Bathtub

by Kathleen Stevens.

Do you want to know what
happens in the story?
Ask me!

©The Education Center, Inc. • *THE MAILBOX*® • *Preschool* • Oct/Nov 1995

**I learned
about helping
others when
I heard the
story**

The Little Red Hen.
Ask me to help you with a
chore tonight!

©The Education Center, Inc. • *THE MAILBOX*® • *Preschool* • Oct/Nov 1995

243

Hen Bag-Puppet Patterns

Use with *The Little Red Hen* on page 233.

Finished Project

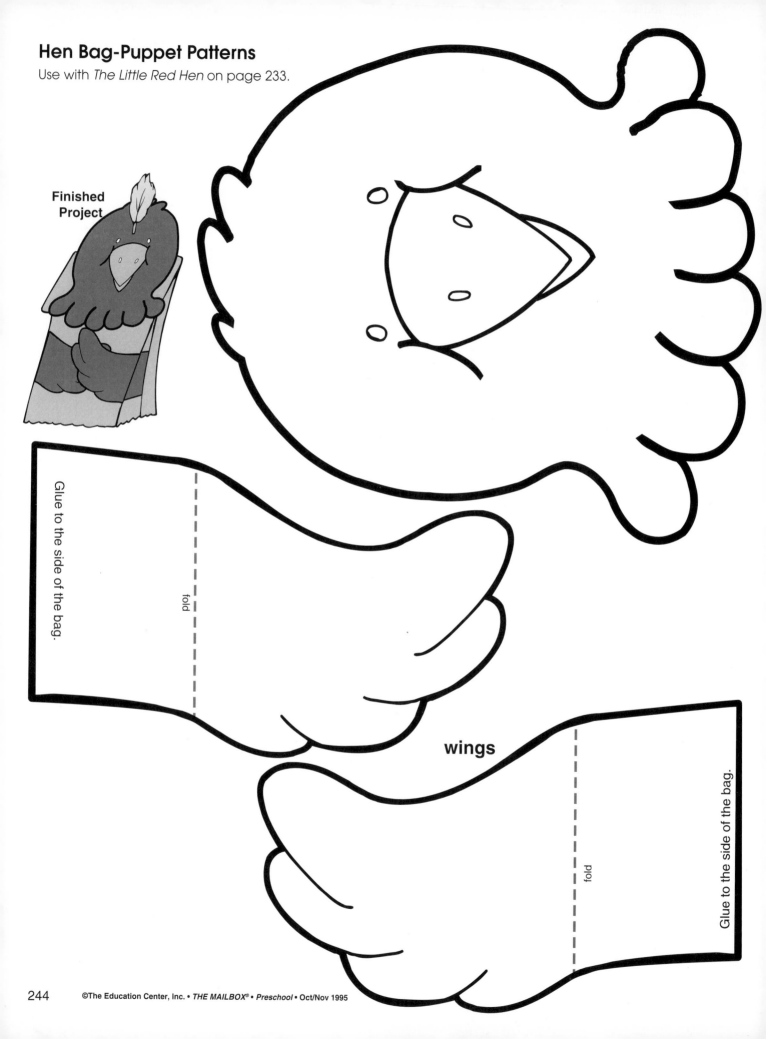

Glue to the side of the bag.

fold

wings

fold

Glue to the side of the bag.

After reading each of the books mentioned below and on pages 234 and 235, send home copies of the corresponding note.

I heard a bedtime story today. The book was *Ira Sleeps Over* by Bernard Waber.

Wonder what other bedtime stories I could listen to? Let's check some out at the library!

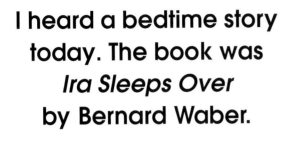

I listened to a story about an elephant that wanted to be different. The story was *Elmer* by David McKee.

Ask me what makes me unique and different!

Runaway Mittens by Jean Rogers was a good story.

X X X X X X

Ask me to tell you about it!
Maybe we can go to the library sometime and get other books about mittens.

I heard the story of *The Gingerbread Man* today.

Ask me to tell you the story.

Book Notes

After reading each of the books mentioned below and on pages 236 and 237, send home copies of the corresponding note.

I heard the story

Goodnight Moon

by Margaret Wise Brown.

Let's look at the moon tonight when it gets dark!

©1996 The Education Center, Inc.

Today I listened to a story about a mouse who was very hungry. It was called

Lunch

by Denise Fleming.

Ask me about all the foods that the mouse ate.

©1996 The Education Center, Inc.

IF YOU GIVE A MOOSE A MUFFIN

by Laura Joffe Numeroff

is a funny story!

Ask me to tell you what happened when the moose got a muffin.

Maybe we could make muffins together!

©1996 The Education Center, Inc.

I listened to the story of

The Three Billy Goats Gruff

today.

Let me tell you how the billy goats fooled the troll.

©1996 The Education Center, Inc.

246

After reading each of the books mentioned below and on pages 238 and 239, send home copies of the corresponding note.

**1, 2
Buckle my shoe.
3, 4
Shut the door.
5, 6
Pick up sticks.
7, 8
Lay them straight.
9, 10
A big fat hen!**

The book *Big Fat Hen* by Keith Baker is "eggs-cellent"!

Let's go to the library and check it out!

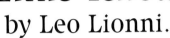

I heard the story ***Little Blue And Little Yellow*** by Leo Lionni.

Do you know what happens when blue and yellow hug?

Give *me* a hug and I'll tell you!

Uh-Oh!

There was a hungry cat in the story

Feathers For Lunch

by Lois Ehlert.

Don't worry—he only ate feathers. Ask me why!

How many birds can we find together in our neighborhood?

Today I listened to a story called

The Ugly Duckling.

Ask me what the duckling looked like when he grew up.

Let's look in the mirror. What do you think I'll look like when I grow up?

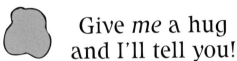
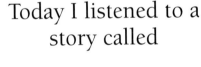

Duck Pattern

Use with *The Ugly Duckling* on page 239, "How Many Ducklings?" on page 260, and "Our Ducklings" on page 261.

Book Notes

After reading each of the books mentioned below and on pages 240 and 241, send home copies of the corresponding note.

The Rainbow Fish

by Marcus Pfister
is a story about sharing.

Ask me what the
Rainbow Fish shared.

Will you help me think of
ways I can share
with my friends?

©1996 The Education Center, Inc.

Today we read
Dinosaurs, Dinosaurs
by Byron Barton.

Let me tell you about
the different kinds
of dinosaurs.

If you were a dinosaur,
what would you
look like?

©1996 The Education Center, Inc.

The Day Jimmy's Boa Ate The Wash

by Trinka Hakes Noble
is a silly story!

Wanna slither down
to the library to
find some more
silly stories?

©1996 The Education Center, Inc.

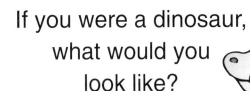

Today I listened to a
story called

The Tortoise And The Hare.

Let's race!
Would you like to
be the tortoise
or the hare?

©1996 The Education Center, Inc.

Tortoise And Hare Patterns Use with *The Tortoise And The Hare* on page 241.

Book Features

The Little Mouse, The Red Ripe Strawberry, And The Big Hungry Bear

Written by Don & Audrey Wood • Illustrated by Don Wood
Published by Child's Play (International) Ltd.

Irresistible! The mouse can't resist the strawberry. The children can't resist the mouse. And you won't be able to resist hamming it up as you read aloud this sweetly suspenseful story. This perfectly preschool tale, by Don and Audrey Wood, is available in paperback and hardcover and on videotape and audiotape (Child's Play: 1-800-639-6404). A big book and teaching guide are also available (Scholastic Inc.: 1-800-325-6149).

Ripe It Is

In preparation for reading aloud *The Little Mouse, The Red Ripe Strawberry, And The Big Hungry Bear,* bring ripe and unripened fruits to school. Show your preschoolers the fruits; then ask them what *ripe* means. Have them decide which of your fruits are ripe. Cut the fruits and give youngsters opportunities to touch, taste, smell, hear, and see the differences between the ripe and unripened fruits. Find out whether your little ones prefer ripe fruits and why or why not. As students talk, reiterate the benefits of ripeness.

The Little Mouse, The Red Ripe Strawberry, and THE BIG HUNGRY BEAR

by Don and Audrey Wood · illustrated by Don Wood

Child's Play

Toe-Tappin' Tune

Set the stage for reading the story by teaching your students the first verse of this bouncy song. Then, just prior to reading the story, ask the students to listen to the story to determine what frightened the mouse. When the story is over, have them talk about the mouse's scare. Discuss the story's happy ending. Then teach your students the last verse of the song.

Little Gray Mousie
(sung to the tune of "Short'nin' Bread")
Little gray mousie loves strawberry, strawberry.
Little gray mousie sees one that's ripe.
Little gray mousie loves strawberry, strawberry.
Little gray mousie has quite a fright.

Little gray mousie loves strawberry, strawberry.
Little gray mousie gives half to me.
Little gray mousie loves strawberry, strawberry.
Little gray mousie rests dreamily.

Sniffing Out Strawberries

Prepare for this follow-up to the story by placing a strawberry drawing or sticker and something strawberry-scented (such as chewing gum or potpourri) beneath a fabric leaf cutout. At different locations around the room, prepare several leaf-covered, strawberry-scented stations in the same way. Also prepare some stations with scents other than strawberry—omitting the strawberry drawings or stickers. In chatting about the story after reading it, ask how that big, hungry Bear was supposed to know where the red, ripe strawberry was. Find out how many of your youngsters think they would be good at sniffing out strawberries; then send all volunteers off to sniff out the strawberry scents. Students may lift the leaves to check their responses. That big, hungry Bear has a fine sniffer for sure—but so do your youngsters.

Putting Words In His Mouth

In this story, the mouse remains silent. Ask your students to imagine what the mouse might have said in each picture. As students dictate, write the mouse's comments on Post-It™ Brand notes trimmed to resemble speech balloons, and attach the notes to the corresponding pages. Reread the book, reading the mouse's comments as well as the authors' words.

Body Language

In *The Little Mouse, The Red Ripe Strawberry, And The Big Hungry Bear,* the mouse's expression and posture are constantly in a state of change. As you flip through the pages of the book, have students comment on each of the postures and facial expressions of the mouse. Explain that the mouse's face and body are telling us something about the feelings that the mouse is experiencing. Reread the story and ask the children to tell what the mouse is feeling in each illustration and to explain how they came to that conclusion.

Half For You And Half For Me!

The mouse is convinced that he can save the strawberry by halving it. If strawberries are available for this activity, have a student use a plastic knife to cut a strawberry in half. (Substitute another fruit if necessary.) Talk about the fact that to halve something, it must be separated into two parts and each part must be the same size. Have each child cut a strawberry in half and share one half of it with a partner. Before eating the fruit halves, have the students talk about whether the fruit was actually halved or not. Ask them how they could tell.

Pumpkin Pumpkin Pumpkin

Written & Illustrated by Jeanne Titherington
Published by Greenwillow Books

If autumn seems like one giant "Pumpkin-fest" to you, then make sure you've got several copies of Jeanne Titherington's *Pumpkin Pumpkin* on hand. Soft, detailed illustrations bring the reader right into the garden for a boy's-eye view of the life cycle of a pumpkin plant. From this vantage point, your preschoolers can delight in and learn about the wonders of nature. *Pumpkin Pumpkin* is available in hardcover and paperback. A big book and teaching guide are also available (Scholastic Inc.: 1-800-325-6149).

Setting The Stage

Before students begin to arrive, put a few pumpkin seeds on one tabletop and a pumpkin on another. Invert a cardboard box on the tabletop to cover and hide the seeds, and use another box to hide the pumpkin. In preparation for reading aloud *Pumpkin Pumpkin*, give students opportunities to guess what's covered by each box. Lift the box covering the pumpkin seeds. Being careful to reveal neither that they are seeds nor what kind of seeds they are, have students speculate about what the seeds are. Once it has been determined that the objects are seeds, find out what students think will grow from the seeds. Ask students what seeds need to grow. Find out, for example, if students think the seeds would begin to grow if they were left on a windowsill. Then read aloud *Pumpkin Pumpkin*. Afterward have a student lift the remaining box to see if youngsters' predictions about its contents were right. Encourage students to give a step-by-step description of how the seed was transformed into a pumpkin.

Rolling Along

That was some pumpkin that Jamie grew! Show students the picture in the book of Jamie hauling his pumpkin in a wagon. Find out why your preschoolers think that the wagon was used. In turn, have each child experiment with the best ways to move three pumpkins that vary in weight from very light to heavy. Ask that the child move each pumpkin in three different ways to find out which way is best for moving that particular pumpkin. The first time, have him carry the pumpkin in his arms. The second time, have him put the pumpkin in a box and push or pull it. And finally have him put the pumpkin in a wagon and pull it. When each child has had a chance to experiment with moving the pumpkins, talk about which pumpkins were easiest to carry and which were easiest to haul. Find out what your students think there is about a wagon that helps minimize the effort needed to move a really big pumpkin.

Audrey Englehardt & Ruth Stanfill

Pick Of The Crop

If you're looking for blue-ribbon pumpkin books to use along with *Pumpkin Pumpkin*, look no further.

It's Pumpkin Time!, Written by Zoe Hall, Illustrated by Shari Halpern, Published by Scholastic Inc.

The Pumpkin Patch, Story & Photographs by Elizabeth King, Published by Dutton Children's Books

Growing Pumpkins, Written by Melvin Berger, Published by Newbridge Communications, Inc.

Pride Of The Patches

Visiting a local farm for a look at a real pumpkin patch is a great way to follow up a reading of *Pumpkin Pumpkin*. While at a farm, students can examine the sizes, textures, and colors of pumpkin plants and pumpkins. And, hopefully, they can see pumpkins in varying stages of development. If there are no pumpkin patches nearby, take youngsters to a produce stand or market. Photograph students with pumpkins of varying sizes—especially some really large ones. (Be sure to make a few pumpkin purchases too. If possible purchase pumpkins in a variety of sizes for later use.) When your photos are developed, have students compare the sizes of the pumpkins they saw with the size of Jamie's pumpkin in *Pumpkin Pumpkin*. Is Jamie's pumpkin larger or smaller than the biggest one they saw? How do they know?

Audrey Englehardt & Ruth Stanfill
South Roxana Elementary
Roxana, IL

Seedy Situation

If you're preparing a jack-o'-lantern for Halloween this year or making the recipe on page 23, you'll no doubt have your youngsters scraping the seeds from a pumpkin. Have students wash the pumpkin seeds and dump them on several layers of paper towels to dry. Reread the last page of *Pumpkin Pumpkin*. Ask your preschoolers how many seeds Jamie kept for planting next spring. Give each student an opportunity to count out six seeds and put them in an envelope to take home. So that he will remember what the seeds produce, have him draw a pumpkin on the envelope. Plant a few seeds in a large container in the classroom. Encourage students to tend the seeds and comment on what happens.

THE SNOWY DAY

Written & Illustrated by Ezra Jack Keats
Published by Scholastic Inc.

Set the mood for wintertime by showcasing this classic story, the 1963 Caldecott Medal winner. You and your little ones will find these follow-up activities to be fun and frosty as can be. *The Snowy Day* is available in paperback and as a big book with teaching guide (Scholastic Inc.: 1-800-325-6149).

by Jayne Gammons

Imagine That!

After reading the story aloud, ask students to recall Peter's adventures in the snowy city. Then encourage youngsters to act out some of those adventures, such as making a snowman and climbing a mountain of snow. If the weather in your climate already resembles a winter wonderland, bundle up your little ones and reenact the story outside. Need some help creating the feeling of winter due to the warm temperatures outside your classroom? Spread lengths of polyester batting over the floor to resemble snowdrifts. To create a snowstorm, cut white tissue paper into small pieces and pile the pieces onto a tray. Hold the tray in front of a fan and turn the fan on. After the blizzard, give children resealable bags to fill with the pretend snow. Be sure to keep a camera handy so you can capture all of this snowy-day silliness on film!

Softly Colored Snowdrifts

Your preschoolers will create a softly colored snowdrift with this cooperative art idea. Ask the children to look closely at the colors on the snow in *The Snowy Day*. Explain that Ezra Jack Keats used chalk to add color to his collage illustrations. Cut a large piece of white bulletin-board paper. Gently tear the top of the paper so that the length of paper resembles hills of snow. Provide students with pastel colors of chalk and encourage them to rub the sides of the chalk on the paper. Lightly spray the paper with hairspray; then hang the snowdrift in a hall or on a long bulletin board. On the paper, mount the developed pictures that were taken during the outdoor and/or indoor activities described in "Imagine That!" Title the display "Our Snowy Day."

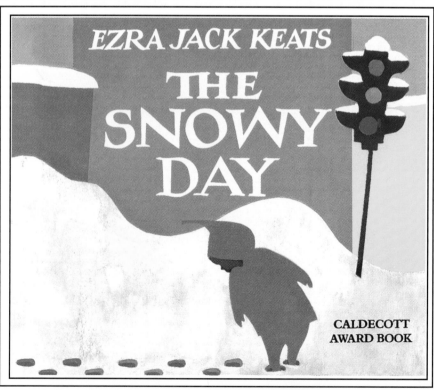

Disappearing Snowball

Peter wanted to keep a snowball as a remembrance of the snowy day. If it's snowy where you are, make a snowball and put it in a coat pocket. Ask youngsters to make predictions about what will happen to the snowball. Then hang the jacket up so everyone can observe what happens to the snowball as time passes. Later ask students for their explanations as to why the snowball melted. Give students an opportunity to make snowball keepsakes that are guaranteed not to melt. For directions, see the "Snowballs" idea on page 96 of our "Crafts For Little Hands" section.

Footprints In The Snow

Crunch, crunch, crunch! Can you hear the sound of Peter walking in the snow? First he walked with his feet pointing out, then with his feet pointing in, and finally with his feet dragging to make tracks. As a class, observe the illustrations of Peter's footprints in the snow. Then have students make some permanent footprint tracks of their own. Place a length of white bulletin-board paper on the floor. At one end of the paper, place a tub containing a mixture of light blue paint and dishwashing liquid. At the other end, place a towel and a tub containing warm water. Have each student, in turn, step barefoot into the paint. While holding his hand, encourage him to take several steps with his feet pointing in, several steps with his feet pointing out, and several steps dragging his feet. Have him rinse his feet in the tub of water; then dry his feet. When the tracks are dry, post the paper on a bulletin board along with a drawing of Peter.

Creative Collages

Chances are that your children, like many other young children, will find Keats's simple, collage-style illustrations appealing. Give youngsters an opportunity to be creative with this simple art activity that will also help develop fine-motor skills. Provide each student with a sheet of construction paper and a supply of construction-paper scraps. Encourage him to tear the scraps and glue them on his sheet of paper as desired. Ask each child to tell you about his collage; then write his dictation on a snowflake cutout. Display the collages and snowflakes where they can be seen and enjoyed by parents as they visit your school.

Let It Snow!

When the weather outside is frightful, you'll find the wintry movement ideas on page 135 simply delightful! Use the ideas to extend the story. Hurry! Winter will be over in a flurry!

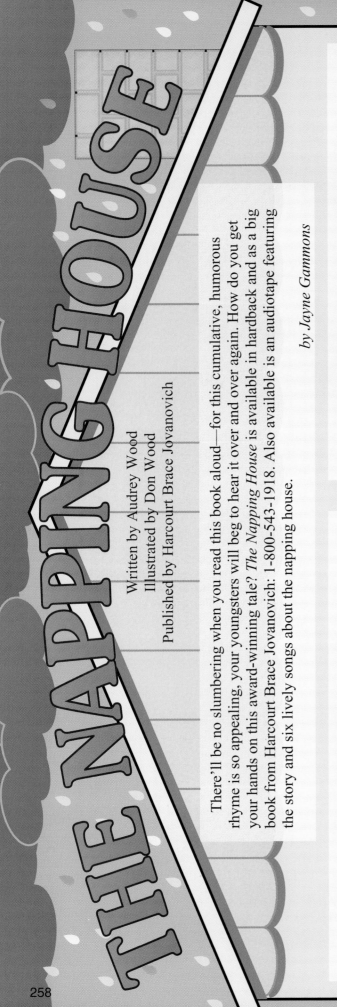

THE NAPPING HOUSE

Written by Audrey Wood
Illustrated by Don Wood
Published by Harcourt Brace Jovanovich

There'll be no slumbering when you read this book aloud—for this cumulative, humorous rhyme is so appealing, your youngsters will beg to hear it over and over again. How do you get your hands on this award-winning tale? *The Napping House* is available in hardback and as a big book from Harcourt Brace Jovanovich: 1-800-543-1918. Also available is an audiotape featuring the story and six lively songs about the napping house.

by Jayne Gammons

Save It For A Rainy Day

Do rainy days have you snoozing, snoring, dreaming, and dozing? If so, it's the perfect time to read aloud *The Napping House.* Have each child bring a pillow, blanket, or resting mat to the group area. When everyone is comfy-cozy, show them the cover of the book. Ask why people or animals might nap during the day. As you read the book through the first time, encourage the children to observe the animals shown on each page and to predict which animal will be the next to make its way to Granny's bed. Little ones will also want to keep an eye on the wide-awake flea who eventually gets to the sleeping stack and starts a zany chain of events that ends with a crashing finale.

Sweet Dreams

Looking at Don Wood's illustrations will lead you to wonder why those sleepy characters seem so content. Perhaps it's because in the napping house where everyone is sleeping, everyone is also dreaming. On chart paper, list and draw a simple picture of each character. Ask students what they think each animal or person might be dreaming about. List their ideas on the paper. Ask each child to select one character. Have her draw a picture of the sleeping character or the character's dream. Write on her paper as she dictates her ideas. If you have the audiotape, be sure to conclude this activity by listening to the song "Sweet Dreams."

It's Raining, It's Pouring

The whole class is snoring. Of course taking a nap is the natural follow-up activity to this story. Set the mood by playing an audiotape of a rain shower (available at nature products stores). Take a picture of each child as he is resting. Then have double prints of the pictures developed. Or push two chairs together so that the seats are touching, add a pillow, and cover the seats with a blanket to resemble a bed. In turn ask each child to lay on the bed and pretend that he is sleeping. Take a picture of each "snoozing" child and have double prints developed. (Save the second set of prints for "The Napping Class" display.) Provide each child with a sheet of art paper; then have him glue his photo to the bottom. Ask him to draw the animal of his choice on the paper above his picture. Then add this poem to the paper, completing it with the child's dictated response. If desired compile the pages into a class book and send it home for parents to enjoy.

Look, oh, look!
What can it be?
Something strange
Is napping on me!
It is a [animal].

The Napping Class

This display is a snore-stopper! In advance cut out a large house shape and mount it onto a dark blue background. Add the title "The Napping House." Then mount the second print of each child's picture from "It's Raining, It's Pouring" (page 258) on the house. Give the children an opportunity to add to the display. Ask them to press raindrop-shaped sponges into white paint, blot the sponges on newsprint, and press them onto the background paper.

Play Along

After reading the story aloud several times, the rhythmic verse will begin to sound like music to your ears. Why not add instruments to the narration for surprisingly effective sound effects? Collect six different types of instruments such as a tambourine, a triangle, sand blocks, a maraca, a drum, and a set of step bells. With each subsequent reading of the story, select a child to play each different instrument. Ask each child to play his instrument after a specific phrase in the story such as "And on that bed there is a granny," or "And on that granny there is a child." As you read, each child plays his instrument on cue. Sounds delightful!

From *The Napping House* by Audrey Wood. ©1984 by Audrey and Don Wood. By permission of Harcourt Brace & Company.

A Flea! Can It Be?

Is nap time over? Let your little ones know—napping-house style. Once everyone is awake but still lying down, instruct each child to place one open hand on the floor. Place a small, black pom-pom (to represent the flea) in one child's open hand. Have him jump up, pass the pom-pom to another resting child, and remain standing. When each child has been given the pom-pom and is standing, sing this song (a modified version of "Old MacDonald").

There is a house,
A napping house,
Where everyone is sleeping.

And in that house, there is a bed,
Cozy, cozy, cozy.

And in that bed, there is a granny,
Snoring, snoring, snoring.

And on that bed, there is a child,
Dreaming, dreaming, dreaming.

And on that child, there is a dog,
Dozing, dozing, dozing.

And on that dog, there is a cat,
Snoozing, snoozing, snoozing.

And on that cat, there is a mouse,
Slumbering, slumbering, slumbering.

And on that mouse, there is a flea,
Biting, biting, biting.

With a cat here,
And a dog there,
And a child here,
And a granny there.

There is a house,
A napping house,
Where no one now is sleeping!

Have You Seen My Duckling?

A Caldecott Honor Book
Written & Illustrated by Nancy Tafuri
Published by Scholastic Inc.

Have you seen *Have You Seen My Duckling?* by Nancy Tafuri? In this tale, a mother duck searches for a wayward duckling who has decided to explore his home, the pond. Where can you find this darling duckling book? *Have You Seen My Duckling?* is available in both English and Spanish from Scholastic Inc.: 1-800-325-6149. A big-book version with teaching guide is also available.

Tafuri's Tale

The first time you share this delightful book with your little ones, refrain from any dialogue other than reading aloud Tafuri's small amount of text. Encourage youngsters to examine the pictures carefully and quietly as you slowly turn the pages. Then turn on a tape recorder and read the book again, this time asking youngsters to describe the scenes on each page. Ask clever viewers to describe where the missing duckling is, as well as what they think he might be doing. Have youngsters express what they think the other characters—such as the mother duck, other ducklings, or additional pond animals—might be thinking or saying. Stop the tape recorder; then, during another group time, replay the tape for youngsters to hear. Place the book-and-tape set in a listening center or send it home for families to enjoy.

How Many Ducklings?

With these ducky math manipulatives, the question won't be, "Have you seen my duckling?" but instead, "How many ducklings have you seen?" To prepare, reduce the duck pattern on page 248. Use the pattern to cut eight ducks from yellow felt; then cut eight ducks for each child from yellow construction paper. Also cut a large circle from blue felt; then cut a large circle from blue construction paper for each child. If desired, laminate the construction-paper ducks and pond shapes for durability. During a small group time, encourage youngsters to count the ducklings on each page of the book. Then provide each child with a pond cutout and eight duck cutouts. Place the felt pond on a flannelboard. Pose a question such as "Have you seen [*four*] ducklings?" Then count aloud as you place four felt ducks on the felt pond. Challenge youngsters to count the specified number of ducks to place on their ponds. Provide assistance as needed.

Have You Seen These Ducklings?

There's more than one story about a duck who lags behind. Read aloud *Rebel* by John Schoenherr (Philomel Books) or *The Story About Ping* by Marjorie Flack (Puffin Books). Ask youngsters if they have ever been accidentally left behind or separated from their parents. Encourage them to talk about how they felt. If desired, use this opportunity to discuss safety concerns with the young children in your class.

During your read-aloud time, be sure to make way for *Make Way For Ducklings* by Robert McCloskey (Viking Children's Books). See if your little ones can find the wayward duckling in this story. Compare the number of ducklings in this book with the number in each of the other stories. Which family has more, less, or the same number of ducklings?

Our Ducklings

It's no wonder that the little duckling wanted to explore. Tafuri's illustrations show that the pond is a very busy place! As a class, make a list of the other animals that live in the story's pond environment (butterfly, heron, turtle, beaver, fish, frog, salamander, crayfish, water bug, merganser, snail, fireflies) and discuss what they are all up to. Have your youngsters assist you in searching through nature magazines such as *Ranger Rick* or *National Geographic* for pictures of animals that live in or near a pond. Cut the pictures out. Prepare a bulletin board by mounting a blue, bulletin-board-paper pond shape onto a green background. Mount the pond-animal pictures on the board.

Have your little ones make ducklings to add to the display. Depending on the size of your display, enlarge or simply duplicate the duck pattern on page 248. Reproduce a copy of the pattern on white construction paper for each child. Using a small sponge and yellow and brown tempera paints, have each child paint his duck pattern. When the paint is dry, have him cut out his duck. Then have him glue feathers to the duck. Mount the ducks on the board along with the title "Have You Seen Our Ducklings?"

The Search Is On

Introduce youngsters to a purchased, stuffed duck toy. As a class, name the duck and include it in your story-extension activities. Before your students arrive one day, hide the duckling in a special location in your school. Then prepare for a duck hunt. Plan the stops—such as other classrooms, the office, etc.—that your class will make during the hunt. Give a feather to the adult who will be at each different location. When your children arrive at school, inform them (or allow them to discover) that the duck is missing. As you travel around your school, encourage the children to ask, "Have you seen our duckling?" When the question is posed, cue the adults to then show the feather and communicate that the duck must be nearby. Once you arrive at the location where you hid the duck, congratulate your youngsters on a successful duck hunt. To celebrate, serve a snack any duck would love—fish-shaped crackers and lemonade.

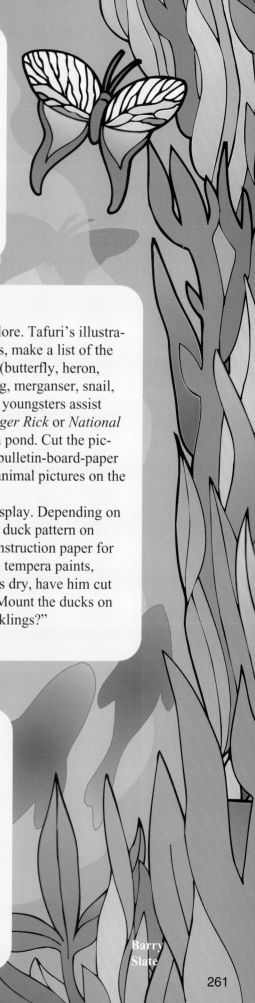

Barry Slate

Jamberry

Written & Illustrated by Bruce Degen
Published by HarperCollins Children's Books

Your storytime will be jammin' when you read this deliciously delightful rhyme about a boy, a bear, and a bunch of berries. *Jamberry* is the pick of the season and is available in paperback, as a board book, and as a big book from HarperCollins Publishers: 1-800-242-7737. The paperback, the big book, and an audiocassette are available from Scholastic Inc.: 1-800-724-6527.

Buried In Berries

Prior to reading *Jamberry* aloud, fill each of four berry baskets with blueberries, strawberries, blackberries, or raspberries. Also prepare a small name card for each child. If you have a bear puppet, have him "read" the story to your listeners. As a tasty follow-up, encourage each child to taste the four types of berries and place his name card by the basket of his favorite fruit. Count the cards and discuss the results.

Since your little ones are sure to want to hear the rhyme again, vary subsequent storytime readings of the book by encouraging youngsters to tap a steady beat as you read. Or play the lively recording of the rhyme that includes both a reading and singing of the berry adventure.

Nancy Jo Mannix
Orlando, FL

A Berry Hunt For Berry Jam

Get your berry-lovin' berry pickers ready for a jam jamboree! Prepare for a class berry pick by spreading artificial foliage at different locations around your room (such as across window ledges and over bookshelves). Determine the type of jam that the class would like to make; then gather and wash the amount of berries indicated on the "Berry Jam" chart. Fill a classroom supply of small, plastic bags with the type of berry chosen. Hide the berry bags in the foliage. Then supply each of your little ones with a berry basket and direct each child to hunt for one bag of berries. Have each child eat a berry or two from his bag. (What's a berry hunt without nibbling?) Then have him contribute to the jam by pouring his berries into a large pot.

With the children's assistance, crush the berries. (If using blackberries or raspberries, sieve half of the pulp to remove some seeds, if desired.) Stir one box of SURE•JELL® Fruit Pectin into the fruit; then add 1/2 teaspoon of margarine. Measure the indicated amount of sugar into a separate bowl. Bring the fruit mixture to a full rolling boil; then quickly add the measured amount of sugar. Boil one minute, stirring constantly. Remove the jam from the heat and allow it to cool. Later serve the jam with bread and butter.

After your class jam jamboree, divide the remaining jam into airtight containers. Send the jam home with a note indicating that the jam should be stored in the refrigerator and enjoyed within three weeks.

Berry Jam

Blackberry (2 qt.)	5 cups crushed berries + 7 cups sugar
Raspberry (2 qt.)	5 cups crushed berries + 6 1/2 cups sugar
Blueberry (3 pt.)	4 cups crushed berries + 4 cups sugar
Strawberry (2 qt.)	5 cups crushed berries + 7 cups sugar

"Hatberry" Toss

Take a good look at the cover of *Jamberry* and you'll hanker for some giant blueberries of your own. Prepare giant blueberries by painting large, Styrofoam® balls with blue tempera paint. Provide youngsters with straw hats or top hats and a bucketful of the giant berries. Then encourage individual students or pairs of students to toss the berries and catch them with the hats.

Umbrella-Berry Dance

Your little ones might not be able to dance in meadows of strawberries like the boy and the bear in the story, but they can participate in an umbrella dance in your own classroom. In advance tie lengths of ribbon streamers to each spoke of an umbrella. Also cut a classroom supply of construction-paper strawberries. Have youngsters describe the page in the book depicting this scene. Give as many youngsters as you have streamers a paper strawberry; then invite them to join in a berry dance. Stand in the center of an open space and hold the umbrella over your head. Have each child hold his strawberry with one hand and the end of a streamer with the other hand. Direct the group to form a circle around you. Play the song version of the rhyme (or any lively instrumental music) as youngsters dance and prance around you in a merry, berry way!

Welcome To Berryland!

Transform your reading or listening center into Berryland. Need a "canoeberry"? Cut a canoe shape from brown bulletin-board paper and secure it to the side of a large cardboard box. How about a "shoeberry"? Fill a large boot with the giant blueberries described in " 'Hatberry' Toss." Bury your readers in berries by making giant berry pillows from felt. To make a pillow, simply trace and cut two large, identical berry shapes from felt. Sew or fabric-glue the berry pillow, leaving a small opening for stuffing. Stuff the pillow and sew or glue the opening closed. Use a black marker to add features and attach green felt leaves if desired. Of course, you'll want to include in the center as many forms of the book as you have available. Enhance the center by displaying raspberry banners similar to those in the book. Finally suspend a "Welcome To Berryland" sign from the ceiling to announce that the center is ripe and ready for readers.

More Berry Fun

For more fun related to berries and other types of fruit, turn to the fruit unit on pages 84-87.

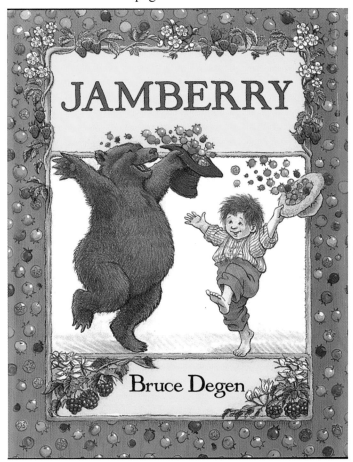

From *Jamberry* by Bruce Degen. ©1983 by Bruce Degen. By permission of HarperCollins Publishers.

263

Out And About

Bubbles

Here's an idea to blow around. Develop the spatial awareness of your little ones with a bubble-blowing activity. On a warm, sunny day, go outside with a portable cassette player and enough bubble solution and wands for each child in your class. As the children blow bubbles, play a selection of instrumental music. The album Music Of Cosmos (available from Collectors' Choice Music™ Catalog at 1-800-923-1122) has several selections suitable for this activity. After an appropriate length of time, gather the children together and talk about how the bubbles moved in the air. Discuss what happens when one bubble bumps into another bubble. Once again, play the selection of music. Encourage youngsters to move like the bubbles as the music plays. Remind them to be careful not to bump into other bubbles! POP!

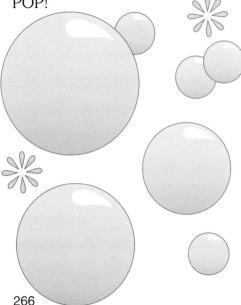

Dirt Dig

Get down in the mud and dirt with this ooey, gooey activity. Take youngsters to a spot where there is plenty of loose dirt. Or fill a large tub with potting soil. Provide each child with a small bowl or margarine tub and a spoon. Have each youngster fill his container with dirt. Then guide him in his exploration of the dirt by asking him to look at, feel, and smell the dirt. Give each child a small cup of water. Have him slowly mix the water into the dirt. Discuss the changes. Give each child a real or artificial flower to top off his mud mess. Looks like a mud pie—mmmmm, delicious!

Pebble Projects

For this creative activity, you will need a box of small rocks for the class and a sheet of construction paper for each student. Help each child find his own sitting space on a sidewalk or in the grass. Have him select a handful of rocks from the collection. Using his paper as a background, ask him to arrange his rocks on the paper. Some children may choose to make pictures while others choose to arrange the rocks in a pleasing design. Provide listening time for each child as he talks about his creative work.

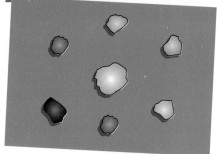

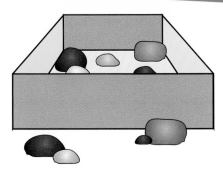

Wild Animals

Is the energy of your little ones too much to contain in a classroom? Take them outside and let them act like wild animals! In advance, cut pictures of different wild animals from magazines. Mount the pictures on tagboard squares and laminate them for durability. Punch a hole in the top of each square; then thread it with yarn to create a necklace. Take youngsters outside and give each child a necklace. Encourage each child to act like the animal shown on his necklace. After an appropriate length of time, collect the necklaces; then redistribute them. Continue in this manner until each child has had the opportunity to act like several different wild animals.

Our Tree

This activity will help little ones appreciate the world around them in a "tree-mendous" way. Seat youngsters by a tree that is located near your school or classroom. Read aloud *A Tree Is Nice* by Janice May Udry (published by HarperCollins Children's Books). After reading the book, have the class look carefully at the tree they are sitting under. Ask students to share what they observe about the tree and reasons why the tree is nice to have around. Explain that the class will watch the tree throughout the year to see how it changes. Have the class name the tree; then encourage each child to give the tree a hug. Conclude the activity by taking a picture of the class by the tree. Then take pictures again at various times during the year.

Fun In The Sun

Have some fun in the sun with these ideas. While soaking up the sun's rays, lead youngsters in singing favorite songs about the sun such as "You Are My Sunshine" and Raffi's "One Light, One Sun." Then discuss some reasons why the sun is important (such as *for light, for heat, and for plant growth*). Provide each child with a large piece of art paper, a paintbrush, and yellow paint. Encourage him to paint freely to create a sun painting. "Sun-sational!"

Flowers And Seeds

The Tiny Seed by Eric Carle (published by Picture Book Studio) is a story about the life cycle of a flower. The story begins in autumn as a tiny seed is blown through the air. After reading the book aloud, share pictures of flowers with your students. Then, as a class, try planting seeds in a variety of mediums such as sand or potting soil. Chart the growth activity of the plants. Remind students that in the story when the wind blew, the seeds flew through the air. Then take the class outside to a grassy area. Help each child find a milkweed plant with a dried pod, or a dandelion. Encourage each child to blow into the pod or onto the dandelion. Children are sure to experience great delight as they watch the seeds blow away.

Cathie Pesa—Pre-K
Youngstown City Schools
Youngstown, OH

Harvesttime

The scarecrows have been guarding the cornfields all summer. Now that harvesttime has arrived, the corn can finally be picked. If possible, take your youngsters to a cornfield to observe the height of the corn and to pick a bushel. Or purchase an ear of corn for each child from a farmer's market or grocery store. In advance, place a large tub of water outside near the area where the class will be working. To begin the activity, take the class outside and give each child an ear of corn. Demonstrate how to pull the green husks away from the corn and wash the corn in the tub. After each child has shucked and cleaned his corn, assist him in using a plastic knife to scrape a small amount of the corn into a bowl. (Wrap each child's corncob in plastic wrap and send it home with suggested cooking directions.) Later mix the scraped corn with a package of cornbread mix and the required ingredients listed on the package. Bake and eat the cornbread for a delicious harvest treat.

Sleeping Beauties

Not all beautiful flowers grow from seeds that are planted in the spring of the year. Planting bulbs with children in the fall will produce a surprise crop of joy in the spring. To plant bulbs, you will need a patch of ground with good drainage. Show children the bulbs and explain to them that sleeping inside each bulb is a flower waiting for spring. Share with them that the bulb will need a snug space in a flower bed and a long winter's nap. Follow the directions included with the package for planting the bulbs. In the spring watch for tips of green to push their way through the ground. Wake up! It's spring!

See pages 218 and 219 for more bulb-related activities.

Things To Do Outdoors

Scurrying Squirrels

Hurry, scurry, little squirrels! Winter's on its way! Get your little ones ready for winter with an acorn hunt. From brown bulletin-board paper, cut out a tail shape for each of your youngsters. Tape or pin a tail to each child; then provide him with a small bucket or lunch bag. Next send your little squirrels out to find acorns. When the hunt is over and the tails have been removed, return to the classroom to examine the acorns and use them for various manipulative activities. For example, you might ask youngsters to sort all the acorns with tops and the acorns without tops, or to count the acorns into sets.

Everybody Needs A Rock

Kids dig rocks! Here's a book and related activity your little rock hounds are sure to enjoy. Read aloud *Everybody Needs A Rock* by Byrd Baylor (published by Charles Scribner's Sons). Then take youngsters outside for a rock hunt. As students are hunting, remind them of the suggestions given in the book for finding the perfect rock. Although the author of the book suggests that "Nobody is supposed to know what's special about another person's rock," provide time for student volunteers to talk about why they chose their rocks.

Jennifer Barton
Elizabeth Green School
Newington, CT

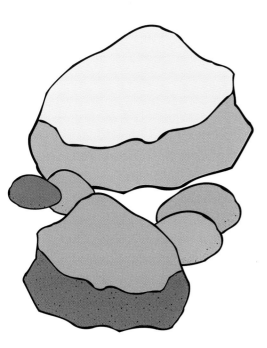

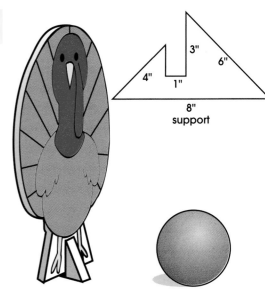

3"
6"
4"
1"
8"
support

Let's Bowl!

Using Styrofoam and a little imagination, you can have safe and fun bowling pins for *every* season or theme. To make a pin, draw an 18-inch-tall seasonal shape, such as a tree or turkey, on a one-inch-thick sheet of Styrofoam (available from hardware stores). Cut the shape out using an X-acto® knife; then cut a 1" square from the center bottom. Use permanent markers to color and add detail to the shape. Also cut from the Styrofoam a support in the size and shape shown. Assemble each pin by placing the seasonal shape in its support. Set several of these bowling pins on a sidewalk or flat surface outside. Provide children with Nerf® balls to use as bowling balls. There will be fun to spare with this striking idea!

Linda Crosby
Hill Crest Community School
Fort Vermilion, Alberta, Canada

269

Out And About

For The Birds

This holiday season have your little ones assist you in decorating a tree as a gift for local birds. Here are some suggestions for ornaments that will be feasts for your fine-feathered friends:

- Assist children in scooping the pulp out of orange halves. Poke holes in opposite sides of the orange halves and thread them with yarn. Knot the yarn and fill the halves with birdseed.
- Using large plastic needles threaded with yarn, have students create dried fruit, cranberry, and popcorn garlands.
- Have students use cookie cutters and your favorite recipe for bread dough to create dough cutouts. While the dough is soft, have students press birdseed into the shapes and poke a hole near the top of each cutout with a straw. When dry, thread each cutout with a length of yarn.

Once the delectable decorations have been prepared, trim a live tree near your classroom or decorate a purchased evergreen tree to display outdoors. Consider inviting a wild bird expert—perhaps a member of the local Audubon Society—to visit your class.

Alice Fiore—Four-Year-Olds
Monica Ros School
Ojai, CA

I like this tree.
You like it, too!
Please tell me where
It goes with you!

Share your holiday
experiences with
Mikki
at
Tiffany Creek School
Route 9, Box 777
Boyceville, WI

Tree Travels

For a terrific field trip, plan to visit a tree farm or a site where Christmas trees are sold. In preparation for the trip, duplicate a note similar to the one shown on green construction paper. Before laminating the notes, ask each child to personalize one. Punch a hole in each note and thread it with yarn. While visiting the tree farm, encourage each child to find a tree that he particularly likes and to tie his note to the tree. In January, messages will begin to arrive at school telling students about the trees' travels. This idea is sure to keep the spirit of Christmas alive and well into the new year!

Loree Austrum and Janine Klaustermeier
Tiffany Creek School
Boyceville, WI

Snowball Olympics

Snowed under with the winter blahs? These snowball activities will be a blizzard of fun. For super snowballs that are guaranteed to last through the winter, make white, circular beanbags or collect Styrofoam balls in several sizes. Bundle up your little ones in their winter coats and hats, and head outdoors. Let the games begin!

Snowball Spooning: Provide each child with a Styrofoam ball to carry on a large spoon. Encourage each child to try walking as slowly and then as rapidly as he can without jarring the ball from the spoon.

Snowball Shoot: In this event, give youngsters opportunities to toss beanbags into baskets.

Snowballs In The Bucket: Group students in pairs; then provide each pair with a small container and a pile of Styrofoam snowballs. Position a bucket at an appropriate distance from all of the partners. Ask the partners to work together to fill their container with snowballs, carry it to the bucket, and empty their container of snowballs into the bucket. Since the snowballs won't melt, there'll be plenty of time to work together!

Snowball Swap: Group students in pairs; then provide each pair with a beanbag. Encourage the children to gently throw the snowball beanbag back and forth.

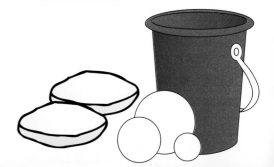

270

Things To Do Outdoors

Puffs And Magic Dragons

Once upon a time in the land of Far Away there lived magic dragons. On frosty winter days, these somewhat fearsome (but mostly friendly) dragons enjoyed huffing and puffing their dragon breath into the air. Give your little ones the opportunity to become dandy, little dragons themselves by making these magic dragon headbands. For each child, cut three green construction-paper triangles. Have each child decorate his triangles using glitter, scraps of aluminum foil, and green tissue-paper squares. Fold a length of a green crepe-paper streamer in half lengthwise. Slide the triangles into the fold, leaving a portion of the streamer free at one end. Staple them in place. Fit a green construction-paper band to the child's head and staple the ends together, creating a headband. Unfold the streamer at the free end and staple it to the headband. Make a dragon headband for each child in the same manner. Encourage youngsters to put on their dragon attire and run around outside, breathing dragon breath in the air.

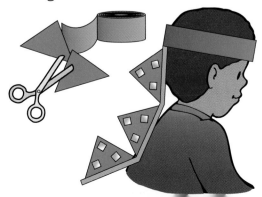

Keep Looking!

Read aloud *Keep Looking!* by Millicent Selsam and Joyce Hunt (Macmillan). Review the story with the youngsters, asking them to name the animals from the story that were "sleeping" and those that were active. Take a walk with the children around your school to find out where they think some animals may be tucked away for the winter. What evidence, if any, can your little ones see that indicates that active animals are wintering there? Students may notice such evidence as animal tracks, or they may observe birds feasting on evergreen berries or on the seeds of dead grasses. How many animals can they find?

Let's Go On A Dinosaur Hunt

If your theme is dinosaurs, why not take your little ones on a dinosaur hunt? Enlarge a dinosaur pattern; then cut it into as many pieces as there are children in your class. Ask an adult volunteer to hide the pieces on a playground area outside. (As a variation, ask the volunteer to hide a dinosaur-shaped cutout or dinosaur-shaped notepad page for each child in the class.) While the parent is hiding the dinosaur pieces, provide each child with his copy of an official dinosaur hunting license. Direct him to draw a picture of himself and write his name. Then go outside and let the hunting begin! Once each child has found a dinosaur piece (or dinosaur cutout), go back into your classroom. If pieces of a large dinosaur were found, encourage the class to cooperatively put the pieces together. Little ones are sure to exclaim with excitement, "We found a dinosaur!"

Michele Reigh
St. Peters School
St. Charles, MO

271

Out And About

Growing In And Out

Start this garden indoors in February and it'll be ready to transplant outdoors by mid-March! Purchase several aluminum cupcake pans and punch a few small holes in the bottom of each section. Fill each compartment with dirt and plant a different type of seed in each section. To label the compartments, cut pictures from seed catalogs or from the seed packets. Glue the pictures onto craft sticks; then insert each stick in the appropriate compartment. Later transplant the sprouts to a location outdoors. Wait patiently, attending the garden with care. Before long, you'll have a harvest to share!

Doris Peiffer—Preschool
Head Start
Anamosa, IA

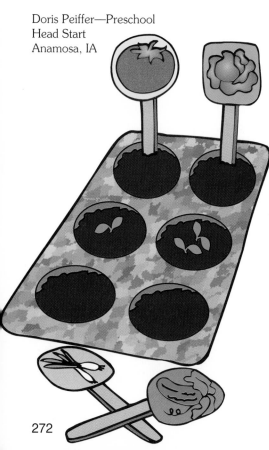

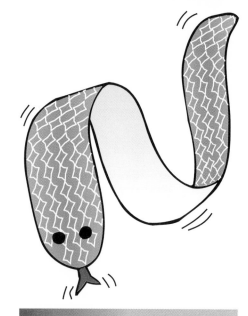

Slithery, Sensory Snakes

For goodness snakes! This is one outdoor project your students *will* get tired of—and for good reason. They'll use a playground tire! To make a sensory snake, measure the tread width and circumference of a tire. Then cut a piece of white bulletin-board paper accordingly. Wrap the paper around the tire and secure it with tape. Have the students rub the entire piece of paper with the sides of green and brown crayons so that the pattern on the tire is transferred to the paper. Remove the paper from the tire and cut the ends so that the corners are rounded. Draw features on the paper snake and add a red paper tongue. Slithering snakes! What a super idea!

Eileen Montemurro—Preschool
Schering-Plough Supertots
Union, NJ

Billions And Billions Of Bubbles

Follow this recipe to make your own bubble solution for a fraction of the cost of commercial solution.

Bubble Solution
3/4 cup dishwashing liquid
1/4 cup glycerin (available from a pharmacy)
2 quarts of water

For the best bubble makers, use plastic flyswatters. (Wire swatters will rust.) Pour the prepared bubble solution into a shallow dish or Styrofoam meat tray. Encourage youngsters to dip the flyswatters into the liquid and wave them through the air. For a related song and movement activity, pop on over to page 136.

Dayle Timmons—Three- And Four-Year-Olds
Alimacani Elementary School
Jacksonville, FL

We're Going On A Leprechaun Hunt

We're telling you no blarney—this St. Patrick's Day shenanigan is one that students will long remember! To prepare for a leprechaun hunt, cut foot shapes from green paper. Cover the shapes with glue and sprinkle on green glitter if desired. Create a path that leads outside by taping the foot shapes to the floor and securing them to the ground or outside walls. For each child, prepare a goodie bag of gold-foil-wrapped chocolates, green candies, or green-tinted popcorn from a popcorn specialty shop. Place the goodie bags in a black cauldron—or a pot covered with black paper—and place the cauldron where the trail of foot shapes ends. Before the hunt, remind students that every leprechaun has a secret pot of gold. Then lead your students as you follow the leprechaun's trail. Well, shimmering shamrocks! Is that gold ahead?

Lida Mills—Preschool Supervisor
Hodgkins Park School District
Hodgkins, IL

How Long?

How long until your little ones can be scientists? Not long at all with this outdoor activity that introduces beginning concepts of measurement. To make a scientific measurement kit for each child, label a small paper bag "Scientist [child's name]." Place a craft stick in each bag. Take a small group of children outside and direct them to find objects such as leaves, twigs, and grass that are as long as the craft stick. Encourage youngsters to break twigs or tear grass to match the length of the stick. Have each child put the objects he finds in his bag. Once inside the classroom, assist each child in gluing his objects and his craft stick onto paper to show that all of the lengths match. To vary this activity, ask children to find objects that are shorter than or longer than the craft stick.

Wilma Droegemueller—Preschool
Zion Lutheran School
Mt. Pulaski, IL

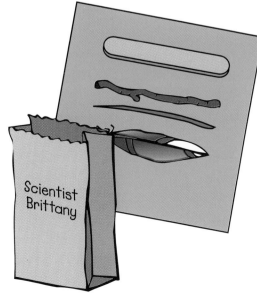

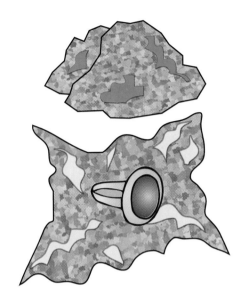

Adventures In Space

Blast off into the great outdoors with these very "space-al" ideas. In advance make several moon rocks for each child by wrapping a small trinket or penny in aluminum foil and scatter them outside. To create a rocket ship in your classroom, place chairs together in a group or in a row. Have each child sit in the rocket ship and together count backwards from ten. When the rocket ship has "landed on the moon," encourage the children to disembark from the rocket ship and step outdoors to explore the moon. Encourage each child to find a predetermined number of moon rocks; then return to the rocket ship. Blast off again and return safely to Earth. Once you have landed, direct the astronauts to study their rocks to discover the prizes inside. Out of this world!

Lida Mills—Preschool Supervisor

273

Out And About

Hoppin' Down The Bunny Trail

Increase the coordination of your bunny buddies with this outdoor springtime activity. Prepare a bunny trail in a grassy area of your school's playground. Position two lengths of rope on the ground parallel to each other and about two feet apart. Arrange the ropes so that the path has both straight and curvy sections. Along the path, place baskets filled with plastic eggs. Provide each child with a small basket and encourage him to go hopping down the bunny trail. Along the way, have him stop and pick up an egg from each basket to put in his own basket. After completing the trail once, have him repeat the activity, this time returning an egg to each basket along the way. "Hoppy" trails to you!

On The Move

You won't have to be a wheeler-dealer to get youngsters excited about this outdoor activity. During a transportation unit, designate a day as Vehicle Day. Invite each child to bring a vehicle—a bike, tricycle, etc.— to school on that day. (Arrange to have extra vehicles for children who may not have brought one.) As each child arrives at school with his vehicle, ask him to park it outside your door. Inside the classroom, show the class a real license plate. Then have each child make his own plate by tracing and coloring numerals onto a tagboard rectangle. Punch holes in the top of each plate; then thread it with a length of heavy yarn. Assist each child in tying his license plate to his vehicle. Encourage the children to ride their registered vehicles on a paved area outside. Beep, beep! Honk, honk! Here we go!

Sue Lewis Lein
St. Pius X
Wauwatosa, WI

Give It A Squirt!

Is it a warm and sunny day? Take this game out for some water play! To prepare the game, you will need six different-colored balloons, six tacks, a large piece of cardboard, and a squirt bottle full of water. Inflate each balloon, knot it, and tack it to the cardboard. Prop the cardboard against a wall outside. To play, a child stands in front of the board and holds the squirt bottle. Depending on the child's ability, state a series of one, two, or three directions. For example to reinforce colors, you might say, "Squirt the blue balloon, then the yellow balloon, then the red balloon." To reinforce counting, you might say, "Squirt the green balloon three times." Go ahead—give it a squirt!

Rachel Meseke Castro
Juneau Elementary
Juneau, WI

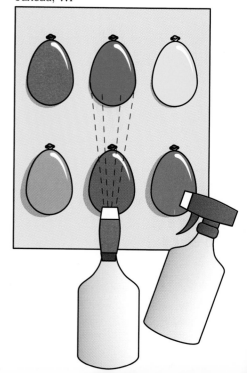

Litter Walk

Children are never too young to learn to take responsibility for the care of our environment. Celebrate Earth Day (April 22) with this early childhood ecology lesson. Have each student personalize and decorate a small paper bag with markers or crayons. Don't forget to decorate a bag for yourself! Then take your class on a litter walk. As a child spies litter, encourage him to pick it up and put it in his bag. (Caution children about the danger of picking up sharp objects such as glass and aluminum can tops. Provide kitchen tongs for picking up these and other potentially dangerous objects. In addition, request that these items be placed in your bag.) Upon returning to the classroom, have each child empty his litter bag into a larger trash bag. Save the decorated bags for future litter walks. After all, *every* day is Earth Day!

adapted from an idea by Carole Watkins—
    Four- And Five-Year-Olds
Holy Family Child Care Center
Crown Point, IN

Picnic Pals

The warm sun and the spring breeze let you know it's perfect weather for a picnic. Decide on a date for your picnic. Ask each child to bring a picnic pal (stuffed toy) to school on the designated day. When it's time for the picnic, arrange blankets or quilts on the ground. Invite the children and their picnic pals to gather around. Then enjoy a treat such as apple juice and crackers. You and your picnic pals are sure to have a simply delightful time.

Melissa Epling—Preschool
Panther Creek Elementary
Nettie, WV

Look Up In The Sky

It's a bird! It's a plane! It's a super art activity that youngsters can do outdoors! Take a group of students outside. Ask them to lie on their backs in the grass and to look at the sky. After a few minutes of sky gazing, ask the students to name items that were seen or can be seen in the sky. Then provide each child with a sheet of art paper, crayons, and a smooth writing surface. Ask each child to draw a picture of one or more things that can be seen in the sky. When his picture is complete, have him paint over his crayon illustration with thinned, blue tempera paint. Secure the pictures to a clothes-drying rack or to a fence, and leave them there to dry. If desired, display the pictures by taping them to your ceiling. My, oh my—what a beautiful sky!

Out And About

A Buggy Band

Have your little ones pretend to be noisy bugs with this outdoor idea. In advance collect a classroom supply of baby-food jar lids. (These lids have raised centers that make clicking sounds when pressed.) Provide each child with a lid. Demonstrate how to hold the lid and press the center with your thumb. Ask the children to imagine that the clicking is the sound of bugs hopping about in the summer. Encourage youngsters to click as you recite your favorite rhyme or sing your favorite summer songs. It's a buggy band!

Sr. Carolyn Mary Cossack, S.M.M.I.—
    Three- And Four-Year-Olds
Sts. Peter and Paul Nursery School
Three Rivers, MA

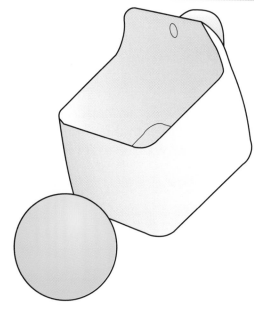

Here's The Scoop

Develop students' gross-motor skills with this fun-filled activity that stresses cooperation. In advance collect a classroom supply of one-gallon milk jugs and foam balls. Cut the top off each milk jug to resemble a scoop. To begin the activity, take your class outside, and provide each child with a scoop and a foam ball. Demonstrate how to toss the ball into the air and catch it using the scoop. Encourage each child to do the same. Then pair students, removing one ball from each pair. Have each pair use the scoops to toss the ball back and forth to each other. To increase the difficulty in this activity, have each pair of students move farther apart before tossing the ball to each other.

Tonie Liddle—Pre-K
Central Baptist Christian Academy
Binghamton, NY

Colorful Sidewalks

Here's an outdoor idea that's really "write" on! Gather your toy cars and trucks and a supply of sidewalk chalk. Take youngsters outside to a concrete area such as a sidewalk. Using the chalk have the class cooperatively draw roads, houses, and buildings on the concrete. Then have students "drive" their vehicles on the chalk roadways. Beep, beep!

Elaine M. Utt—Two-Year-Olds
La Petite Academy
Tampa, FL

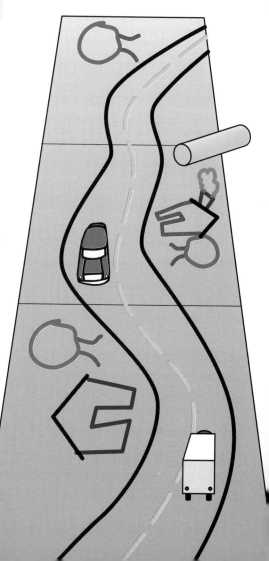

276

Things To Do Outdoors

Wispy Wands

Wispy wands are sure to put lots of color in summer skies. To make a wispy wand, cut 36-inch lengths of colorful paper streamers. Gather several streamers together; then wrap a twist tie around the center of the streamers. Use a pencil to insert the twist tie two inches into one end of a cardboard tube from a clothes hanger. Have each child embellish his wispy wand by coloring the handle and adding stickers to the streamers. Take your youngsters, the wispy wands, a battery-operated tape player, and musical recordings outside. Provide each child with his wispy wand and play the movement song of your choice. As the music plays, encourage students to dance and move freely to the rhythm so that their streamers move expressively.

Lorrie Hartnett—Pre-K
Tom Green Elementary
San Marcos, TX

Bubble Painting

Colored bubbles everywhere! That's the effect of this creative art project. In advance pour commercial bubble solution into several pie plates or shallow pans. (Or prepare bubble solution using the formula on page 78.) Squeeze a different color of food coloring in each pan. Take youngsters, the bubble solution, white construction paper, and bubble wands outside. Provide each child with a wand and a sheet of construction paper. Have each student dip his wand in the bubble solution, then blow bubbles on his paper. Pop, pop!

Pamela Vance—Preschool
Lake Geneva Cooperative Preschool
Lake Geneva, WI

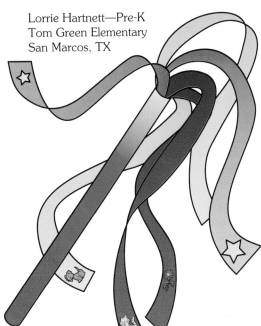

Sunny Days

Use this activity to teach your students that the sun is hot and that its rays produce heat. On a sunny day, fill two small, aluminum pie tins with water. Place one tin in full sunlight and the other in a shaded area. Later take your students on a walk outside the school. Stand with your faces turned toward the sun. Ask students if they feel warm standing in the sun. Then step into the shade and ask if they feel cooler. Encourage youngsters to put their hands in both tins of water and to compare the temperatures of the water in both tins.

Bulletin Boards And Displays

Youngsters' contributions will add a colorful touch to this door display. Before the first day of school, send each child an introductory letter along with a personalized crayon shape cut from white construction paper. Ask each student to color, paint, or otherwise decorate the crayon shape his favorite color and bring it to school on the first day. After using the crayons for various activities, mount them onto a door covered with brightly colored paper.

Sandy Whicker—3-year-olds
Kernersville Moravian Preschool
Kernersville, NC

Cut a toaster shape out of aluminum foil and add construction-paper details. Mount the cutout onto a bulletin board. For each child, mount a personalized toast cutout near the toaster. Take a candid picture of each child participating in a different activity in the room. Attach a developed photo to each child's toast shape. For a terrific twist, replace existing photos with pictures taken on a field trip or while participating in a special outdoor activity.

Tanya Bator—Toddler Teacher, Mont Marie Childcare Center, Holyoke, MA

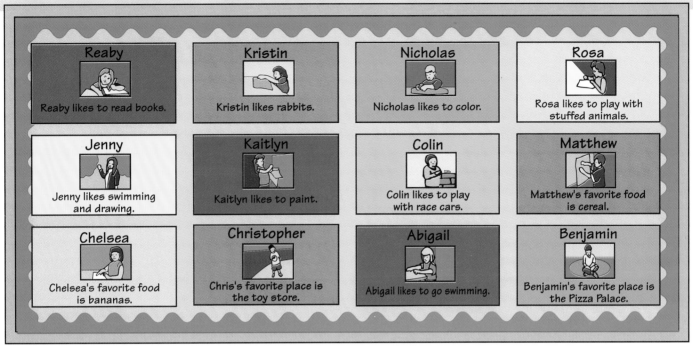

This picture-perfect display is sure to draw interest from youngsters, teachers, and parents alike. During the first week of school, take candid photos of your little ones in action as they participate in activities around the room. Mount the photos onto brightly colored sheets of construction paper; then write information about each student (such as name, favorite place, and favorite food) on the paper around the picture. Laminate the pictures, if desired, before attaching them to the board.

Susan Merkle—Pre-K, Westbury Baptist Day School, Sugar Land, TX

Here's an autumn display that's just as sweet as the children who help to make it. Mount a basket cutout along with a cutout of a cute character onto a wall or bulletin board. Using red, yellow, and/or green paint, have each student sponge-paint an apple cutout. Once his apple is dry, have him glue a torn construction-paper stem and leaves onto it. Cut an oval from each child's apple and attach a photo of the child so that his face is centered in the opening. Mount the apples near the tilted basket.

Barb Johnson and Dona Peck—ECSE Preschool, John Cline Elementary, Decorah, IA

Deck the hall or bulletin board with this sparkly wonder. Have each child squeeze a glue design onto a green sheet of construction paper; then sprinkle the glue with glitter. When the glue is dry, shake off the excess glitter; then mount the glue designs in the shape of a pine tree. Add the finishing touch by attaching a glitter star to the very top of the tree. "Oh, Christmas tree! Oh, Christmas tree!"

Brrr! This wintry bulletin board will get flurries of attention! Provide each student with construction paper, scissors, glue, two craft sticks, and a penguin pattern if desired. Have each child trace or draw a penguin, then cut on the resulting outline. Have him glue craft sticks on the penguin to represent skis. Mount the penguins on a dark blue background along with cotton-batting snowdrifts and snowflake cutouts. Let it snow!

Use this bulletin-board window display by itself or as a background for your housekeeping area. Cover a board with paper; then drape and secure large pieces of lightweight fabric on both sides of the bulletin board to resemble pull-back curtains. Mount a brown construction-paper tree trunk and branches, clouds, and snow-covered construction-paper hills on the bulletin board. Attach student-made snowmen to complete the winter scene. This versatile display can be changed with each season.

Sherry Sanders, Yorktown, TX

The Preschool Express!

Here's a cooperative project in which everyone pulls his own load! Have each child paint a picture on colored construction paper. When the paint dries, attach two construction-paper wheels to each painting. Mount all of the paintings as train cars behind an engine cutout. Attach a class photo in the engineer's place. All aboard the Preschool Express!

We're As Sweet As Candy!

This display is as sweet as can be! Glue lace trim to a large, red heart shape; then mount the heart and a title on a wall. To make delicious-looking chocolates, provide each child with a personalized, tan construction-paper shape. Have him paint his paper with brown tempera paint and top it with real chocolate sprinkles. When each shape is dry, glue it to a larger piece of crinkled black paper to represent the candy wrapper. Mount the finished projects on the heart.

Brandi Kimball—One-, Two-, And Three-Year-Olds
Growing Years, Inc.
Basalt, CO

Faith and begorra! With this door display, your children will walk right under a rainbow! Hang varying lengths and colors of crepe-paper streamers from the top of your classroom door frame. Mount a sun cutout above the door; then add a large, cloud-shaped cutout atop the streamers' ends to complete the dazzling display.

Cindy Goodrich
Forestbrook Elementary School
Myrtle Beach, SC

Promote good nutrition with this display that is just in time for March—National Nutrition Month®. Cut out or have your children cut out magazine pictures of healthful foods. Have each child glue a collection of the pictures to a sheet of paper. When the glue has dried, cut a body shape from the paper. Mount the body shapes on a background along with a title. A tasty treat for the eyes!

Betsy Ruggiano—Three-Year-Olds, Featherbed Lane School, Clark, NJ

Say, "Hurrah!" with this hands-on display. Mount a brown bulletin-board-paper tree trunk and branches onto a white, paper background. Have youngsters use green tempera paint to create handprint leaves on the paper. Welcome spring by adding student-made art projects, fringed paper grass, and a snappy title.

Tracy Tavernese—Four-Year-Olds, Holy Child School, Old Westbury, NY

Your little ones will hippity-hop right over to help you make this bulletin-board display. Have each child crumple her choice of brown, gray, or white tissue-paper squares and glue them on a rabbit-shaped cutout. Add wiggle eyes and paper whiskers if desired. Next have her crumple orange tissue-paper squares and glue them on an orange, carrot-shaped cutout. Tape green curling ribbon to the carrots and mount them as a border on a blue background. Attach the rabbits and a title to complete the display.

Betsy Ruggiano—Three-Year-Olds, Featherbed Lane School, Clark, NJ

A downpour of smiles will appear when your little ones help in making this April display. Provide each child with two sheets of art paper. Have him completely paint each sheet a different chosen color. When the paint dries, have him trace and cut out a triangle from one sheet and an umbrella shape from the other sheet. Have each child glue the shapes together along with black, boot-shaped cutouts. Mount the finished projects with a title on a wall or bulletin board. Splish, splash!

Betsy Ruggiano—Three-Year-Olds

Spring is in the air with this eye-catching display. Mount a large, paper flower—complete with title—on a wall. Have each child draw his face on a skin-toned, construction-paper circle. Have him glue his picture on a colorful piece of construction paper; then have him cut out a flower shape from the paper. Attach a long, paper stem to each flower. On leaf cutouts, write each child's dictation of things he enjoys doing in the spring; then attach the leaves to the stems. Mount the flowers on the wall.

Betty Jean Kobes—Preschool, West Hancock Elementary School, Kanawha, IA

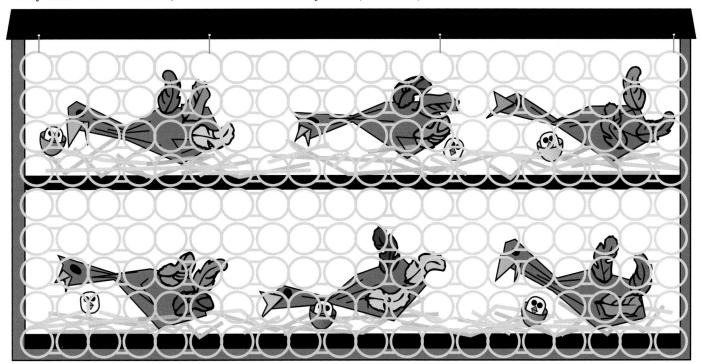

This bulletin board is something to cluck about! Tape a quantity of plastic soda rings together to resemble chicken wire. Mount a poster-board roof to the top frame of the board. Fold and staple poster-board shelves across the middle and bottom of the board. Glue straw atop the shelves. Mount student-made hens and chicks (see page 100) on the shelves. Punch holes across the width of the roof and hang the rows of soda rings with fishing line. Tape the rows to the sides and bottom to complete this three-dimensional chicken coop.

Audrey Englehardt—Preschool Hearing Impaired, South Roxana Elementary School, South Roxana, IL

BULLETIN BOARDS

You've Come A Long Way, Baby!

My feet and hands are big now!
Terry

I have lots of teeth in my smile.
Lorna

I don't have little fingers anymore.
Steve

My hair is darker now.
Julie

My hair grew. I was bald.
Gracie

I have gotten very tall.
Annette

I can run fast now!
Kara

Ask each child to bring a baby picture to school. Mount the photo on a colorful piece of paper along with a recent picture taken at school. On the paper, write as each child describes how he has grown. Share the pictures with the group before mounting them on a wall or bulletin board.

Michelle Castonguay—Preschool, Someplace Special Preschool, Holyoke, MA

Take A Bite Out Of Summer!

I'm going to Grandma's.

I'm going to play in Britt's yard.

I will play with my cousins.

I'll be jumping in my pool.

Sarah Francis will come play.

My sister and I are going to visit my Auntie.

My daddy is taking me on a trip.

No matter how you slice them, these watermelons make a luscious display. When each child has enjoyed a slice of real watermelon, have him wash and dry the seeds. Have him glue a pink half-circle to a slightly larger green half-circle; then glue the real seeds onto the paper slice. Write on his watermelon slice as each child dictates his summer plans. Before attaching it to a background, tear a bite out of the slice. Add paper vines and a title to complete the display.

Andrea Esposito—Preschool, VA/YMCA Child Care Center, Brooklyn, NY

Chances are you're pretty proud of your class of rising stars. Let everyone know with this stellar display. Add gold glitter to a classroom supply of construction-paper stars. Attach each child's picture to a star; then personalize the star. Mount the stars on a foil-paper background along with a border of decorative star garland.

Mary McDonald—Pre-K, F. X. Hegarty School, Island Park, NY

With this blooming display, your budding artists can show off the art techniques they have learned this year. Set up a station in your class for each art technique—such as painting, coloring with chalk, and cutting and pasting—with which your students are familiar. Provide each child with a construction-paper flower-shape to embellish at the station of his choice. Display the flowers atop thick yarn stems; then add construction-paper leaves and grass.

Terry Hyder—Three-Year-Olds, University Park United Methodist Church Weekday School, Dallas, TX

The Second Time Around

THE SECOND TIME AROUND
Recycling In The Preschool Classroom

Special Delivery

Do you have a stash of greeting cards that are just too special to throw away? If so, why not reuse them as postcards? Cut each card on the fold. Recycle the back portions of the cards, but convert the card fronts into postcards. To do this, draw a line down the middle of the back of each card front. If desired, program each of these postcards with a different student's address, and stamp and store the postcards for later use. Whenever you have an opportunity to jot a quick positive note to a child and his parent, use one of the postcards you've prepared. Now that's a special delivery!

Bonnie Howard—Grs. PreK/K L.I. • Apollo Beach Elementary • Apollo Beach, FL

HOORAY!

Jacob builds the most magnificent highways our sandbox has ever had!

Ms. Howard

Jacob Prillaman
Route 5
Martinsville, VA

Naturally Curly Hair

fde

Do you have a few worn-out or broken cassette tapes in your classroom? Well, it's nice to know that when they're no longer usable as audiotapes, you can reuse them in an entirely different way. Unwind each broken tape from its plastic cassette. Then curl lengths of the tape using a pair of sharp scissors, much like you would curl curling ribbon. Place the curled lengths of audiotape in your art area for students to incorporate into their artistic creations. You may be surprised to see all the different ways your students can think of to use these curlicues.

Chris Picanso • Windham, NH

Stackable Storage Compartments

There never seems to be enough storage space that the children can have easy access to. Alleviate this problem by asking your colleagues and the parents of your students to collect a specified type of container for you. (Cylinder-shaped cardboard or plastic ice-cream containers work well for this.) When you have a collection of at least six containers, cover each of them with Con-Tact® covering, if desired. Staple or hot-glue them together to form a storage pyramid. To keep small items from falling out of the compartments of the pyramid, attach half-circles that have been cut to fit the fronts (or tops) of the containers. Label each compartment so that students can observe what type of thing is stored there. Place the filled storage pyramid where students can help themselves to the contents.

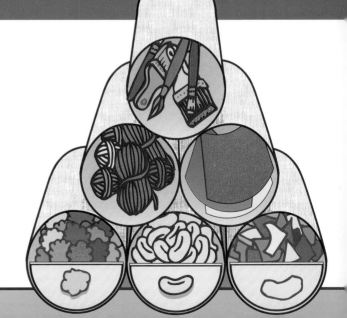

Maria Cuellar Munson—Preschool • Unity Caring Club • Garland, TX

THE SECOND TIME AROUND
Recycling In The Preschool Classroom

For The Love Of Books

What to do with old, ripped storybooks? Don't throw them away—use them in your classroom! Cut out the illustrations and photographs from each old book. Attach felt to the back of each picture; then place the pieces from each individual story in a resealable plastic bag and position the bags near a flannelboard. Encourage your youngsters to use the pieces on the flannelboard to retell their favorite stories or make up new ones.

Sharon Otto
St. Elizabeth Child Development Center
Lincoln, NE

Boxes, Boxes, And More Boxes!

Different sizes, colors, and shapes of cardboard boxes from cereal and other packaged foods have many classroom uses. For example, when construction paper isn't sturdy enough, cardboard boxes can be cut and used as backgrounds for two-dimensional projects, such as collages. A variety of different-sized boxes can be used for lots of hands-on fun for students, such as gluing and painting cardboard structures, or sequencing a collection of boxes from smallest to largest. Another use is to turn boxes into art stencils. Draw a simple design on a panel cut from a box; then cut out the design using an X-acto® knife. Save both the cut-out cardboard design and the stencil to be used for crayon rubbings.

Kelley Sharrock—Pre-K
Church Of Redeemer United Methodist Preschool
Columbus, OH

Lights, Camera, Action!

Old shower curtains can add to your classroom's sense of make-believe when you use them as scenery when role-playing. Simply lay a shower curtain on large sheets of bulletin-board paper or newspaper. Add liquid detergent to different colors of tempera paint. Then paint a scene or item from a book—such as a pond, garden, or forest—onto the shower curtain and allow the paint to dry. Use the curtain as a prop or background when retelling the story. It's also convenient to fold the curtain and store it for next time!

Bonnie B. Boyd
Coquina Elementary School
Titusville, FL

THE SECOND TIME AROUND
Recycling In The Preschool Classroom

Magnet Board Fun

Do you have wooden puzzles with missing pieces? Then you'll find this recycling idea attractive! Transform the remaining pieces from an incomplete puzzle into magnet board manipulatives. Simply affix a strip of magnetic tape to the back of each puzzle piece. Place the pieces and a magnetic surface in a center. Encourage students to use the pieces from thematic puzzles (such as farm, transportation, or alphabet puzzles) for sorting or sequencing activities. They'll soon be stuck on this fun activity!

Susan Cooperider—Four-Year-Olds
The Learning Nook
Springfield, IL

Matching Coupon Shapes

Clip some coupons to help little ones practice visual discrimination skills. Gather coupons in different sizes or shapes. Use a pencil to trace the shape of each coupon onto a piece of cardboard or tagboard. Then use a fine-tip marker to draw dotted lines over the pencil lines to resemble the dotted lines around the coupons. Laminate the coupons and cardboard for durability, and cut out the coupons. To use these, have a child match each coupon to its outlined shape on the cardboard.

Kathie DeAnn Thornton—Preschool
Private Educational Child Care
Wake Forest, NC

Don't Trash Those Tops!

Get some punch out of old plastic tops when you use them for lacing activities. Collect plastic tops from small microwave meals or from peanut, coffee, or potato-chip cans. Using a hammer and nail, punch holes in each top to create a simple design. For each lid, thread a shoelace through one of the holes; then secure one end of the lace with a knot. Have children weave the shoelace through the holes to discover the design.

Kathie DeAnn Thornton—Preschool

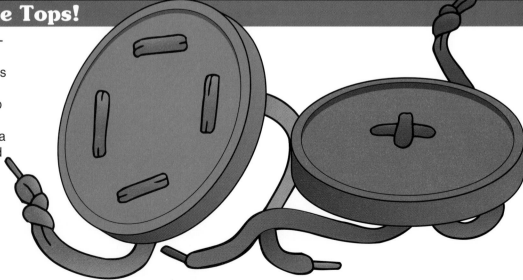

Building Bridges Between Home And School

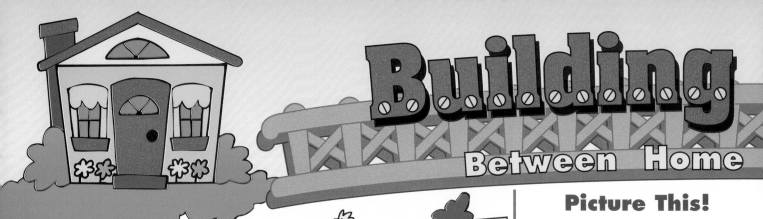

Building
Between Home

Fancy Family Footwork

Your children and their families will be doing some fancy footwork with this homework assignment. With each child, send home a large black piece of construction paper, several smaller sheets of brightly colored construction paper, and a letter explaining this project. In the letter, ask each parent to help his or her child trace, on the colored construction paper, a foot of each person who lives in their household. Request that the parent and child together cut out the feet and attach them to the black sheet of paper. Encourage them to creatively decorate the feet as desired. As the feet posters are returned to school, ask each child to share how he made his poster and who he made it with. To finish your foot fun, punch holes in the posters and bind them together to create a "Foot Book."

Tammy Lutz—Preschool/Head Start
George E. Greene Elementary
Bad Axe, MI

You're Invited To A Letter Picnic!

Invite parents to a picnic of alphabetically appetizing foods. Before the picnic, help each child choose one letter he has learned about; then brainstorm a list of foods that begin with that letter. Have each child make an invitation for his family. On each invitation, request a specific food from the brainstormed list for that parent to bring or send. Before the big event, help each child make a placemat that also reinforces his chosen letter. For example, if *C* is the selected letter, he may want to decorate a cat to glue to his placemat. After the picnic, assist children in making thank-you notes to send to their parents.

Tammy Clark—Pre-K
Polly Panda Preschool
Indianapolis, IN

Picture This!

Parents are sure to get the picture when you send home a class photo album. In your photo album, place a collection of pictures showing children participating in classroom activities. Label the pictures with students' names and explanations about the learning goals of the activities shown. After each child has had an opportunity to take the album home, update the album with current photos. No one will feel left out of the picture with this terrific idea.

Melissa Epling, Summersville, WV
Nettie Elementary Preschool

Bridges
And School

Family Projects Bulletin Board

Encourage parents to spend quality time with their children by sending home family projects every season or holiday. Simply attach a letter to several sheets of construction paper and send a set home with each child. Consider also sending home a small bottle of glue and a pair of scissors that can be returned with the completed project. In your letter, explain that you would like for as many members of the family as possible to work together to create a piece of artwork. You may want to suggest a theme, such as "Apples," or a topic, such as "What Makes Grandparents Special." Encourage parents to have fun and be creative—emphasizing that the important part will be the process rather than the product. As the projects are returned, ask each child to share his family's creation and tell how his family helped. Display each unique masterpiece on a bulletin board titled "Fabulous Family Projects."

Bernie Bussacco—Early Intervention Pre-K
R. D. Wilson Elementary School
Waymart, PA

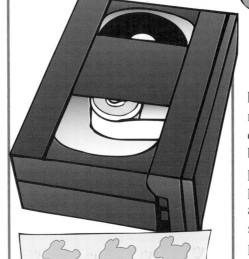

Thought you might like to see what our trip was like.

Mrs. Adams

Video To Go

Today's busy parents are not always able to attend school plays or chaperone field trips. Make sure they don't miss a thing by videotaping these special school events. Ask a volunteer who is able to attend to videotape the occasion. Then send the video home with a different child each night. It's sure to be a blockbuster!

Joan Adams
Montgomery, AL

Fun Box

Prepare a "Fun Box" to be sent home with a different child each night. Using paint pens, label and decorate a lunchbox. Inside the box include a variety of art supplies such as crayons, markers, paper, a pair of scissors, glitter, and glue. Also include small snacks such as pudding cups or packs of hot chocolate mix. Consider taping a note to the inside lid of the box, requesting that parents spend time with the child exploring the contents of the box and then creating a project. Little ones will be proud to share their family's work of art with their classmates.

Melissa Epling—Preschool
Nettie Elementary Preschool
Summersville, WV

Creating artwork as a family can be relaxing, fun, and rewarding. Create some artwork and share a treat!

Pam Crane

297

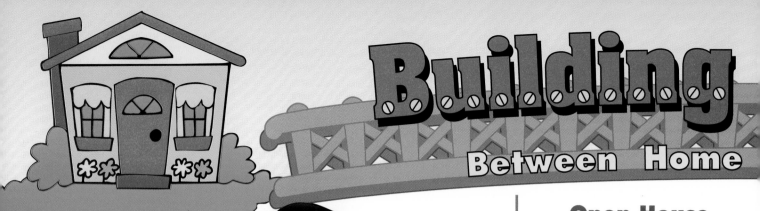

Building
Between Home

Parent Recognition

Let parents know how much you appreciate them with this special display. In advance, ask each parent to donate a picture of himself with his child. Mount each picture on a piece of construction paper, leaving space to label each picture with the parent's and child's names. Display all of the pictures around the title "Preschool Parents Are Special!" This is sure to be a hit with parents and children alike.

Open House Video

Lights, camera, action! Capture excerpts of your youngsters' first few months of school on video. Videotape your students involved in their daily activities, such as their arrival, instructional time, snack, recess, learning centers, storytime, and dismissal. Feature the video at Open House. Then let each child in turn take the video home overnight. This wonderful keepsake is bound to make a big hit.

A Day In The Life Of Your Child

Try this idea to give your Open House or PTA visitation a new twist. Have each parent experience what his child does in school, by having him go through portions of your daily routine. For example, have parents participate in circle time and work in centers under the direction of their youngsters. Parents will see what their children do in school and will be tickled to watch their little ones in action.

Michelle Armstrong—Pre-K
West Side Elementary
West Point, MS

Bridges And School

Holiday Parent Workshop

Invite parents to a holiday workshop with activities that are not only fun, but also provide opportunities for positive interaction and language development as well. Prior to the workshop, have your students help you decorate your classroom. Then organize learning centers with a holiday theme. For example, you might want to prepare centers in which parents and children listen to a story, make ornaments, and follow directions to decorate cookies. Encourage all of the children and parents to use the ornaments they made to decorate a tree together. Conclude the workshop by eating the cookies and by singing holiday songs. As they are headed out the door, provide parents with a copy of any patterns or recipes that they used in the centers. A good time will be had by all!

Cathie Pesa—Preschool Special Needs
Youngstown City Schools, Youngstown, OH

I work at a publishing company as an in-house artist. I draw all day and get paid for it.

Mr. Crane

I work at home taking care of Susie's little brother.

Mrs. Young

A "Work" Book

Children are proud to talk about their parents and their understanding of what they do at work. Create a class book about jobs by requesting that one parent or caregiver for each child write a brief description of his or her occupation. Copy each description on construction paper; then ask each child to illustrate her parent's job description. Bind the pages between covers; then read the book aloud. This project is sure to do a good job of involving parents!

Mary E. Maurer, Caddo, OK

News Of The Month

Get into publishing if you want to inform parents about the activities in your busy classroom. Each month write a newsletter which includes information about your class and school activities. Also include simple recipes, book reviews, activities for home, and information about child growth and development. Information about community offerings, such as museums and parks, makes an excellent addition to your newsletter as well. Extra! Extra! Get your preschool news here!

Mary E. Maurer

Preschool News

Miss Maurer's Class

Class News

School News

Holiday Cookies

At The Park

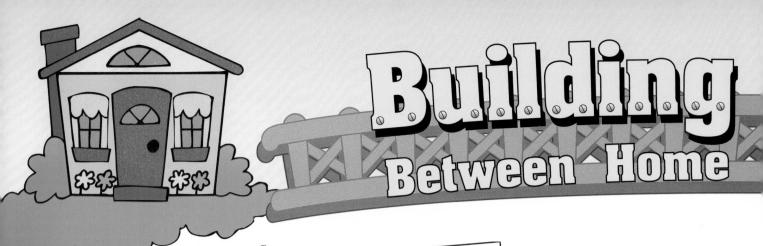

Building
Between Home

Pocket Folder

Do you have a problem with getting notes from school to home? If so, try this terrific tip. Purchase a two-pocket folder for each child. Have each child decorate his folder. Personalize each folder; then laminate it if desired. On one side of the folder, place items such as notes, student work, school announcements, and calendars. On the other side, enclose a daily report. Parents can get in the habit of referring to the folder for classroom information and using the folder to transport their notes to school. Family members are sure to feel well-informed when you use these folders!

Samita Arora—Pre-K and Kindergarten
Richmond, IN

A Sticker A Day

Caregivers will be in the know and your little ones will love keeping up-to-date with this calendar idea. Each month list the upcoming school events, holidays, and activities on a calendar. Duplicate a copy for each child. Attach a sheet of small seasonal stickers to each calendar; then send the calendar home with each student. Ask each parent to assist his child in attaching a sticker to the appropriate space on the calendar each day. This routine will not only help parents keep up with the scoop in school, it will also help students practice left-to-right progression, number recognition, and one-to-one correspondence. Now that's eventful!

Sally Greiner—Early Childhood Special
 Needs Teacher
Metzenbaum School
Chesterland, OH

A Helpful Placemat

This placemat will certainly supply each of your students with food for thought! Supply each child with a large sheet of white construction paper. Have each youngster use crayons to draw or trace shapes on both sides of his paper. Personalize each sheet; then laminate it for durability. Have each child take his paper home and use it as a placemat. Encourage each student to ask a parent or family member to review the shapes and colors on his placemat before or after mealtime.

Donna Cohen—Special Education
Pine Ridge Elementary
Stone Mountain, GA

Bridges
And School

Share-A-Book

Book-sharing between home and school will be in the bag with this smart idea. Purchase or make a canvas bookbag. Using fabric paints, decorate one side of the bag with the school name or mascot. On the other side, paint the phrase "Share-A-Book." Prepare a note to parents explaining the purpose of the bag. In the note, encourage each parent to help his child select one book to put in the bag. Attach the note to the inside of the bag; then send the bag home with a different child each night. Each day when a child returns the bag, have him share his book with the other students.

Mary C. Warren—Three-Year-Olds
Kiddie College School, Inc.
Prattville, AL

Dear Caregiver,
It's your child's turn to share a book. Place one in the bag, and we'll have a look!

Thanks,
Ms. Warren

Please send the book and bag to school tomorrow.

Ask Me About My Week!
What funny thing did Miss Debbie wear to school? (sunglasses)

What did you do outside? (planted seeds)

What materials did you use at the art center?

Ask Me About My Week

Use this unique idea to help parents and children communicate with one another about classroom activities. At the end of each week, send home a list of suggested questions about school that parents can ask their children. For example, when you're studying ocean animals, you may suggest that they ask, "Can you name one ocean animal you learned about?" Also provide questions about daily activities, such as "What game did you play outside?" For selected questions, include additional information so parents can guide their children to answer. Both parents and children will enjoy the exchange of information that results.

Debbie Brown—Four- And Five-Year-Olds
Corson Park Day Care
Millville, NJ

Spring Art Show

Throughout the school year, date and save some of your students' special artwork to display in a spring art show. Prior to the show, group the art by theme or season. Then display the art by taping it to your classroom walls, covering the room with art from floor to ceiling. As parents view the work of their little artists, they will be able to see the development of creativity and fine-motor progress. After the show, have each child decorate a large paper bag. Remove each child's artwork from the walls and place it in his bag to be taken home.

Cathy Schmidt—Three-, Four-, And Five-Year-Olds
De Pere Co-op Nursery School
Green Bay, WI

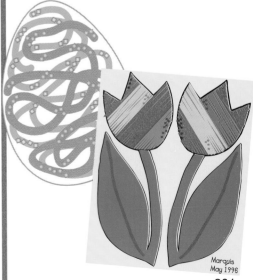

Marquis
May 1996

301

Getting Your
Ducklings In A Row

GETTING YOUR DUCKLINGS

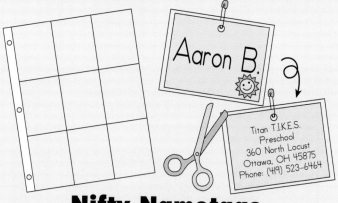

Big Books For Little Hands

Making big books accessible to little hands will be easy with this tip. For each big book you'd like to display, hot-glue two wooden clothespins onto a wall. Then clip the books to the wall. Now all of your big books are easy to view and easy to use!

Esther S. Wert
Children's Place Preschool
Sayre, PA

A BUTTON FOR BEAR
by Dan Foreman

Squared Away With Carpet Squares

To ensure a calm start to your day, try this management technique. Before children arrive at school, place a carpet square and a book on the floor for each child. After you welcome each child, ask him to sit on the carpet square of his choice. As the children quietly browse through the provided books, you'll have a chance to get your administrative tasks all squared away.

Claudia Pinkston—Four-Year-Olds
Lexington, SC

Nifty Nametags

Do away with torn and tattered nametags with this nifty idea. Cut clear, plastic, three-ring binder pages used to display baseball cards into nine individual pockets each. For each nametag, cut a 3 1/2" x 2 1/2" rectangle of construction paper. Print a child's name on the rectangle; then attach decorative stickers if desired. (If the nametags are to be used on field trips, consider putting the child's name on one side of the tag and the school's name and phone number on the other side.) Slide the paper into the pocket. Punch a hole in the top of the pocket. Using a large safety pin, attach the nametag to the child's clothing. For trips, pin the nametags on with the school name showing. (Public safety officers believe that labeling a child with his name can work to the advantage of a would-be abductor.)

Brenda Berger—Three-, Four-, and Five-Year-Olds
Titan T.I.K.E.S. Preschool
Ottawa, OH

IN A ROW

Colorful Paintbrushes

Get a handle on messy paint centers with this colorful suggestion. Use enamel paint to paint the handles of brushes and the paint cups in matching colors. Fill each cup with its corresponding color of paint. As students paint their masterpieces, they'll be able to replace the brushes in the correct cups by matching the colors.

Vickie Zalk—Three-Year-Olds
Hope Creative Preschool
Winter Haven, FL

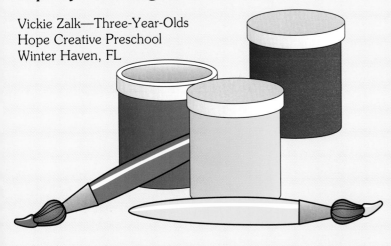

Who's Helping?

Need an easy-to-change classroom helpers chart? Use a behind-the-door shoe organizer that has clear pockets. For each pocket label a piece of tagboard with a different classroom job. Place a tagboard label in each pocket. Then place a different child's photo or nametag in each pocket to designate your daily or weekly helpers. When it's time for new helpers, simply rearrange or replace the pictures or nametags in the pockets.

Kimberly Filip, Oakman Preschool, Dearborn, MI

Rack 'Em Up!

A colorful, plastic file crate makes the perfect puzzle rack for a preschool classroom. Simply turn the file crate on its side and slide the puzzles in! Little ones can put away puzzles quickly and easily with this attractive organizational method.

Debra Holbrook
Southern Baptist Educational Center
Olive Branch, MS

GETTING YOUR DUCKLINGS

Center Signs

Create colorful signs to help your youngsters remember how many children are allowed at each of your centers. For each center, label a sheet of colored construction paper with the center name. Then cut a number of shape cutouts (such as stars or hearts) from a complementary color of construction paper. Determine the number of students you wish to visit a particular center. Glue the corresponding number of shape cutouts to that center's sign. Laminate all the signs and post them near your centers. Students can tell at a glance how many children are allowed and can count heads to figure out if there is room for one more!

Tracy Tavernese—Four-Year-Olds
Holy Child School
Old Westbury, NY

Busy Bodies

Use this rhythm activity to keep little bodies busy while waiting in line. Perform a movement for children to imitate, such as clapping. After a while, change to another movement such as head nodding. Then let students take turns selecting and leading the activity. No more fidgeting in line!

Sherri S. McWhorter—Pre-K
Franklin County Head Start
Carnesville, GA

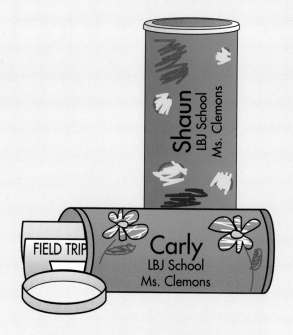

Let's Get It Home!

Is it difficult for your preschoolers to get important papers home? Try this unique solution! For each child, provide an empty potato-chip can with a plastic lid. Cover the cans with colored construction paper. Use a permanent marker to personalize each one with a child's name, school, and teacher name. Then let students decorate their cans using a variety of art materials. When important papers need to go home, simply roll them up and place them in the appropriate cans. Put the lids on to keep the papers safely inside.

Anna N. Clemons—Preschool
LBJ Elementary
Jackson, KY

IN A ROW

Tips For Getting Organized

Memory Jogger

Keep track of important reminders with this simple idea. Type a list of all the children in your class. Make several copies. Laminate one copy and post it near your door. Use a dry-erase marker to jot down notes about transportation, medications, or other reminders next to children's names. Erase the notes at the end of each day and the list will be ready to use again. You'll find many uses for the other copies of the list, such as keeping track of which children have brought in permission slips for a field trip.

Sally Greiner—Early Childhood Special Education
Metzenbaum School
Chesterland, OH

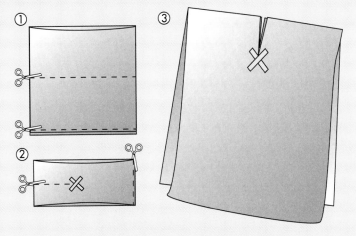

> Joey–ride home with Amy
> Andy
> Mark–absent
> Sue
> Amy–will take Joey
> Sandy–Mom will be late

Mystery Boxes

Here's an activity that will keep little ones busy while you handle morning routines. Collect a supply of empty baby-wipe boxes. Fill each box with a different set of toys such as dominoes, counters, toy cars, or beads and laces. As children enter the room, allow them to choose a "mystery box" from a special shelf. When a child finishes with one box of toys, he may return it and take another. As children discover and play, you'll be free to take care of last-minute notes and answer parent questions.

Barbara M. Marks—Pre-K
Kinderplace
Oshkosh, WI

Painting Aprons

These easy-to-make art aprons will help youngsters stay neat and clean when painting. Simply cut the bottom seam off a large garbage bag. Then cut the bag in half horizontally. You now have the makings of two painting aprons. For each one, cut a slit about eight inches long into one side seam as shown. On each side of the apron, tape the end of the cut with two pieces of masking tape placed in an X shape. (The Xs will help little ones find the head opening easily.) Trim off the opposite side seam to the desired length. These aprons are inexpensive, disposable, and easy for children to put on and take off on their own.

Eva Chinn, August School, Stockton, CA

(Note: The National Health and Safety Performance Standards state that all plastic bags should be stored out of reach of children. Permit youngsters to use these painting aprons only while they are being closely supervised by an adult.)

GETTING YOUR DUCKLINGS

Wallpaper Nametags

Try this alternative to construction-paper nametags. Cut sheets of wallpaper into 8 1/2" x 11" rectangles so that they fit into your copy machine. Choose a favorite nametag pattern and duplicate it onto the wallpaper. Cut out the shapes, punch holes in the tops, and thread with lengths of yarn. Voilà! You have nametags with delightful designs! For added fun, look for wallpaper with thematic designs that correspond to your field trips or special events.

Jackie Wright—Preschool
Summerhill Children's House
Enid, OK

"1-2-3. That's Enough For Me!"

Do your youngsters linger at the water fountain after outdoor play? Speed things along with this simple rhyme. As each child takes her turn at the fountain, have the waiting children say, "1-2-3. That's enough for me!" The end of the rhyme is the drinker's signal that it's someone else's turn at the fountain.

Doris Porter—Preschool
Headstart
Anamosa, IA

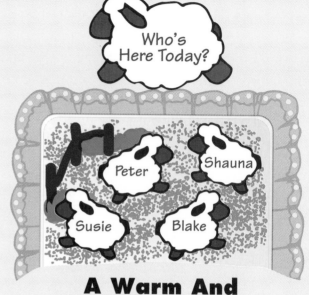

Who's Here Today?

A Warm And Woolly Welcome

Let little lambs welcome your little ones to school each day! Begin by using craft paints to create a meadow scene on a large, rectangular cookie sheet. Hot-glue eyelet lace trim around the edges of the pan. Hang the cookie-sheet meadow on your classroom wall. From construction paper, cut one large lamb shape and a classroom supply of smaller lamb shapes. Laminate the cutouts. Write on the large cutout "Who's Here Today?" Mount the larger lamb above the cookie sheet. Label each smaller lamb with a different child's name. Attach a piece of magnetic tape to the back of each lamb. Place the lambs on a table or store them in a container. As each child enters the classroom, have her find her lamb and place it in the cookie-sheet meadow to let you—the mother lamb—know she is present.

Martha A. Briggs
Rosemont Tuesday/Thursday School
Fort Worth, TX

308

IN A ROW

Flannelboard Story Storage

Keep flannelboard stories and pieces accessible with this nifty storage idea. Insert each story into a clear, top-loading sheet protector. Put the accompanying pieces in the protector with the story. Then place all of the sheet protectors in a three-ring binder. Organize the binder seasonally or thematically to suit your needs.

Mary Anne Liptak—Four- And Five-Year-Olds
Lollipop Co-operative Preschool
Macedonia, OH

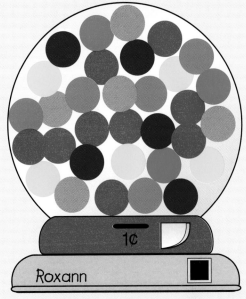

A Bubble Gum Bonus

Inspire youngsters with this motivational bubble gum display. For each child, cut a bubble-gum machine shape from construction paper. Label each cutout with a child's name. Laminate the cutouts if desired. Then post them on a classroom wall. When you spy a child exhibiting good behavior or achieving a goal, reward him with a round sticker to attach to his bubble gum machine. When his machine is full, have him take it home to show his family.

Roxann Reed—Preschool
Tri-City Christian School
Lee's Summit, MO

Cleanup Freeze

Turn cleanup time into fun time! Play a song as children clean up from an activity or from playtime. Throughout the song, stop the music and have everyone freeze. Restart the music to get little ones moving again. Cleanup will be a breeze when you play the freeze!

Debbie Brown—Four- And Five-Year-Olds
Corson Park Day Care
Millville, NJ

309

Our Readers Write

Our Readers > Write

Fun Dough

Who would have thought a great thirst quencher could become the secret ingredient in a wonderful homemade play dough? Grab a package of Kool-Aid® and the other ingredients listed to see for yourself!

Kool-Aid® Fun Dough

2 1/2–3 c. flour
1/2 c. salt
1 pkg. unsweetened Kool-Aid®
1 tbsp. alum

2 c. boiling water
3 tbsp. corn oil
1 c. additional flour

Mix the first six ingredients into a dough. Using some or all of the additional flour, knead the dough until it reaches the desired consistency. Store the dough in an airtight container.

Linda Lopienski
Bellmore, NY

Stuck On Colorful Glues

If you love the looks of colored-glue art projects, but hate to think of what the colorful name-brand glues cost, then you've come to the right place! Collect and clean empty, plastic squeeze bottles such as the ones glue and mustard come in. Put a few drops of food coloring in each bottle; then gradually add plain white glue and use a drinking straw to stir the glue until it's evenly tinted. Since colored glues don't have to be expensive, they can become one of your most frequently used art mediums.

Kimberly A. Calhoun—PreK
MacGregor Creative School
Cary, NC

Communicating With Parents

One sure way to increase communication with parents is to keep a log, such as a spiral or loose-leaf notebook, in your entryway. Each day before students arrive, date a clean page in the notebook and write a message to the parents. If there's no pressing business, you may elect to write a positive or inspirational message or a thought for the day, rather than an announcement or reminder. As the parents come and go, they can read your message and leave messages of their own. It's surprising that such a simple habit can do a marvelous job of keeping the channels of communication open. But it does!

Gail E. Joseph-Joireman
Bellingham, WA

August 29, 1995
Field trip tomorrow...
Old shoes and
clothes are suggested.
We're going to milk

Any messages for Ms. Joseph-Joireman?

If so, add them to today's page. Thank you!

Cozy Reading Corner

Make your reading corner especially inviting with these novelty pillows. Supply each child with a small white T-shirt, or ask each child to bring one from home. Using fabric crayons (and the directions from the crayon manufacturer) or fabric paints and sponges, have each child creatively decorate her shirt. When the shirts are ready for use, have parent volunteers stitch up all but the neck opening of each shirt, stuff each one with fiberfill, and stitch the neck opening closed. Store these novelty pillows in a laundry basket. When youngsters are ready to "read" or listen to a story, these billowy pillows will be just right for reclining in the reading corner.

Debbie Jones—PreK, Lorton, VA

A Perk For Your Helper

For most children, being the teacher's helper is a thrill in and of itself. But here's a suggestion to add to the fun for your Helper of the Day. From a fabric store, purchase preprinted pillow pieces (both fronts and backs) that feature juvenile designs. Cut out the pieces and machine stitch to hem the bottom edge of each pillow design. Then, with the pillow pieces' right sides together, stitch around three sides of the fabric—leaving the bottom edge open. You may want to create several chair covers in this manner, so each helper may select the design he prefers. As soon as the Helper of the Day is identified, he may slip a chair cover over the back of his chair and begin his duties.

Dawn Hurley, Child Care Center, Bethel Park, PA

Welcome To Preschool!

Help your youngsters (and their parents) ease into preschool by inviting small groups of students to get-acquainted sessions. Several weeks before school begins, mail each child a letter (indicating his scheduled time to visit), a school supplies list, and a nametag to wear on the first day of school. When each child arrives with his parent, ask them to work together to complete a simple craft that they can display in the room or take home. Ask your teacher's assistant to supervise the children as they begin to explore the room. Meanwhile, share information with the parents and answer any questions they might have.

Wilma Droegemueller—Preschool, Zion Lutheran School, Mt. Pulaski, IL

What's Inside An Apple?

Show two apples to your class and ask the youngsters what might be inside. Cut one apple in half vertically and the other in half horizontally. Discuss how the two apples look the same inside and how they look different. Then have youngsters make apples to open. To make an apple, color the bottoms of two white paper plates red, yellow, or green. With white sides facing, put the plates together, punch holes in one side, and tie them together with matching string. Open the apple and glue seeds onto the inside. Attach stem and leaf cutouts. What's inside an apple? Open it up and see!

Connie Harget—Preschool
Liberty Childcare, Powell, OH

Ruffle Away Clutter

Your room will look as pretty as you please when you use a dust ruffle to cover your shelves. Cut out the flat section of a dust ruffle, leaving an inch along the edge next to the ruffle. Place the ruffle edge under a shelf; then use tacks or a staple gun to attach it to the shelf. Decorate your shelves in this manner and watch classroom clutter disappear!

Lisa Fox
Smyrna West, Smyrna, TN

Fingerplays At Your Fingertips

Keep fingerplays at your fingertips. Put your favorite fingerplays onto index cards. On each card, attach a sticker or draw a picture of an item that relates to that fingerplay. Laminate the cards; then punch a hole in the top corner of each one and place them on a metal ring. When it's fingerplay time, ask a child to flip through the cards and make a choice. You'll be surprised at how quickly your youngsters will be able to find their favorites just by looking at the pictures.

Rosalie Sumsion
Home Day Care/Preschool
Monument Valley, UT

Five little kittens standing in a row,
They nod their heads to the children so.
They run to the left; they run to the right,
They stand up and stretch in the bright sunlight.
Along comes a dog who's in for some fun.
ME-OW! See those kittens run!

Apple Tree

This welcome-to-school bulletin board will introduce students and parents to your school staff. On a bulletin board, mount a blank calendar and a large tree cutout with a branch for each department in your school. Label each branch with a department name; then label the roots with the names of your administrators and support staff. Cut out an apple shape for each teacher and teacher assistant. Label each apple with a different teacher's name and attach a photo of that person. Place the apples on the appropriate department branches. As the year continues, move the apples onto the calendar to indicate each staff member's birthday.

Lauren C. Hinton—Preschool Special Start
Dawson County Primary School
Dawsonville, GA

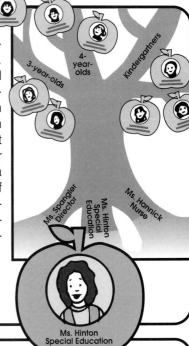

3-year-olds
4-year-olds
Kindergartners
Ms. Spangler Director
Ms. Hinton Special Education
Ms. Hannick Nurse

Ms. Hinton
Special Education

Make A Circle

Using tablecloths is a wonderful way to help little ones form a circle. Simply spread a round tablecloth on the floor and ask your children to stand along the edge. With the tablecloth, directions such as "Walk around the circle!" or "Step inside the circle!" will be easy to follow.

Teresa Hanak—Preschool, Fenton Preschool, Fenton, MI

Picture This!

Get counting and number recognition in focus with this idea. In advance, prepare a large cutout of each number from one to nine. Photograph the appropriate number of children holding each cutout—one child holding the number one, two children holding the number two, and so on. Place the pictures in an album. Youngsters will enjoy looking at the pictures and counting their friends.

Janet Strickland—Preschool
ABC Learning Center
Corinth, MS

Beanbag Toss

This versatile game idea can be adapted to reinforce a number of language and math concepts. Decorate an old bedsheet or large piece of bulletin-board paper with shapes, numbers, or letters. To play, have each youngster toss a beanbag and name the shape, number, or letter that the beanbag landed on. Or have each child call out one of the choices, then throw the beanbag to see if he can get it to land at the announced location.

Linda Lopienski
Asheboro, NC

Color Match

Here's a quick time filler that will reinforce color recognition. Lay different colors of construction paper on the floor. Encourage each child to find an object in the classroom that matches one of the colors; then have him lay the object he found on the appropriate sheet of paper.

Maria Cuellar Munson—Preschool
Garland, TX

Bath Towel Paint Smock

Change an old bath towel into a paint smock in less than one minute! Simply fold down one-third of the towel. Starting at the fold, cut a half circle from the towel to create an opening big enough for a child to put his head through. A child can easily slip this paint protector on without the frustration of buttons or fasteners.

Teresa Hanak—Three-Year-Olds
Fenton Preschool
Fenton, MI

I printed big and small bears.

"Beary" Big And "Beary" Small

Use a retelling of *"Goldilocks And The Three Bears"* along with this art project to emphasize the concepts of big and small. In advance, label each child's paper as shown. Using a die-cutting machine or a bear pattern, cut several large bear shapes and several small bear shapes from sponges. Have each child make large and small bear prints on his paper using the sponges and brown paint. Assist him in counting the number of big and small bears that he printed on his paper. This activity is sure to be big fun for small hands.

Betsy Ruggiano—Three-Year-Olds
Featherbed Lane School, Clark, NJ

Special Words

Here's a helpful hint for getting the attention of busy children. Each day announce a special word that relates to the current theme. For example, if the theme is transportation, the special word of the day might be "trucks." Each time you say the word, students stop and listen for directions. What a fun way to get their attention quickly!

Keitha-Lynn Stewart—Four-Year-Olds
Little Kids Day Care Center, Inc., Sissonville, WV

Scissor Smiles

Getting a handle on how to hold a pair of scissors can be tough for a three- or four-year-old. By drawing a happy face on his thumbnail, a child can quickly learn how to hold his scissors correctly. Simply remind him to make sure that he can see the smiling face when using his scissors.

Cynthia J. Wunderlich—Preschool
St. Luke's United Methodist Child
   Development Center
Orlando, FL

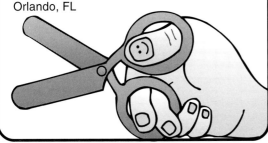

Once Upon A Holiday Book...

What could be better on a winter's day than settling down with a good book? Designate a day during the holiday season for students to come to school in their pajamas or wear pajamas under their clothes. (Don't forget to put on your own bathrobe and slippers!) Encourage youngsters to also bring stuffed toys, pillows, and blankets to school on that day. To create the perfect atmosphere for a cozy reading time together, dim the lights and play soft music. Gather all of your youngsters around you and, once everyone is cozy, read aloud selections of holiday literature such as *The Polar Express* and *'Twas The Night Before Christmas.* After several selections, everyone can settle down for a long winter's nap!

Marsha Feffer—Pre-K
Salem Early Childhood Center, Salem, MA

Handy Magnets

Mom and Dad will treasure these keepsake magnets when their preschooler is all grown-up. To make a magnet set, have a child place her hands on the copy machine. For better results, cover the child's hands with a white cloth. Photocopy her hands. To the copy of one hand, attach a picture of the child. On the other, have the child write her name and the date. Laminate and cut out the hands. Attach a piece of magnetic tape to the back of each hand cutout. These magnets are sure to be a hands-down favorite among parents.

Cheryl Chacka
Eagle Point School
Oakdale, MN

Holiday Necklaces

After you have trimmed the tree, trim yourself with these easy-to-make holiday necklaces. Simply restring the novelty beads from wooden or plastic tree garlands onto dental floss. (Check after-Christmas sales for great buys on these garlands.) String small ornaments along with the beads to create a truly unique necklace. Since each garland can provide a large quantity of beads, consider making several necklaces similar to your own to place in your class dress-up area. You're sure to receive compliments from admiring students and adults when you accessorize with these seasonal necklaces.

Wilma Droegemueller—Preschool
Zion Lutheran School, Mt. Pulaski, IL

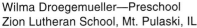

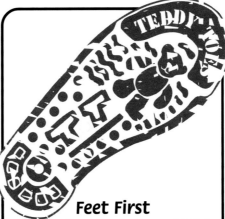

Feet First

Checked out the bottom of kids' shoes lately? Well, if you do, you'll find a variety of interesting designs just waiting to be discovered! Read aloud *The Foot Book* by Dr. Seuss (published by Random House). Then pair students. Have each child use crayons to rub the designs on the soles of his partner's shoes onto paper. Encourage students to compare the designs and sizes of the shoes while looking at the rubbings.

Beth Lemke—Head Start
Coon Rapids, MN

Shaving Cream Cleanup

Wipe away your blues (and greens and yellows and reds) with this tabletop-cleaning method. After creating a design (such as the letter *C* or a cat shape) on each tabletop with shaving cream, have students spread the cream around with their fingers. As the children make their own designs on the table's surface, the shaving cream will remove built-up glue and crayon marks. When the shaving foam disappears, wipe the tables with a wet cloth. My, what supersmelling, superclean tables you have!

Judy Elliott—Pre-Kindergarten
St. Michael's Catholic School, West Memphis, AR

Index